chayil

חָיִל

[Heb. 2428]

khah'·yil

"a force"

an army or host

English translations:

1. might, strength, power, capable
2. valiant, virtuous, valor
3. riches, substance, wealth
4. noble, worthy, excellent, praiseworthy

Royalty free image credits from 123rf.com stock photos:

front cover (sword and Bible): <a href='https://www.123rf.com/profile_balazschristina' >balazschristina / 123RF Stock Photo</a>

dedication page and p. 238 (lion image): <a href='http://www.123rf.com/photo_19359021_sepia-toned-black-and-white-striking-lion-face-portrait.html'>cd123 / 123RF Stock Photo</a>

back cover (praying woman): <a href='https://www.123rf.com/profile_halfpoint'>halfpoint / 123RF Stock Photo</a>

God's Chayil Women

Moving Beyond Tradition to Embrace Truth and God-given Purpose

❦

K.P. Taylor

DOULOS BOOKS
Rapid City, South Dakota

God's Chayil Women

Copyright © 2014 by K.P. Taylor

Published by Doulos Books, Rapid City, South Dakota

Boldface words in passages were added for emphasis by author throughout the book. **Scripture quotations** were taken from multiple English versions and are marked as follows:

AMP: Scripture quotations marked **AMP** taken from the Amplified® Bible, Copyright © 1954, 1958, 1962, 1964, 1965, 1987 by The Lockman Foundation. Used by permission. (www.Lockman.org)

CEV: Scripture quotations marked **(CEV)** are from the Contemporary English Version Copyright © 1991, 1992, 1995 by American Bible Society, Used by Permission.

CJB: Scripture quotations marked **CJB** are taken from the Complete Jewish Bible, copyright 1998 by David H. Stern. Published by Jewish New Testament Publications, Inc. www.messianicjewish.net/jntp. Distributed by Messianic Jewish Resources Int'l. www.messianicjewish.net. All rights reserved. Used by permission.

ERV: Scripture quotations marked **ERV** are taken from the Holy Bible: Easy-to-Read Version™ Taken from the HOLY BIBLE: EAST-TO-READ VERSION™ © 2006 by World Bible Translation Center, Inc. and used by permission.

ESV: Scripture quotations marked **ESV** are from The Holy Bible, English Standard Version® (ESV®), copyright © 2001 by Crossway, a publishing ministry of Good News Publishers. All rights reserved.

EXB: Scripture quotations marked **EXB** are taken from The Expanded Bible. Copyright © 2011 by Thomas Nelson, Inc. Used by permission. All rights reserved.

GNT: Scripture quotations marked **(GNT)** are from the Good News Translation in Today's English Version - Second Edition Copyright © 1992 by American Bible Society. Used by Permission.

GW: Scripture quotations marked **GW** are taken from GOD'S WORD®, © 1995 God's Word to the Nations. Used by permission of Baker Publishing Group.

HCSB: Scripture quotations marked **HCSB** are taken from the Holman Christian Standard Bible®, Copyright © 1999, 2000, 2002, 2003, 2009 by Holman Bible Publishers. Used by permission. Holman Christian Standard Bible®, Holman CSB®, and HCSB® are federally registered trademarks of Holman Bible Publishers.

KJV: Scripture quotations marked **KJV** are from the Holy Bible, King James Version. 1987 printing. Public Domain.

MOUNCE: Scripture quotations marked **MOUNCE** are taken from THE MOUNCE REVERSE-INTERLINEAR NEW TESTAMENT Copyright © 2011 by Robert H Mounce and William D Mounce. Used by permission. All rights reserved worldwide.

NASB: Scripture quotations marked **NASB** taken from the New American Standard Bible®, Copyright © 1960, 1962, 1963, 1968, 1971, 1972, 1973, 1975, 1977, 1995 by The Lockman Foundation. Used by permission. (www.Lockman.org)

NCV: Scripture quotations marked **NCV** are taken from the New Century Version®. Copyright © 2005 by Thomas Nelson, Inc. Used by permission. All rights reserved.

NIV: Scripture quotations marked **NIV** are from THE HOLY BIBLE, NEW INTERNATIONAL VERSION®, NIV® Copyright © 1973, 1978, 1984, 2011 by Biblica, Inc.™ Used by permission. All rights reserved worldwide.

NKJV: Scripture quotations marked **NKJV**™ are taken from the New King James Version®. Copyright © 1982 by Thomas Nelson, Inc. Used by permission. All rights reserved.

NLT: Scripture quotations marked **NLT** are taken from the *Holy Bible*, New Living Translation, copyright © 1996, 2004, 2007 by Tyndale House Foundation. Used by permission of Tyndale House Publishers, Inc., Carol Stream, Illinois 60188. All rights reserved.

PHILLIPS: Scripture quotations marked **PHILLIPS** are taken from J. B. Phillips: The New Testament in Modern English, Revised Edition. Copyright © J. B. Phillips 1958, 1960, 1972. Used by permission of Macmillan Publishing Company.

THE MESSAGE: Scripture quotations marked **THE MESSAGE** are taken from *THE MESSAGE*. Copyright © by Eugene H. Peterson 1993, 1994, 1995, 1996, 2000, 2001, 2002. Used by permission of NavPress Publishing Group.

VOICE: Scripture quotations marked **VOICE** are taken from The Voice™. Copyright © 2008 by Ecclesia Bible Society. Used by permission. All rights reserved.

ISBN 978-0-9838102-1-6

All rights reserved. Permission granted to copy portions of this book for nonprofit noncommercial use with proper bibliographical citation and link for purchasing a new book from Amazon.com or other online bookseller listing the book for purchase. Any other electronic or commercial use is limited to brief quotations or reviews with proper bibliographical citation.

Library of Congress Control Number: 2014904249

Subject Headings: 1. Biblical Studies   2. Women   3. Church and Ministry

Cover design and graphics by K.P. Taylor and C.G. Taylor.

Printed in the United States of America

Father,

Thank you for the wisdom
You freely give to all
who diligently seek it,
and for Your Holy Spirit,
Who guides us into all truth
and reveals the things to come.
Amen.
Come Lord Jesus.

Call to Me,
and I will answer you,
and show you **great** and **mighty** things,
which you do not know.

Jer. 33:3, NKJV

For

every chayil woman of God,

whose heart burns with zeal for the

purposes of God,

who has heard the trumpet sound

and cannot stand still,

this book was written for you.

I believe the Lord says to you in this hour:

"Daughter, you run your race,
for I am for you,
not against you."

The **Lion** has **roared**…
who can but **prophesy**?
Amos 3:8

Sketch on spine

While contemplating the themes of this book, I drew this sketch as a rough idea of what I believe embodies the notion of a *chayil* woman. The youthful grace and dignified bearing characterize the noble spirit resident in every woman of God, regardless of her age.

I also wanted the sketch to convey a woman who stands fully equipped and soberly vigilant at her post. Only part of her face is showing, reflecting her desire to be out of the limelight so that her King alone receives glory. Her gaze remains fixed on Him and her hope in His promise to return and establish a wise, just, and righteous government on the earth.

She looks to the distant horizon, searching for her Beloved with longing in her heart. Her spiritual armor defines her readiness to take on whatever challenge her Commanding Officer gives her. She holds her shield ready to protect herself from the arrows

sent to discourage or dissuade her from her authority and position as part of God's army. Her unswerving love for, loyalty to, and trust in her Beloved drives away all fear. Though never lacking in zeal, she restrains herself from marching out on her own. She patiently waits for the word from her Captain.

She will not stand still when the trumpet sounds.

This is the legacy of every *chayil* woman of God. It is a call to every daughter of the King to remember who she is and to discern why she has been called to be a part of God's kingdom for this hour in history. With vision and purpose ignited in her spirit, each daughter of God can wholeheartedly pursue her calling, unhindered by the fear of man or the doubt of double-mindedness. She must be set free to take her place.

Kathy Taylor

Table of Contents

	Preface	15
Chapter 1	Musings from the Pew	19
Chapter 2	Leprosy on the Wall	30
Chapter 3	Preunderstandings	40
Chapter 4	Spiritual Identity	52
Chapter 5	A Wife of Noble Character	73
Chapter 6	Wisdom Personified as a Woman	91
Chapter 7	Scriptural Precedents	103
Chapter 8	Moving Forward	123
Chapter 9	1 Corinthians 14:34-36	135
Chapter 10	1 Timothy 2:11-15	150
Chapter 11	Shifting Paradigms	180
Chapter 12	*Chayil* Spirit of Women	203
Chapter 13	The Perfect Timing of God	217
Chapter 14	Closing Argument	228
Chapter 15	Restoring Women and *Koinonia*	239
	Epilogue	260
	Addendum	263
	End Notes	266

Note: Hebrew (**Heb.**) and Greek (**Grk.**) word references use Strong's numbered index throughout

Preface and Acknowledgments

> *But Amos replied, "I'm not a professional prophet, and I was never trained to be one. I'm just a shepherd, and I take care of sycamore-fig trees."* Amos 7:14, NLT

I want to be clear at the outset. Like Amos, I have no claim to academic authority nor do I have an official position in any local church. I tend a flock, like Amos. I love the Lord and His Word. I love the Body of Christ, and I love hearing and reading what other believers have to say on any biblical topic.

I have learned a great deal from the hundreds of books and articles I've read, and the thousands of messages I've heard from Baptists, Catholics, Charismatics, Evangelicals, Four Square, Lutherans, Messianic Jews, Methodists, Non-denominationals, Pentecostals, Presbyterians, Wesleyans—clergy and lay people alike (this list is alphabetical and not all-inclusive or prioritized). Now I find myself burdened and compelled to contribute.

For decades, I have been in agreement with the complementarian view of women's roles in the church and family. Recently, however, I've felt distracted about this issue. I realized I had become double-minded… a state the Bible warns leads to instability in all our ways. I began my search to understand this issue as revealed in God's Word to rid myself of this doubt and confusion.

I have read dozens of books and articles on this subject over the past two or three decades, trying to come to some solid conclusion about which view correctly captures God's heart and Word on the matter. Almost everything I read, whether taking a stance on one side of the issue or the other, came from sincere believers searching for truth. I was impressed by the writers' efforts to make sure the church walks out compliance to the Word. This is the right heart posture for every believer—to grasp the truth and live in obedience to the Word as a sign of our love and respect for the Savior who reconciled us to God. Even so, I still lacked the solid, cohesive thought I needed to be able to operate from a posture of faith—in one direction or the other.

While in prayer one morning this past January, I felt the Lord's burden and urgency for His daughters. Specifically, the Lord turned my attention to the many women's conferences that will be taking place this year. I thought of the women who would be attending these gatherings, many struggling with the double-mindedness I, too, experienced. While these conferences serve a wonderful purpose and provide a time for connecting with other like-minded believers, my heart longed to see these women empowered with a ready defense when they returned home. After being invigorated by the messages and *koinonia* experienced at the conferences, these women would need to remain on fire without wavering in their conviction when back in their local communities.

The burden to see women and the church freed from instability on the issue of women in ministry intensified. I wondered what I could possibly do to help free women from double-mindedness and lack of conviction on this issue. 'Lord, what can I do? I still have questions myself.'

'You give them something to eat.' When the disciples saw the vast crowd in need of something to eat, Jesus gave this directive. His request dumbfounded the disciples because they had little more than nothing. I found myself in the same position. All I had was incomplete understanding, a bunch of disconnected thoughts, and a handful of Bible verses—hardly enough to bring cohesion to a controversial topic that needs stability.

In obedience, I sat at the computer to write. Each day that I sat before the Lord to learn from Him, I found greater revelation in the Word on this issue than I could have imagined beforehand. What started out to be a ten- to twenty-page article expanded into the book you hold in your hands. I discovered that my former allegiance with the complementarian view was only partly correct in a limited context—the husband-wife relationship. I now have conviction that God is no respecter of persons when it comes to the many different believers who make up the body of Christ. Neither my nor anyone else's opinion about and preferences for leadership matter to God. He will send whomever He wills.

Acknowledgments

I am indebted to Dr. Gary L. Nebeker, Professor of Theology at Grace University in Omaha, Nebraska. His article on preunderstandings, which I have referenced throughout the book, provoked me in a profound way. Meditating on his work allowed the Holy Spirit to open a window in my mind that somehow empowered me to write what is contained in this book.

I also want to thank J. Lee Grady, Craig Keener, Catherine Kroeger, Cindy Jacobs, Susanna Krizo, Wade Burleson, Loren Cunningham, David Hamilton, Gilbert Bilezikian, and a host of other authors who dared to confront tradition. They have functioned as forerunners who have opened the door for the church to experience the oneness that burned in the heart of Jesus as He prayed for His followers before going to Gethsemane. The *koinonia* for which Jesus and the apostles prayed can only manifest when believers are of one mind and heart, each doing his or her part to build up the body so we can reach unity and maturity.

My sister Patti, Th.M. (and currently finishing work for her Ph.D.), took time out of her busy schedule to help with the first four chapters of the manuscript. Her contributions and suggestions were targeted and thoughtful—very much appreciated. She is an amazing and brilliant woman and I love her dearly.

My husband, Max, not only helped with the manuscript by proofing and giving excellent suggestions, he very patiently waited as I focused my time and energy in writing this book—stacks of books and papers everywhere, talking to myself, forgetting to buy bread and other necessary items, laundry in heaps, hogging the computer, constantly asking, 'What day is it, anyway?' The kids have all been great as well. Christy donated her graphic arts talent to help with the cover and document preparation. At her young age, she has already learned what it means to work through frustration. Everyone contributed by keeping the house running smoothly, providing many laughs along the way, and waiting patiently for a turn at the computer (usually not until my eyes started burning and I could no longer work). I love them all—I am truly blessed.

I cannot fail to thank my friends Agatha Dawson, Nancy Berg, and Pastors Gaylord and Sharon Lemke. These are long-distance friends that I rarely see. I have lately been so preoccupied that I have had very few conversations with any of them. But I know these are eternal friends. We pray for each other, and when we do reconnect, we always just pick up where we left off. Just reading their names fills me with affection—I really love and cherish these people.

I apologize if I have forgotten anyone. I have read so much that oftentimes another author's ideas become so entrenched in my own spiritual thought that I've lost track of where the ideas originated. This is completely unintentional. I have endeavored to give credit where credit is due, but hope the reader will allow me grace for those thoughts that may have originated elsewhere but which have not been footnoted to designate this.

Closing Remarks

Many women are currently suffering not only with double-mindedness on this issue, but with the restrictions and censorship some in the church have placed on them. When one part suffers, the whole body suffers. We need to move forward with clarity and with every member honored, recognized, and set at liberty to run unhindered the race specifically marked out for them.

It is my hope and prayer that what is written here will take us one step closer to the unity Jesus prayed for as we release every member to do what God has called them to do.

Until the King returns,

Kathy Taylor

Chapter 1

Musings from the Pew

> *Indeed, God has put the body together in such a way that he gives greater dignity to the parts that lack it, so that there will be no disagreements within the body, but rather* **all the parts will be equally concerned for all the others. Thus if one part suffers, all the parts suffer with it**; *and if one part is honored, all the parts share its happiness.* 1 Cor. 12:24b-26, CJB

Many women in the church are currently suffering with uncertainty about their role in the body of Christ. Double-mindedness on the issue of women in ministry causes them to be unsure or hesitant about their callings, or worse, to abandon a calling that contradicts their church's accepted parameters. Lack of solid understanding on certain portions of Scripture clouds our ability to discern the direction the Holy Spirit desires to impart.

I would like to share a few lines from a sermon I heard in a church we attended. The pastor is a man who loves the Lord and has unswerving loyalty to God's Word. He also has genuine concern for the lost and the welfare of those he shepherds. I want you to understand this at the beginning because I am using some of his teaching to demonstrate doctrine in the church that places women in the position to experience confusion regarding their callings and giftings in the church; teaching that prevents women from being resolute in running the race God has ordained for them; teaching that brings wavering between steadfast zeal toward a specific goal and ambivalent indecision leading to spiritual inertia. The result is that many women suffer, giving up purpose and vision to accept silent mediocrity and chains.

The pastor who gave this teaching did not have this intent—he was merely trying to remain true to the Word as he understood it. But we can unintentionally hurt the ones we serve by having incomplete or faulty understanding on this or any other biblical issue.

Jesus came to set the captives free. He also told us to ask the Lord of the harvest to send laborers into His harvest field. What if the Lord sent an army of women laborers for this purpose, as He has in many mission fields and underground churches abroad in our day? The present day Western church is stuck in a mindset that not only rejects the laborers God sends but also causes division and an anemic state. The body of Christ needs to have unity of mind on this issue so we can move forward. Pastors, leaders, and those who have a voice must energetically exert themselves to wake up the sleepers because when the harvest comes in, the church will need all the help she can get.

The hour has already come for us to shake off slumber (Rom. 13:11). When driven by love and divine purpose with the zeal of the Lord blazing within, we will operate as David did (Psalm 132:4-5): *"I will not give sleep to my eyes or slumber to my eyelids until I find a place for the* LORD, *a dwelling place for the Mighty One of Jacob."* Having clarity on the issue of women's roles in the church will free God's daughters from hesitation. They will be able to hear with no misgivings the voice of the Holy Spirit, calling them to run the race *God* has ordained for them.

> *[F]or the **light makes everything visible**. This is why it is said, "**Awake, O sleeper**, rise up from the dead, and **Christ will give you light**." So **be careful how you live**. Don't live like fools, but like those who are wise. **Make the most of every opportunity** in these evil days. Don't act thoughtlessly, but <u>**understand what the Lord wants you to do**</u>*. Eph. 5:13b-17, NLT

The Sermon

The pastor began his informal midweek adult Bible class on the subject of husbands and wives. *"Husbands, likewise, dwell with them with understanding, giving honor to the wife, as to the weaker vessel, and as being heirs together of the grace of life, that your prayers may not be hindered."* (1 Pet. 3:7)

He continued, 'Why are women weaker? He's not talking physically here, but Peter is referring to her weak emotional nature. Men are more decisive, which gives them the edge as leaders. Decisions are to be made by the husband, because women are more easily deceived, as we learned from Eve.' A widow raised her hand. 'What about someone like me?' The pastor replied, 'This doesn't apply to single women...'

I drifted off in thought to the natural conclusion. When women get married, their brains become impaired by emotions and they are no longer capable of making a quality decision. Wow. I married a man and now I am an idiot. But absurd conclusions aside, we have to conclude there must be more to this than meets the eye. I thought of all the women believers who are currently suffering in this same cloud of confusion, struggling to understand how they really fit in the body of Christ. 'When one part suffers, the whole body suffers.'

Asthenes

Asthenes (Grk. 772), the word Peter used to describe women in the passage discussed in the Bible class, means 'without strength.' Spiros Zodhiates, Th.D., a Greek scholar and author, wrote, "In Classical Greek [it is] never used with the meaning of moral weakness, but only in a physical sense, weak, powerless, without ability."[1] In the Bible, we see it used in reference to man's weak nature (Mark 14:38; Rom. 6:19), weak conscience/faith (Rom. 14:1-2; 15:1; 1 Cor. 8:7-12), weak discernment (Rom. 8:26), weakness financially (Acts 20:35), weak health/infirmity (Matt. 25:44; Acts 5:15; 1 Cor. 11:30), inability to save himself (Rom. 5:6), and weak understanding (implied, Heb. 5:2).

These uses speak of humanity in general, neither singling out men or women as the weaker in these areas. If one is adamant that the personal pronoun 'him' means men and excludes women, then only men have weak consciences in 1 Cor. 8:7-10 (cf. also Mark 14:38, spoken only to the disciples). It seems obvious, however, that ascribing gender is not the authorial intent in these passages.

While *asthenes* is used in various applications in the NT, the use in 1 Peter 3:7 clearly imparts its most common use, since it is a well known fact that as a whole men are physically stronger than women. To assume it implies anything else would initiate a never-ending debate, something the apostles warned against repeatedly. In several of our English translations, the word has actually been translated to show this:

- "... honoring the woman as [physically] the weaker..." (AMP)
- "Although your wife may be weaker physically..." (CJB)
- "... she isn't as strong as you are..." (CEV)
- "... since they are ·weaker than you [the weaker sex; *or* the less empowered one; the weaker vessel; women are typically physically weaker, but in Greco-Roman and Jewish society, they also had less power and authority]." (EXB)
- "... honouring them as physically weaker..." (PHILLIPS)

So why would a pastor read *'emotional'* weakness into the text? I thought of King Xerxes and the little tension he had with Queen Vashti (see Esther 1 if you are unfamiliar with the story).

The Way It Has Always Been

In the first chapter of the book of Esther, we see a king and his advisor plotting to prevent the loss of their long held cultural tradition of absolute authority over their wives. When Queen Vashti defied her husband by not responding to his request, the king and his advisor sought to prevent the whole kingdom from collapsing by the ripple effect this would cause. "There will be no end of disrespect and discord (v. 18)."

> *"Then when the king's edict is **proclaimed throughout all his vast realm**, all the **women will respect their husbands**, from the least to the greatest." The king and his nobles were pleased with this advice, so the king did as Memukan proposed. He sent dispatches to all parts of the kingdom, to each province in its own script and **to each people in their own language**, proclaiming that **every man should be ruler over his own household**, using his native tongue. Est. 1:20-22, NIV*

I learned that this concern was not without its valid points, though the magnitude of the effect seems based more on paranoia than on reality in this case. Patriarchal governments, particularly those exercising absolute control, are sustained by prescribed gender roles in order for the socioeconomic machine to run smoothly. If patriarchal authority collapsed within the household, the socioeconomic structure of a likewise patriarchal government could potentially erode simultaneously. This threat of gender role erosion, perhaps including the prospect of being the 'weak link' responsible for loss of power, incited the king and his advisor to take extraordinary measures for its prevention.

This Persian cultural tradition was enforced not only in Persia, but in every nation they had conquered—a law to enforce respect in order to maintain control. This mindset continues to this day, whether blatant and practiced openly or subtle and only inwardly discerned.

Quest to Know God's Truth

Solomon instructs us to seek wisdom and understanding as precious above all else (Prov. 2). He admonishes the reader to 'search for it as for hidden treasure' (v. 4). By describing wisdom as hidden, Solomon points out that we only find wisdom as we plumb the depths of God's Word by the illumination of the Holy Spirit. Taking the Bible at only face value will not yield this hidden wisdom. Memorizing passages of Scripture without understanding the meaning the Lord desires to impart will benefit us far less until such time that we gain deeper understanding. Mysteries can only be known and understood through revelation by God in His timing to humble students of the Word.

> *It is the **glory of God to conceal** things, but the **glory of kings is to search** things out.* Prov. 25:2, ESV

Paul spoke of God's hidden wisdom given to the mature (1 Cor. 2:6-16). Wisdom and understanding do not come to us automatically just because we are believers or because we have read the Bible. Similar to children who must be trained to think and behave properly, so also believers need to be trained in the ways and mind of God. Our thoughts are not His thoughts. We have been given the Word, the Holy Spirit, prayer, and the community of believers to help us in our quest to mature and understand truth (John 16:13; 2 Tim. 3:15-17; James 1:5).

There is also the matter of God's revelation of mysteries at the appointed time. Prophesying of Christ, Asaph foretold that the Messiah would 'utter hidden things' (Psalm 78:2). God spoke through Isaiah, stating He would 'tell new things that were once hidden and unknown' (Isa. 48:6b). The prophet Daniel explained that God alone 'reveals deep and hidden things' (Dan. 2:22).

Jesus reminds us that God hides things from those who think themselves wise or learned and reveals them to those who are not (Matt. 11:25). Some of the things Jesus taught were hidden even from the disciples (Luke 9:45; 18:34). Paul spoke of the mystery of Christ, which had been 'hidden for long ages past' (Rom. 16:25).

Paul also stated that God hides mysteries because they are destined to be revealed at specific times for God's preordained purposes (1 Cor. 2:7; Eph. 3:9-11). Paul reminds us that the riches of complete understanding, wisdom, and knowledge are hidden in Christ, who John called the Word (Col. 2:2-23; John 1:1,14). The apostle also stated that in this age, we only know and understand in part (1 Cor. 13:9-12).

These hidden treasures do not only pertain to the revelation of Christ. After the Messiah had been revealed through His death, resurrection, and ascension, and after the outpouring of the Holy Spirit at Pentecost had taken place, John recorded Jesus' words to the church at Pergamum. This fact is important, because it reveals that there are still hidden things to be learned.

Jesus rebuked this church for tolerating immorality and eating food sacrificed to idols, two of the four injunctions the Jerusalem council determined all believers are to uphold (Acts 15). They also followed the teaching of the Nicolaitans, the content of that teaching remaining open for debate. Many believe this teaching pertained to the oppression of the people through a dominating/hierarchical leadership model based on the Greek word roots *nikos* (Grk. 3534; victorious conqueror) and *laos* (Grk. 2992; the people).

Jesus made the following promise to those who turned from sin and error. The 'hidden manna' in the following passage can be understood as the treasure hidden in God's Word that has not yet been revealed. Jesus is the Word (John 1:14) and the manna from heaven (John 6:35-59). Hence, we can conclude that the manna from heaven provides knowledge and understanding of the treasure hidden in God's Word.

> *Whoever has ears, let them hear what the Spirit says to the churches. To the one who is victorious, I will give some of the* **hidden manna**. Rev. 2:17a, NIV

There is still hidden manna to be discovered in God's Word. From these passages, we have an idea of the conditions for obtaining this wisdom. God reveals the treasure hidden in His Word:

- to those who diligently seek it
- to the humble, not those who think highly of themselves, their education, and their accomplishments
- to those who turn from sin and error
- in His timing and for His purposes

Seek Wisdom

In the second chapter of Proverbs, Solomon urges us to seek God's wisdom diligently throughout our lives. Only *then* would we understand the fear of the Lord and find the knowledge of God (v. 5). Wisdom from God is the only means we have to 'understand what is right and just' (v. 9). God's wisdom delights our soul and guards us from error (vv. 10-11). Solomon exhorts us to:

1. accept the Word and store it in our hearts (v. 1)
2. turn our ears to wisdom (v. 2)
3. apply our hearts to understand (v. 2)
4. ask for insight (v. 3)
5. cry aloud for understanding (v. 3)
6. look for it as something more precious than earthly wealth (v. 4)
7. search for it as for hidden treasure (v. 4)

> *For **the Lord gives wisdom**; from his mouth come **knowledge and understanding**. He holds **success in store for the upright**, he is a **shield to those whose walk is blameless**, for he **guards the course of the just** and **protects the way of his faithful** ones.*
> Prov. 2:10-11, NIV

Wisdom, righteousness, and justice are inherent in God's nature and linked with God's protection and guidance (success). God desires that His children reflect His nature in these three traits—**wisdom, righteousness, justice**—by asking and searching for wisdom, putting on the righteousness of Christ, and renewing our minds and walking humbly before Him so that we will love mercy and do justly (Mic. 6:8). Remember this, as it is key for later discussion.

As believers pursue knowing, understanding, and living the Truth, they must at some point examine whether they have the resolve to persevere. This pursuit may entail replacing or tweaking cherished and long-held beliefs and practices when faced with eternal, unshakeable truth that may subvert established paradigms or worldview. Dr. Gary Nebeker, Ph.D., Professor of Theology at Grace University, wrote, "[W]e must hold the Scripture to be true and seek to understand it rather than conforming the Scripture to our understanding or preunderstandings."[2] *Selah.*

Renewing the Mind Includes Turning from Error

In His grace, God does not want us to remain mired in sin and error. He will do whatever it takes to let His children know if they have stepped onto the path leading to destruction, or that they have been thinking in a way contrary to His order and truth. This may come as the gentle conviction of the Holy Spirit as we read the Word or hear a sermon, or as the counsel of a close friend or someone we look to for guidance. If we dismiss these channels, the Lord may try to get our attention in a dream or vision. He may send a complete stranger with a prophetic word. Stronger still are judgments sent to discipline us and dire circumstances to get our attention (see Job 33:14ff).

> **Trust in the LORD** with all your heart and **lean not on your own understanding**; in all your ways **submit to him**, and he will make your paths straight. **Do not be wise in your own eyes**. Prov. 3:5-7a, NIV

True believers are primarily interested in conforming to what the Word describes as truth rather than seeking to find passages of Scripture that justify their worldview. Yet no matter how hard we try, some ideology reversal takes a long time to accept. It is easier and requires less effort to establish a quick foundation from which to operate and to keep that foundation no matter if we later discover it is counter to Scripture.

Many believers are unaware of the baggage permeating their worldview. This worldview creates a subconscious grid or filter that affects interpretation of Scripture. Every believer approaches Scripture colored by his or her particular context. The unsettling point at play in hermeneutics (principles of interpretation) is epistemology—

unpacking and bringing to self-awareness what we know, how we know it, and how what we know affects how we approach Scripture.

What we discover in the process of 'unpacking our preunderstandings' are then the presuppositions that color our understanding of any particular text. Once we grasp this concept, we become more deeply aware of our limitations, which should provoke growing humility and the acknowledgment that we are flawed and can be shortsighted in our understanding of what the Bible teaches. Safeguards from error of this kind include spiritual discernment and the thoughtful evaluation of the corporate church (cf. 1 Cor. 14:29).

Why I Wrote This Book

It is not the purpose of this book to address the husband-wife relationship, though it will be briefly discussed in chapter five. Nor was this book written to reinvent the wheel by repeating what has already been written on the widely debated subject of men's and women's roles in the church. Merely rehashing the debate in which most believers have already taken sides would serve little purpose. I am writing to serve those in my circle of influence—my children, my family, my friends, and the believing women I encounter who are in need of answers and don't have the time or resources to research this topic.

The primary 'proof texts' used so often to determine how we govern our churches will be compared to the whole of Scripture. This must entail grammatical-historical context if we are to reconcile the lack of congruency these passages pose with Scripture as a whole. This is what Solomon meant by searching for hidden treasure. Even the disciples, who took Jesus' words literally on many occasions when Jesus meant something completely different (e.g., Matt. 16:11; Mark 8:17), had to learn the deeper truths concealed in the words Jesus spoke.

We will look briefly at some of the examples of women given in the Word for our edification and instruction (1 Cor. 10:11).

> *(All)Scripture is God-breathed and is <u>useful for teaching</u>, rebuking, correcting and training in righteousness, so that the servant of God may be **thoroughly equipped for every good work**.*
> 2 Tim. 3:16-17, NIV

> For ⟨everything⟩ that was written in the past was **written to teach us**... Rom. 15:4a, NIV

I am immediately reminded of Loren Cunningham's (co-founder of YWAM with his wife, Darlene) statement that at least 886 verses in the Bible came through women.[3] According to Paul's own testimony, these verses are there to **teach**, reprove, correct, and train in order to equip believers for their work. Paul reminds us that *everything* recorded in the past in the Word is written to **teach** us.

The recorded words and actions of these ancient heroines are included in the Word to *teach* us, an activity part of the current day church does not allow women to do. We must keep this in mind if we are to come to any cohesive conclusion about the intended meaning of those controversial passages in Paul's letters and what they were meant to teach us about church governance and leadership.

Our study will first examine how God gets our attention to show us that we have strayed from the truth. From there we will go deeper in our discussion of preunderstandings, followed by an overview of God's original intent for men and women. Next, we will take a quick tour of biblical examples of women and the roles in which they were called to function. After this foundational survey, we will then have a closer look at the two most widely used passages in the Bible to teach that women are to remain silent in the church, neither teaching nor operating in any leadership capacity.

This may seem like a circuitous route to get to our goal of understanding two controversial passages, but I believe this is the strategy of the Lord to erect a stable and sure foundation. When building a case, an attorney will often pull together seemingly unrelated testimony to establish a convincing argument. In the end, the relevance of each testimony and piece of evidence can finally be understood in light of the attorney's blueprint or plan to reach a stated objective.

In other words, the relevance becomes apparent when the attorney ties all the evidence and testimony together to make his or her closing argument. I pray that we will hear what the Spirit is saying to the church, grow in our understanding of God's Word, and love His truth more than our own views, reputation, or love of tradition.

***The unfolding of your words gives light**; it gives understanding to the simple... **Give me understanding**, so that I may keep your law and obey it with all my heart... May my cry come before you, Lord; **give me understanding <u>according to your word</u>**.*
Psalm 119:130,34,169, NIV

Chapter 2

Leprosy on the Wall

> *[E]ach one should build with care... If anyone builds on this foundation using gold, silver, costly stones, wood, hay or straw, their work will be shown for what it is, because the Day will bring it to light. It will be **revealed with fire**, and **the fire will test the quality of each person's work**. If what has been built survives, the builder will receive a reward. If it is burned up, the builder will suffer loss but yet will be saved—even though only as one escaping through the flames.* 1 Cor. 3:10b,12-15, NIV

Believers must diligently search the Bible to see if what they have been taught is found in the Word. This enables us to build on our foundation with something precious and eternal. If we give a denomination, pastor, or teacher carte blanche authority, believing all they say without question, we display laziness and indifference to the Word and Spirit of God. If these truly mattered to us, we would search the Scriptures diligently to verify teaching, as the noble Berean Jews did (Acts 17:11).

For those who have precious little time to do this on their own, the Holy Spirit will often lead us to just the right people, message, or written materials that will help us in our quest to know Truth. We only need to ask in faith and be sober and watchful for the answer.

Some believers are more introspective; they may hear a series of sermons and then require some time away from the church to consider what they've heard. Extroverted church leaders often misunderstand their introverted brothers and sisters in this regard. I have heard many leaders, for whom I have a great deal of respect, caution against isolation for even short periods. In most cases this is wise, especially for newer converts still in the process of training a weak will or awakening a seared conscience to truth.

In other instances, however, this injunction grates against the inclination of those believers who seek solitude away from the noise of typical church life in order to hear God's voice as they seek to understand the Word in all its depth. We have the examples of Elijah, John the Baptist, and other prophets who spent a good deal of time away from the crowd. Leaders should guard themselves from being too critical of these believers. For the introvert, church activities can, at times, hinder their faith and relationship with the Lord rather than make it grow.

Research has documented that while people in the West prefer the human dynamism of extroverted, charismatic leaders, it also demonstrates in study after study that extroverts make more mistakes than introverts. They are not less intelligent—just less careful. They will spend less time trying to figure out how all the pieces of a puzzle fit together in favor of just going with one stance or another so they can move on. Extroverts are the risk takers.

Introverted believers are very uncomfortable with this. They are compelled to see how every piece fits. Famous introverts include Albert Einstein, Sir Isaac Newton, and (arguably) Abraham Lincoln.[4] We need to guard ourselves from offense if the Lord works differently in the lives of these introverted believers. The church should not demand that they join in everything and be visible at all times like their extroverted counterparts. God designed the different temperaments for His purpose and pleasure. Pastors should not expect their congregants to express their faith as a carbon copy of the leadership.

[Note: Introversion does not necessarily mean shy and/or unsociable. Many introverts are very sociable, but require more down time than extroverts to process and link all the information received. Generally, introverts like to see all details in their proper place.]

Current State of the Church

The Barna Group conducted a study on younger believers' faith issues. "When asked what has helped their faith grow, 'church' does not make even the top 10 factors. Instead, the most common drivers of spiritual growth, as identified by Millennials themselves, are prayer, family and friends, the Bible, having children, and their relationship with Jesus."[5]

I personally know several individuals, couples, and families who spent a season away from church. They continued to flourish in their faith among the people they knew and through concentrated time in Bible study and prayer. One young woman, who has a vibrant faith and reads the Word regularly, stated, 'It bothers me to hear a pastor proclaim his version of truth, ridiculing those who believe differently, when I know Bible verses that state otherwise.' Most Christians have been taught to follow their church leaders *faithfully* but not necessarily *thoughtfully*.

Pastors are not always faithful in equipping their congregants with the necessary interpretive tools for studying the Bible on their own. Their focus typically turns to doctrinal prescriptions and absolutisms, often based on what they were taught in seminary. Pastoral humility, demonstrated by allowing those who listen to carefully weigh what is said and give feedback, is sometimes lacking. Pastoral leadership tends to prefer tighter control in the arenas of teaching and authority. This can open the door to corruption, vainglory, and a domineering control over those who come every week to be spoon-fed.

Some pastors believe that if someone leaves their church, that individual will eventually be lost or slip into error. Pastors often equate leaving their church with leaving God. In some cases, this may be true. In others, however, nothing could be further from the truth. One comedian commented, "Every day, people are straying away from the church and going back to God."[6]

This incitement to fear of consequences may be viewed as a misuse of ecclesial power and thus devolves into a form of pastoral self-idolatry. It is a negation of Romans 8:38-39 that states that nothing can separate us from the love of God, not even powers or principalities. The hierarchical church is seen by some as holding the power of salvation rather than understanding that the Holy Spirit empowers the priesthood of all believers. Sadly, pastoral judgments that provoke this type of fear may have underlying financial aspects in some cases.

With so many leaving the church in the past decade, though not necessarily forsaking their faith, should we not consider that this might be 'leprosy on the wall,' sent there to get our attention?

Levitical Law: Spiritual Truth for Our Day

The Lord implanted corollaries of spiritual truth in Levitical law. Paul used the laws about oxen to teach that we are to support those who labor on our behalf (1 Cor. 9:9-11). Many Levitical laws were written as object lessons for gathering wisdom about living righteously and justly.

One section of Levitical law provides a procedure for cleansing a dwelling defiled by mold. The KJV translated this defiling mold as a 'plague of leprosy' (Lev. 14:33-53). The Bible uses mold and leprosy metaphorically as surface indicators that something has brought contamination. These visual anomalies grab our attention and cause alarm, provoking us to seek out the cause. Mold and leprosy metaphorically indicate the presence of sin, error, or pollution from the world and its ways. Whatever the case, it is a call to prayer for discernment as well as action to remedy the issue. I will use the two metaphors interchangeably in keeping with the two terms translators have chosen for this passage.

The steps required in this procedure establish the spiritual precedent for the action we are to take when we discover that some of the stones in our spiritual dwellings have acquired a 'defiling or spreading mold.' Paul warned us to be careful about the way we build on the foundation we have received. Error or sin can creep in, and the convicting power of the Word and the Spirit alerts us to its presence, described in this passage as mold or leprosy. This conviction may come as a vague uneasiness with a doctrine we hold or confusion when someone teaches something different from what we see in the Word. It could also indicate the presence of hidden corporate or personal sin.

When we read the Word of God, we must keep in mind that the Spirit of God will inform us at the spiritual level which underlying aspect of the poetic metaphors used in a passage He currently wants to emphasize. This demonstrates the dynamic nature of the Word, though caution must be exercised to prevent overstepping the limits of any metaphor. The mold-leprosy metaphor can point to sin (personal or corporate) or reveal error in our thinking, whether erroneous personal views or corporate doctrine out of synch with the mind and heart of God. It could also represent pollution from the world. The Lord will speak to us at the heart level whether He is pointing to personal or corporate issues.

I want to be clear on this issue of defining the mold-leprosy metaphor in this passage. The use is not a case of 'either-or' but of 'both-and.' There are issues of pollution from the world as well as sin and error in the church, on both corporate and personal levels. Understanding that the Word of God is living and requires the Spirit of God to breathe life into the words specific to our situation allows us to understand spiritual metaphors more fluidly, rather than adopt only one specific nuance for rigid adherence.

God Puts Mold on the Wall

Notice in the following passage that the Lord Himself puts the mold in the house. He is letting us know that something is not kosher. When we first notice the mold, our next action is to let the priest know. Under the new covenant, Jesus is our High Priest interceding on our behalf. He inspects our spiritual house, observing the defiled area:

> *The LORD said to Moses and Aaron, "When you enter the land of Canaan, which I am giving you as your possession,* **and I put a spreading mold in a house** *in that land, the* **owner of the house must go and tell the priest,** *'I have seen something that looks like a defiling mold in my house.'* **The priest is to order the house to be emptied** *before he goes in to examine the mold, so that nothing in the house will be pronounced unclean.* **After this the priest is to go in and inspect the house**.*"* Lev. 14:33-36, NIV

Note that the house must be emptied first so nothing else will be pronounced unclean. For our discussion, consider the possibility that the Lord may be removing at least some of the people from our churches to keep these believers from being defiled by error, the pollution of worldliness, or corporate sin.

In a present day context, our first step is to come to the Lord in humility, asking for wisdom and understanding (see also Eph. 1:17; Col. 1:9). This opens the door for the Holy Spirit to work on our mind and heart, granting us wisdom to understand and conviction where needed.

> *If any of you* **lacks wisdom, you should ask God***, who* **gives generously to all** *without finding fault, and it will be given to you.* James 1:5, NIV

> ***The one who gets wisdom loves life;*** *the one who cherishes understanding will soon prosper.* Prov. 19:8, NIV

The second step is to isolate the mold so that it doesn't spread:

> *He is to **examine the mold** on the walls, and if it has greenish or reddish depressions that appear to be **deeper than the surface** of the wall, the priest shall go out the doorway of the house and **close it up for seven days**.* Lev. 14:37-38, NIV

The priest inspects the mold to determine whether it is more than surface deep. The spiritual correlation points to defilement that is entrenched, whether representing false knowledge about God, pollution from the world and its ways, or ingrained personal or corporate sin. Repentance means 'to turn' (Heb. 7725 *shuv*: to turn back, turn around, return). This encompasses issues of the human condition that require turning in order to embrace God: 1.) turning or changing our mind when our thinking and religious dogma do not line up with God's Word, 2.) changing our behavior when confronted with sin, and 3.) recognizing and removing worldly influences and practices.

Entrenched Mold

If the mold is deeper than the surface, the priest seals up the house for seven days. This is the same number of days Miriam was isolated outside the camp in the wilderness when she contracted leprosy by the hand of God for her rebellion (Num. 12). This gave her time to reflect and repent. This is a picture of taking time to seek the Lord in prayer and meditation on the Word by shutting ourselves in and sincerely seeking to hear the Holy Spirit's instruction for conviction and repentance.

The number seven is often representative of completion, for example, the seven days of creation. Spiritually applied, during the 'seven' (figurative) days the house is sealed, the Lord draws us to seek God's heart and the truth in His Word as illuminated by His Holy Spirit (1 Cor. 2:6-16). Jesus described this as space or time to repent (Rev. 2:21). Understanding and revelation are available only to true believers because they have been given the mind of Christ (1 Cor. 2:16b).

When the grace period expires, the second inspection takes place. Either the mold has spread or it has begun to turn back. If we are turning our hearts from sin, our minds from error, and our desires from the lure and entrapments of the world, the 'mold' will begin to abate and the priest will perform the cleansing ritual.

> But if the priest comes to examine it and **the mold has not spread** after the house has been plastered, he shall pronounce the house clean, because the defiling mold is gone. **To purify the house** he is to take **two birds** and some **cedar wood, scarlet yarn** and **hyssop**. He shall **kill one of the birds over fresh water** in a clay pot. Then he is to take the cedar wood, the hyssop, the scarlet yarn and the live bird, **dip them into the blood of the dead bird** and the **fresh water**, and **sprinkle the house seven times**. He shall purify the house with the bird's blood, the fresh water, the live bird, the cedar wood, the hyssop and the scarlet yarn. Then he is to **release the live bird** in the open fields outside the town. **In this way he will make atonement for the house, and it will be clean**. Lev. 14:48-53, NIV

Once again, we see the number seven used for completion. This procedure is not a magical ritual. The physical elements involved speak of:

- **Jesus' atoning work on the cross to bring eternal life** (hyssop, scarlet yarn, bird that was killed, dipping the live bird, cedar)
- **the work of the Holy Spirit to illuminate and set us free from error and sin as well as cleanse our conscience from guilt** (water, hyssop, the bird released)
- **the washing of the water of the Word to cleanse our minds from worldly thoughts by replacing error with truth** (hyssop, water, cedar, the sprinkled blood)
- **the eternal nature of God's loving kindness, grace, and mercy toward us** (cedar, the bird released)
- **our own repentance or turning from what caused the mold** (receiving the sprinkling of the combined elements, the bird that was dipped in the killed bird's blood and freed)

If the Mold Spreads

If God has pointed out that we are on the wrong path but we continue on it without heeding the Spirit's invitation to turn away, the mold will spread. This indicates the presence of deeper and not just surface mold. Roadblocks to true repentance and gaining spiritual understanding include pride, indifference, fear of reprisal, clinging to doctrinal error or tradition because we like it or are comforted by it, subconscious biased preunderstandings, love for the world and its ways, fear of man or desire for man's approval, and unwillingness to relinquish personal sin that we enjoy or from which we derive some benefit. Refusing to relinquish sin or stubbornly clinging to doctrinal error or the world's ways once the issue has been made known results in stricter measures.

> On the seventh day the priest shall return to inspect the house. **If the mold has spread** on the walls, he is to order that **the contaminated stones be torn out and thrown into an unclean place** outside the town. He must have all the **inside walls of the house scraped** and the material that is scraped off dumped into an unclean place outside the town. Then they are to **take other stones to replace these and take new clay and plaster the house**. Lev. 14:39-42, NIV

The defiled stones and the plaster that covered the stones are removed. Our High Priest deals ruthlessly with the contamination. Remember, we must be careful how we build on the foundation we have been given. Building with stones permeated with our own traditional, cultural, educational, psychological, and experiential concepts of God, His Word, and His ways can prevent our spiritual house from being clean and pure before God.

When these issues are brought to our attention, we are to remove the contaminated stones and replace them with God's eternal truth. If we ignore the Holy Spirit on the matter before us, or if we only partially turn, hoping to cling to some of our own ways by creating a hybrid of truth and error, we increase the likelihood that the mold will resurface. This is serious and grievous before God, requiring that the house be torn down and thrown into an unclean place outside the camp.

> **If the defiling mold reappears** in the house after the stones have been torn out and the house scraped and plastered, the priest is to go and examine it and, if the mold has spread in the house, it is a **persistent defiling mold; the house is unclean.** It must be **torn down**—its stones, timbers and all the plaster—and **taken out of the town to an unclean place**. Lev. 14:43-45, NIV

A hybrid of truth and error poses a serious threat. Satan uses this same subtle strategy to lure believers off course. "Whatever is only almost true is quite false, and among the most dangerous of errors."[7]

Is Our House Defiled?

The spiritual house we are building impacts those around us. This is especially true for those in leadership. Paul exhorted Timothy:

> **Watch your life and doctrine closely.** *Persevere in them, because if you do, you will* **save both yourself and your hearers.** 1 Tim. 4:16, NIV

Levitical law declared unclean anyone who entered the defiled house, and those who slept or ate there had to wash their clothes (Lev. 14:46-47). This symbolically sums up the defilement believers can acquire in a church that does not preach sound doctrine or that patterns itself after the world. Consider carefully that teachers are subject to stricter accountability before God and risk the possibility of leading others astray (James 3:1). Jesus warned that some *Torah* experts were hindering seekers from entering the kingdom (Luke 11:52).

Many of these institutions will be 'torn down' by the grace and mercy of God to prevent the spread of error and defilement to Jesus' bride. They may not be physically torn down, but they may cease to bear fruit. Jesus will return for a bride without spot or wrinkle (Eph. 5:27). I need to add that just because a specific church is going through a season of molting or pruning does not necessarily mean it has been defiled or that its lamp stand has been removed. These seasons exist to prepare the church for new growth and fruit bearing in the next season, no matter how uncomely the church may look in the present. It may be a trial sent to test the steadfast faith of those who remain. Each community of believers must seek the Lord for discernment in their unique situation while those outside their particular community must guard themselves against a critical spirit.

Paul reminds us that those who stubbornly cling to error open themselves to the judgment of God (Rom. 2:5). In Proverbs, we are instructed to build and establish our houses with wisdom and understanding, filling the rooms with 'precious and beautiful treasures' (Prov. 24:3-4). Isaiah warned Israel that because they had no regard for God's work or deeds, they would go into exile because of their lack of understanding. Their leaders would go hungry and the common people would be 'parched with thirst' (Isa. 5:12b-13).

From these passages, we learn that the way in which we build our spiritual house matters to God and our own well-being. The Word instructs us to seek and discern God's will and specific direction, and especially to act on His conviction regarding sin and error. Being a leader requires diligently pursuing greater and deeper understanding of God and His ways as well as discerning the current spiritual season. If we ignore God's counsel and the direction given by the Spirit, we not only hinder 'the thirsty' but we invite God's judgment as well.

Paul cautions believers against discarding the discernment and conviction of the Holy Spirit regarding sin and error. Deception often comes through 'empty words,' whether words that excuse sin by preaching a false concept of grace or words that allow us to keep our comfortable worldview and opinions. In either case, disobeying the Spirit's conviction brings God's grief-induced wrath (Grk. 3709, *orge*; Eph. 5:6).

Jesus also warned, 'watch out that no one deceives you, for many false teachers will appear and deceive many' (Matt. 24:4,11; see also Col. 2:4; 2 Tim. 3:13). Zeal alone will not carry believers to the right end. Zeal without knowledge leads to ruin (Rom. 10:2), and the hasty will miss the right path (Prov. 19:2). Praying for discernment and waiting for the Lord's direction may not suit the timetable the impatient have made for themselves, but doing so will safeguard believers from deception and error. Remember, it is the 'glory of God to hide a matter, but is the glory of kings to search out a matter.' Searching out a matter often proves to be a lengthy, involved endeavor, requiring that we strain to hear the still small voice of the Spirit saying, 'This is the way, walk in it.'

Believers depend on the Holy Spirit for conviction as well as for revealing error and illuminating the treasure God wants them to discover concealed beneath the surface (cf. 1 John 2:27). We are exhorted to pay attention to our lives (1 John 1:8) and the things we believe, examining ourselves to see if we are still in the faith (2 Cor. 13:5).

> **But who can discern their own errors?...** *Save us and help us with your right hand, that those you love may be delivered.*
> Psalm 19:12; 60:5, NIV

Chapter 3

Preunderstandings

> *A person may think their own ways are right, but the Lord weighs the heart.* Prov. 21:2, NIV

In order to gain a deeper understanding of the concept of how preunderstandings can taint any believer's interpretation of Scripture, take the time to read Dr. Gary L. Nebeker's excellent online article, *"Who Packed Your Bags?": Factors That Influence Our Preunderstandings.*[8] Dr. Nebeker, Ph.D., is currently on the faculty of Grace University in Omaha, Nebraska. This article effectively summed up everything else I had researched on this subject. The basic premise of his teaching reminds us that 'our thoughts are not the same as God's, nor our ways like His ways' (Isa. 55:8).

In this article, Dr. Nebeker put forth a convincing case for the difficulty scholars face in their attempts to be purely exegetical when interpreting Scripture. Exegesis entails sticking to what the author of a passage desires to convey to the audience for which the message was originally intended, paying attention to the grammatical construction as well as the historical and cultural context of the day. Dr. Nebeker skillfully reasoned that this task is infiltrated by our own parameters of what makes sense based on our traditions (theological and otherwise), culture, personal life experiences, education, and psychological makeup.

The following thoughts have been directly quoted from his article (emphasis added; the lengthy article was not broken down into pages and therefore exact locations of these quotes are unavailable):

- [W]hile it is vigorously argued that Scripture is the embodiment of objective truth, at the same time, such objective truth requires an interpreter. The **interpreter, regardless of his spirituality and exegetical acumen, brings certain subjective apprehensions to the text.**

- **Without an awareness of theological biases**, there can even be **calamitous consequences in the practical outworking of our faith**. Hence, the interpreter needs to be a student not only of the Scriptures, but also as a student of his or her theological tradition.

- One lesson that **church history has taught us is that no Christian is immune to the cultural and social forces of our age**. Try as Christians scholars might to be separated from the sway of secular culture, we invariably are the products of our age. This is not always to the degree where Christianity is corrupted or compromised, but the culture and societies in which we find ourselves nonetheless inform our presentations and practice of truth.

- **Distanciation** entails a self-conscious distancing of the interpreter from his or her point of hermeneutical surveillance and, as such, **is an attempt to survey or understand the text as the biblical author might**. A fusion of hermeneutical horizons begins when the interpreter understands that **there are chronological, cultural, geographical, linguistic, and literary considerations that exist between himself and the biblical author**.

- [D.A.] Carson elaborates on the significance of distanciation as it relates to academic enterprise: "**Whenever we try to understand** *the thought of a text (or of another person, for that matter), if we are to understand it critically—that is,* **not in some arbitrary fashion, but with sound reasons**, *and* **as the author meant it in the first place**—*we must first of all grasp the nature and degree of the differences that separate our understanding from the understanding of the text. Only then can we profitably fuse our horizon of understanding with the horizon of understanding of the text—that is,* **only then can we begin to shape our thoughts by the thoughts of the text so that we truly understand them**. *Failure to go through the distanciation before the fusion usually means that there has been no real fusion:* **the interpreter <u>thinks</u> he knows what the text means, but all too often he or she has <u>simply imposed his own thoughts onto the text</u>**."

- [A] pastor who is concerned with transmitting biblical content that has relevance for the needs of his congregation may not see his aim as teaching his parishioners how to study the Bible critically. **Consequently, the layperson learns content, but is not taught to evaluate.** Within a local church context where the pastor assumes a majority of the preaching and teaching responsibilities, **a lay-person may develop an unswerving loyalty to a pastor's teachings without considering them critically.** Hence, hermeneutical distanciation with the layperson is necessarily controlled and confined. Perhaps this would be so to a lesser degree with the well-read layperson.

- (quoting Vern Poythress): *"We are not to be elitists who insist that everyone become a self-conscious scholar in reading the Bible...* ***We are not to despise laypeople's understanding of the Bible****... sometimes their conclusions may be a result of a synthesis of Bible knowledge due to the work of the Holy Spirit. Scholars cannot reject such a possibility without having achieved a profound synthetic and even practical knowledge of the Bible for themselves."*

- The late Robert McAfee Brown... has maintained that **experience grounds and places an interpreter within a particular viewing location** in life. Regarding one's perspective of reality, he concludes that:

    1. What we see is not necessarily what is there.
    2. What we see depends on where we are standing.
    3. When others tell us what they see, we need to know where they are standing as well as where we are standing.
    4. No matter how much anybody sees, nobody sees it all.
    5. What we see is always subject to correction.

    [Note: Dr. Nebeker points out that Brown's list is not without fault, but points to the overall legitimate nature of considering our own narrow perspective for what it is—limited.]

- As we turn our attention to the task of biblical interpretation, it is incumbent upon us to be **critical students of ourselves**. We must be alert to any elements of our tradition, experience, culture, society, education, and even **our own inner workings that can influence our acquired understandings that we all bring to the biblical text**.

- [Grant R.] Osborne writes, "*Preunderstanding only becomes negative if it degenerates into an a priori grid that determines the meaning of the text before the act of reading even begins*."... [T]here may be times when the interpreter **unconsciously reads his or her preunderstandings into the text**. As regards the professional scholar, this seems most likely to occur as a **consequence of cultural limitations** or other varieties of **distanciation blindness**.

- **Intellectual disturbance** that comes with learning should not come as a surprise. A sage of old once observed, "*For in much wisdom is much vexation, and those who increase knowledge increase sorrow*" (Eccl. 1:18 [NRSV]). Disruption within an educational context must serve the overall aim of building up one's systematized body of beliefs. This may mean that **some mistaken beliefs will be replaced with true beliefs**. Therefore, **intellectual disruption is not of necessity synonymous with destruction of one's beliefs**.

- [Leon] Festinger's proposal of "cognitive dissonance," **the mental conflict that occurs when beliefs or assumptions are contradicted by new information**... maintain[s] that the conflict that the new information provokes can be controlled several ways:
  1. one can **reject, explain away, or avoid** the new information;
  2. one can **persuade oneself that no conflict actually exists**; or
  3. one can attempt to **reconcile the differences** in a way that **preserves the stability or order in his or her worldview**.

Some theologians hastily jumped to the conclusion that the principle of preunderstanding creates a hermeneutic of relativism and is therefore anti-scholarship since it allows Scripture to be understood by the worldview and cherished traditions of the student; that it becomes a hermeneutic of current cultural thought and existential philosophy. This type of reactionary judgment misses the point. The commitment is not to relativism but to searching for truth, all the while cognizant of the inescapable fact that everyone has conscious and subconscious ideas that influence interpretation.

The normative preunderstandings of the dominant voices in biblical scholarship within any homogenous community of faith have commitments to extrabiblical thought and values that must be recognized and deconstructed. Humility comes from acknowledging one's limits rather than assuming the orthodoxy of one's position or opinions. Defending truth is admirable only when motivated by love undergirded with the humility that allows us to truly hear the viewpoints of other sincere students of the Word without transitioning into an angry debate.

This should make us less bullheaded when it comes to the more debatable points of Scripture, allowing others leeway and grace when their views do not match our own. The Lord Himself stated the world would know we are Christians by our love for each other, not our rancorous debate over who is right on certain doctrinal points not expressly made clear or cohesive when taken at face value in the biblical text. The humility in scholarship is that our work is never complete because we are incomplete people. We are people who see through a glass darkly. Those who come after us will critique, nuance, and continue our work. It is an ongoing process and perhaps, one might assert, an act of faith rather than certainty in some instances.

Understanding this gives hope, because Paul stated we need apostles, prophets, evangelists, pastors, and teachers to continually labor to move the church toward maturity and unity **in the knowledge of God**. As the church continues to build on the revelation of the previous generations, we come ever closer to the maturity and unity in the knowledge of God that has historically eluded the church. We stand on the shoulders of those who have gone before us. Whether we are that generation on whom the 'culmination of the ages has come' remains to be seen (cf. 1 Cor. 10:11). But I believe we are really, really close.

Homogenous Viewpoints vs. Multitude of Counselors

Extrapolated further, the points made by Robert McAfee Brown in the bulleted list alert us to the possible hazard of surrounding ourselves only with those who interpret the Bible precisely as we do. This practice may lead not only to shortsighted interpretations of Scripture, but foster elitism as well. The 'us four and no more' convention isolates believers from the wider body of Christ, encouraging divisiveness bordering on cultism in some cases. I don't think this is what the Lord had in mind.

Having lived in five states and taken part in several different congregations, from the older protestant denominations to charismatic non-denominational churches, and from Pentecostal assemblies to Messianic Jewish congregations, our family has experienced a broader continuum of theological thought than most believers have been exposed to. This could be viewed as church hopping if one has a critical bent, but it has served us in acquiring a 'multitude of counselors' (Prov. 11:14; 15:22; 24:6). If we only listen to those trained in our seminary brand and who preach only in our particular branch of Christianity, then we have limited our field of vision because we have selected for ourselves only those counselors standing in our immediate hermeneutical range (Brown's points 1-3).

This essentially confines our view to the teaching we have received and the doctrine with which we are comfortable in our particular Christian brand. Operating in this way constrains or marginalizes one of the checks and balances God has provided believers for staying true to the Word. We have the Bible, the Holy Spirit who will give us a witness or check in our spirit, and the corporate body of Christ where the ones who speak are to let the rest judge (1 Cor. 14:29). If we only surround ourselves with counselors who think as we do because they have the same training we have, we have eschewed wisdom in favor of homogeneity.

In some cases, especially where known heresy exists, it is unwise to consider other views without personal depth in the Word. There is a good deal of mixture in the various doctrines of the church, and it benefits us little to be exposed to these doctrines if our knowledge of

Scripture is so shallow that we cannot discern the difference between the holy and the common.

Paul counsels us to test everything and hold onto what is good (1 Thes. 5:21). Mutual dialogue with others should not bring division but grounded faith—even if we do not agree on every point. Cross-pollination is good for the body of Christ.

We have an object lesson from nature that I believe is worth consideration for the church. Without cross-pollination, most fruit trees will not bear fruit. When cross-pollination is insufficient, the result is small, malformed fruit. The fruit will have very few seeds for reproducing the plant and often falls from the tree before reaching maturity.[9]

I sincerely believe that without cross-pollination, spiritually isolated churches often produce little (if any) fruit and are prone to possess 'leaves only,' just as the fig tree Jesus cursed to be withered (Matt. 21:19). From science, we know leaves have the function of feeding the tree itself. In contrast, fruit has the function of reproducing the tree as well as providing food for passersby. One lesson we learn from the fig tree illustration is that a tree with only leaves to feed itself, with no evidence of accepting cross-pollination in order to bear fruit, is doomed to be judged for providing only for itself (Matt. 21:19). When Jesus returns to evaluate what we have done with the good deposit He has given us, He will be looking for fruit (Matt. 16:27; Rom. 2:6-9; Rev. 2:23b).

Blind Spots

As another object lesson illuminating our need to engage believers with different viewpoints, I would like you to consider an example from human anatomy. The human eye has an optic nerve that transmits messages to the brain. The place where this nerve exits the back of the eye has no light receptors to capture the images that land on it. The absence of receptors causes a blind spot. Dr. Eric H. Chudler, neuroscientist and Executive Director of the Center for Sensorimotor Neural Engineering in Seattle, Washington, has a great website with easy to understand explanations on a number of neuroscience topics for kids—great for homeschoolers. I have adapted the examples in this section from his website.[10]

As a test for this blind spot, hold the book about twenty inches away, cover your right eye, and look at the smiling face with your left eye. Then slowly bring your face closer to the book until the musical notes disappear from view. It is at this point that the image of the notes has landed on your blind spot. To test the right eye, cover your left eye, look at the music notes, and follow the same directions until the smiling face disappears from view.

There is another object lesson from the eye's blind spot that is appropriate for our discussion. Our brain demonstrates an adaptability phenomenon when there is a perceived gap in information. In the following example, cover your right eye and look at the stack of books with your left. Hold the book away from your face about two feet. Slowly bring the book closer to your face until the gap between the two lines disappears and it looks like one long line in your peripheral vision.

The following visual test is a variation of the brain's capacity for filling in information that is not there. Perform the same procedure as in the previous example, this time focusing your left eye on the letter while the right is covered. At the point where the area of missing data lands on your blind spot, the missing data in the center of the patterned box will be furnished by your brain.

These examples are illustrations of the cognitive, psychological, experiential, cultural, and spiritual blindness of which each believer must be aware in his or her quest to understand truth. Not only do we have blind spots, there are also times when we cannot perceive them because our brains may fill in the missing data with something that seems reasonable according to the pattern of thinking established by our personal worldview and traditions. This is where those observing from a different viewing point can help us notice our errors and assumptions. This describes the safety of a multitude of counselors who are viewing from different perspectives.

Part of the strategy of our enemy is to exploit these blind spots and prevent us from obtaining the light of wisdom and knowledge God desires to impart. As a result, we remain a divided and narrowly focused rabble rather than a unified, powerful, like-minded army of vision and purpose. Every moment we waste in disunity provides ground for our enemy to advance.

Closing Thoughts

A friend and former mentor once told me that if there had been an eleventh commandment, he believed it would have been, "Thou shalt not deceive thyself." As I read Dr. Nebeker's article, I reflected on the points made and how obviously difficult the task of objective interpretation becomes. The mental and psychological baggage we carry may blind us to the dichotomy a specific passage poses with the remainder of Scripture.

An example of the power personal experiences exert over our interpretations can be seen in the movie *National Treasure*. When the main character, Ben Gates, discovered a meerschaum pipe providing a clue to the whereabouts of the treasure, the puzzling line "fifty-five in iron pen" appears as part of the riddle. Shaw, one of the men on the expedition, provided a clue to his checkered past. He heard the word 'pen' and automatically assumed the clue was referring to a prison (**penitentiary**) rather than a writing utensil.

For our study, we need to keep the following specific concepts at the back of our minds:

1. No one is immune to cultural influences.

2. Distanciation (consciously removing ourselves from our point of reference in order to take the biblical author's place of surveillance) is essential for understanding Scripture.
3. The Holy Spirit can reveal deeper meaning in passages other than the actual grammatical-historical interpretation of the text, and we are not to dismiss these interpretations. For example, Paul used the law about feeding oxen while they are working to establish the spiritual principle that we are to provide for those who labor for Christ on our behalf (1 Cor. 9:9-10). Matthew took the passage regarding God's deliverance of Israel out of Egypt to confirm that Jesus fulfilled this prophecy when He returned from Egypt as a child (compare Hosea 11:1 with Matt. 2:15).
4. The intellectual disturbance we experience when finding some of our beliefs need tweaking should not destroy our faith.
5. Believers who encounter 'cognitive dissonance' when faced with revealed truth contrary to their previous beliefs may reject or explain away the information, persuade themselves that no conflict exists, or reason the differences away in order to maintain a long-held and cherished worldview.
6. We have the Word, the Holy Spirit, prayer, and the corporate body of Christ as our system of checks and balances for understanding truth and God's will.
7. We need cross-pollination to bear fruit and come to maturity.
8. Everyone has blind spots, sometimes filling in the missing information with cultural views and the reasoning of men without being aware that this is being done. A multitude of counselors can provide protection from this type of blindness.

Guarding ourselves against the tendency to dismiss new information opens our minds to receiving spiritual discernment. It takes diligence to make sure we are walking in God's truth rather than culturally fashioned tradition. It can be stressful to change our thinking on firmly rooted indoctrination. We have to examine ourselves to see if we are imposing our own thoughts, traditions, and comfort on the meaning of any text.

It is important for us to grasp the intended meaning of all Scripture, using all of our mental energy and capability submitted to the guidance of the Holy Spirit. In addition, available scholarship and references should be considered in order to come to an informed conclusion. However, it is naïve to think that there won't be diversity of opinion on some of the more intricate and perplexing discussions on issues unrelated to the existence and deity of Christ, the way of salvation, the resurrection of the dead, etc. This diversity will continue to exist until believers come to maturity with unity of faith and knowledge, having one mind, as Paul described (Eph. 4:13-16; 1 Cor. 1:10; Rom. 15:6; 2 Cor. 13:11; Php. 2:2).

There is a difference between the diversity of thought in doctrinal points and the diversity believers exhibit in the expression of their faith. Matters of religious formalism and expression are quite diverse, and I don't believe the Lord minds this. Unity can be achieved with diversity of expression, providing creative enrichment in the community of believers. I don't believe the Lord intended for us to demonstrate unity through conformity. Creation is diverse, the races of people are diverse—I believe the Lord enjoys diversity in this way.

Diversity in doctrine can be a much greater obstacle in reconciling opposing groups, especially if one group limits the function or full inclusion of another group. Believers must always be wary of causing division in this manner and seek to be of one mind for the cause of Christ without sacrificing truth.

As an additional thought, we should consider that in some cases the biblical authors themselves may not have known the full import of what they wrote under the inspiration of the Holy Spirit (cf. 1 Pet. 1:10-12; Dan. 12:8-9). From this, we may also conclude that knowing only the grammatical-historical context may not give us the underlying truth that the Spirit of God planted beneath the surface. No one knows the deep thoughts of God except the Holy Spirit (1 Cor. 2:10-14). Allowing the Spirit to instruct us opens a door for understanding that includes deeper intimacy with God.

There are topics in biblical study where the variables do not present themselves in a cohesive way, at least not on surface glance. A concrete and cohesive conclusion requires diligence, honesty in dealing with what appear to be conflicting thoughts or examples in Scripture, and the prayer of faith that the Holy Spirit will illuminate the intended meaning. Our conclusions should also be presented to the wider body of Christ for thoughtful, Holy Spirit-inspired evaluation.

Hosea wrote that old and new wine rob the people of understanding and bring them to ruin (Hos. 4:11b,14b). The old wine could be viewed symbolically as representing long held socio-philosophical and theological traditions. The new wine could represent the influence of the world, modern cultural paradigms, and the rampant license and relativism of our present day. Our willingness to set aside all of these for the discernment given from above allows us to truly hear what the Lord wants to teach us.

> *Now we have not received the spirit of the world but the Spirit of God,* ***so that we might understand*** *the things God has so freely given us.* 1 Cor. 2:12, CJB

Chapter 4

Spiritual Identity

> *Then God said, "Let us make mankind in our image, in our likeness, so that they may rule."* Gen. 1:26a, NIV

After reading Dr. Nebeker's article, I became keenly aware that my understanding of women's roles in the church had become a tangled web of isolated Bible verses, tradition, cultural advances, personal experiences, psychological assessment of what seemed reasonable and logical in my own eyes, and the conflicting articles and books I've read on the subject. Because of this matrix of ideas, I found myself leaning toward the complementarian view whenever I read those very convincing works. This view supports the idea that men and women have different but complementary functions in marriage and the family as well as in the church and secular arena.

On the other hand, I could equally relate to and agree with the plausible arguments and valiant efforts of the egalitarians that dug deeply to find the original grammatical-historical context of the difficult passages in question. Egalitarians view men and women as fundamentally equal, advocating equality of authority in every arena.

Agreeing with both views brought double-mindedness. One so inclined is 'unstable in all his ways.' Knowing the truth as God defines it in His Word gives the only reliable means for solving this issue. This first entails rooting out long-held views of women based on faulty premises. Particularly influential in this respect were the Greek philosophers. Their low view of women infiltrated the church's view and theological understanding of women as noted throughout church history.

Greek Philosophy and Early Church Fathers

Dr. Nicholas D. Smith, Ph.D., Professor of Philosophy at Lewis and Clark College in Portland, Oregon, provided the following scholarship for Aristotelian thought on women. Aristotle saw nothing approaching equality in men and women. "[I]n the Politics he flatly declares, "as regards the sexes, the male is by nature superior and the female inferior, the male ruler and the female subject." Aristotle… plainly distinguishes manly from womanly virtues, and sees biology as demonstrating that the generation of the female is no better than that of a "mutilated male," a reproductive failure the same in kind, though of a lesser degree, as those that result in (other) monstrosities."[11]

The Greek philosophers developed a set of ideas about human relationships and hierarchy based on what they observed, experienced, and inductively reasoned from those observations. Inductive reasoning moves from specific observations to construct a broad, generalized conclusion. As with all inductive reasoning, if observations or facts present themselves that contradict previous conclusions, the inductive judgments must be altered to reflect those new findings. We will later discuss the impact modern research findings have on the Greek philosopher's staunchly held inductions regarding women.

The following are quotes from early church leaders demonstrating Aristotle's influence on their views of women.

- **Clement of Alexandria**: "[T]he very consciousness of their own nature must evoke feelings of shame."
- **Origen**: "And do you not know that you are (each) an Eve? The sentence of God on this sex of yours lives in this age: the guilt must of necessity live too. You are the devil's gateway: you are the unsealer of that (forbidden) tree: you are the first deserter of the divine law: you are she who persuaded him whom the devil was not valiant enough to attack. You destroyed so easily God's image, man. On account of your desert—that is, death—even the Son of God had to die."
- **Augustine**: "I don't see what sort of help woman was created to provide man with, if one excludes the purpose of procreation. If woman was not given to man for help in bearing children, for what help could she be? To till the earth together? If help were needed for that, man would have been a better help for man. The same goes for comfort in solitude. How much more pleasure is it for life and conversation when two friends live together than when a man and a woman cohabitate?"

- **John Chrysostom**: This fourth century theologian likened women to "white-washed sepulcher(s)... [F]emales... need greater care precisely because of their ready inclination to sin."
- **St. Albert the Great**: "Woman is less qualified [than man] for moral behavior. For the woman contains more liquid than the man, and it is a property of liquid to take things up easily and to hold onto them poorly. Liquids are easily moved, hence women are inconstant and curious... Woman knows nothing of fidelity. Believe me, if you give her your trust, you will be disappointed. Trust an experienced teacher. For this reason prudent men share their plans and actions least of all with their wives. Woman is a misbegotten man and has a faulty and defective nature in comparison with his. Therefore she is unsure in herself. What she herself cannot get, she seeks to obtain through lying and diabolical deceptions. And so, to put it briefly, one must be on one's guard with every woman, as if she were a poisonous snake and the horned devil... In evil and perverse doings woman is cleverer, that is, slyer, than man. Her feelings drive woman toward every evil, just as reason impels man toward all good."

  "The north wind strengthens the power, and the south wind weakens it... The north wind leads to the generation of males, the south wind to the generation of females, because the north wind is pure and dries out the exhalations and stimulates the natural force... the south wind is moist and heavy with rain."[12]

Some insults last a long time. Hopefully, if you are a woman, you will sufficiently recover from these ill-reasoned conclusions and misogynist statements to tackle the next section.

Thomas Aquinas

The thoughts of Thomas Aquinas, a medieval theologian well known for his blended views of Greek philosophy and biblical thought, have infiltrated church thought for centuries. In several statements in the *Summa Theologica* and elsewhere, Aquinas assumes the inferiority of women, not only in bodily strength but in breadth of intellect. Note the following perceptions Aquinas held of women:

- "By taking the vow of virginity or of consecrated widowhood and thus being betrothed to Christ, **they are raised to the dignity of men**, through which they are freed from subordination to men and are immediately united with Christ."
- "**Woman is defective and misbegotten**, for the active force in the male seed tends to the production of a perfect likeness in the masculine sex; while the production of woman comes from defect in the active force or from some material indisposition, or even from some external influence, such as that of a south wind, which is moist."
- "Good order would have been wanting in the human family if some were not governed by others wiser than themselves. So by such a kind of subjection woman is naturally subject to man, because **in man the discretion of reason predominates**."
- "The reliability of a person's evidence is weakened, sometimes indeed on account of some fault of his... sometimes, without any fault on his part, and this **owing either to a defect in the reason, as in the case of children, imbeciles and women**, or to personal feeling."[12]

In summary, Aquinas viewed women as bearing less dignity than men, having a flawed and misbegotten physical body, and possessing defective reasoning and lesser intellect.

Dr. Marie I. George, Ph.D., professor of Philosophy at St. John's University in Jamaica, New York, wrote:

> Aquinas' views on female inferiority were doubtless influenced as well by Aristotle's reproductive biology, with its understanding of the relation between male and female as one of active (perfect) principle to passive (imperfect) principle. Aristotle saw the sperm as the formative agent; the mother simply supplied raw material to be incorporated into the developing child. He also thought the sperm was directed to producing only male offspring, and that when this did not result it was because something interfered with the active principle within the sperm.
>
> Following Aristotle, Aquinas argues that "perfection" can mean two different things: first, that a being has all the parts and

powers it ought to have; and second, that its parts and powers are greater than those of another being. A plant that has all the attributes and abilities it ought to have (e.g., to grow, to reproduce) is a perfect plant, but compared to a dog, which not only grows and reproduces but also sees and moves about, it is a less perfect being. In the same way, the general intellectual inferiority of women does not make them defective or inferior simply speaking, but only in the particular natural order, in comparison to most males...[13]

Aquinas formulated a system of order or law divided into four subarenas: divine, human, natural, and eternal. For our discussion, we will take a brief look at natural and human law.

Natural law is discovered by 'reason.' "Classically, natural law refers to the use of reason to analyze human nature... **Some early Church Fathers, especially those in the West, sought to incorporate natural law into Christianity.**"[14] The shortcoming is immediately obvious. First, we subject the biblical text to interpretation through a lens of what seems reasonable to us personally in our culture and time. What is reasonable in one mind may not be reasonable in that same mind once new facts have emerged. Personal reasoning is subjective in that it is clouded by the limits of human intelligence and creative thought as well as the confines of the era in which one lives.

Second, social and scientific information become additional factors affecting reasoning because no matter how current, there is always more to be discovered. These newer discoveries typically render previous thought obsolete and incorrect, even if only in part. Our information is ever fragmentary and incomplete, which is easily demonstrated by the continual addition of updated research. We need to take our ignorance and limitations seriously. We only know in part and see in part (1 Cor. 13:9-12).

Although his belief that woman was by nature intellectually inferior pervaded his writings, Thomas Aquinas also constructed argumentation that the soul and physical body are distinct from one another. He stated that the body alone does not comprise the definition of what it means to be human. The soul is the 'substantial form' that determines whether someone is human, as evidenced by the ability to reason. Intellect or reasoning capability are equated with the soul. The physical matter of the body can change and is therefore "only potentially a human being. The soul is what actualizes that potential into an existing human being. Consequently, the fact that a human body is live human tissue entails that a human soul is wholly present in each part of the human."[15] Understanding that God implanted His image in every person, male and female alike, should motivate us to give less concern to the physical (e.g., gender) than to the manifestation of God's image as expressed through an individual's soul/spirit.

For understanding human law as defined by Aquinas, I turned to Dr. Jan Garrett, Professor Emeritus in the Department of Philosophy and Religion at Western Kentucky University. Dr. Garrett wrote the following regarding Thomas Aquinas' views on human law, acknowledging that Aquinas believed that respect for human law **"is largely a matter of custom or habit."**

> Even though laws are general, they are still **adapted to the nature of the community**, which is not everywhere the same, and to the classes of individuals who make up the society... Human laws are **subject to change**, according to Aquinas, because **experience in practical matters may allow us to improve them**... Human law can be changed, and **occasionally should be changed**, but it should not be lightly changed.[16]

Noteworthy among these remarks is that Aquinas posited these laws are not static. They can be changed as the community changes or as new information presents itself.

Certain views on women were based on cultural observation, personal opinion, or research where no effort was taken to level the playing field to render the results meaningful and statistically significant. For example, it is widely understood that students who study for a test will do better than those who have never been exposed to the material covered. Similarly, past research and mindsets that concluded women were mentally inferior did not take into consideration that educated men who dealt with challenges in government and business were being compared with uneducated, sequestered women.

In order to gain clarity on this issue, I looked at historical views held about women that have been invalidated by current medical research. I examined research on the intellectual differences between men and women. I searched for biblical evidence defining any natural propensities of men and women in the arena of sin. I included examination of any biblical indication that one or the other had tendencies to be deceived or teach error more than the other.

By nature, the inductive reasoning the Greek philosophers employed exhibits the typical characteristics of reasoning in the early stages of development, namely that because these inductive conclusions are more open-ended and exploratory, they require adjusting when new information comes to light. We will find that the philosophers' inductive reasoning as it pertains to women would never hold up under modern day research standards and scrutiny.

> *The first to state his case seems right until another comes and cross-examines him.* Prov. 18:17, HCSB

Debunking Myths: Genetics and Intellectual Capacity

Some of the issues raised in the church today on both sides of the woman debate involve historical traditions in the church and society that have no basis in scientific fact. From the Greek philosophers, we have the ancient belief that women were depositories for the little humans men implanted in their wombs, taking the view that women were little more than fertile soil for the next generation. Another widely held belief ascribed blame to the woman if no sons were born. Modern science, however, proves that each parent gives only half of the genetic material required to reproduce another human being. We also now know that the male and not the female contribution to the genetic material determines the gender of the child.

Similarly, women were once viewed as intellectually inferior, incapable of learning. While direct observation may have supported this conclusion in the past, this observational method used subjects insufficiently matched in education and vocational training in order to make the conclusions valid. Research from the past century records that over this period, women have closed the alleged IQ gap between men and women, proving that women and men have comparable IQ's. In a study conducted in 2012 by Dr. James R. Flynn, Ph.D., Emeritus Professor of Political Studies at the University of Otago in Dunedin, New Zealand, the average IQ of the women studied edged slightly above the men in societies where women are allowed to pursue education and employment opportunities similar to men. The only statistically significant difference uncovered was in the extremes on either end of the IQ spectrum. Men were more heavily represented on the obscenely high end of IQ's as well as on the devastatingly low end.[17]

It seems recent research explains this phenomenon of the men being more heavily represented in the extremities. Dr. Christopher Badcock, Ph.D., Emeritus Reader in Sociology at the University of London, stated recently, "Another important factor in sex chromosome expression is the huge dissimilarity between the information carried on the X and Y chromosomes. The Y has a mere 100 or so genes, and there is no evidence that any of them are linked to cognition. This contrasts sharply with the 1,200-odd genes on the X chromosome. There is mounting evidence that at least 150 of these genes are linked to intelligence, and there is definite evidence that verbal IQ is X-linked. It suggests that a mother's contribution to intelligence may be more significant than a father's—especially if the child is male, because a male's one and only X chromosome always comes from his mother. And in females, the X chromosome derived from the father is in fact bequeathed directly from the father's mother, simply setting the maternal X-effect back one generation, so to speak."[18]

I like the way J. Kemp connected and summed up these findings in a post commenting on the article, "Human Intelligence: Cleverer Still" [note: an allele is a DNA coding sequence that occupies a specific position on a chromosome]:

> There are strong indications that a major structural factor at work in male vs. female intelligence is the reality that there are key intelligence-impacting genes on the X-chromosome, of which men have only one while women have two. All female mammals are mosaics with respect to the X-chromosome, meaning that their tissues are a patchwork quilt in which one or the other of their X-chromosomes is turned on (and the other

off) in each patch. This creates a situation where it is easier for males to win the IQ lottery if they happen to get a single very strong version of the relevant genes on their X-chromosome. For a woman to have that same gene in all of her tissues, she would have to inherit the rare, very strong allele/s from both of her parents, which is statistically far less likely to occur. Similarly, males are also far more likely to lose this lottery, and wind up mentally retarded, which is where women pick up the dividend of having two X-chromosomes: X-based mental retardation is far less common among women as their risk is diversified by having two X-chromosomes, and thus a good chance of having one more helpful allele on one of their X-chromosomes to offset any harmful allele.[19]

[Note: While extremely high IQ's are impressive, many studies show they carry with them a predisposition to schizophrenia, bipolar disorder, and self-destructive behaviors like substance abuse. Very low IQ's can be associated with sociopathic behavior and extreme aggression.]

It turns out that children will be better off intellectually if their moms and paternal grandmothers are intelligent since no evidence links the Y-chromosome to intellect. How like our Creator to make sure that even at the cellular level, He demonstrates that we need one another.

[Note: After reading research re: male-to-female birth ratios, which range from 103-110 male births for every 100 females, or a ratio range of 1.03:1 to 1.1:1, two thoughts came to mind. 1.) The males born with devastatingly low IQ's and some with freakishly high IQ's would most likely be rejected as suitable mates (see previous note), reducing the overall ratio of males:females closer to 1:1. 2.) This data also supports God's intention for one man/one woman marriages, not polygamy. If polygamy were God's idea, the ratio would be 1:2, 1:3, or even higher.]

Debunking Myths: Gender Stereotypes

As far as the more emotional nature of women is concerned, it is well documented that fluctuating hormones are at least in part responsible for mood swings—even in men. However, the sections of our jails dedicated to convicted felons who commit *crimes of passion* are predominantly male by no small margin. So are we to accept a blanket statement that the cyclical emotional nature of women makes them too volatile to handle leadership? Could we not make a similar judgment about the male population, whose crimes of passion cause them to make some of the most devastating decisions known to humanity? Men may demonstrate a narrower *range* of emotions, but they are emotional just the same. Anger is still defined as an emotion.

When we look at the widely held belief that women are more easily deceived, we must ensure the playing field is leveled before we make the comparison. In current society, this would entail studying a group of men and women of similar average IQ with similar educational and experiential background. Already it becomes obvious how difficult it would be to control the sample required for this type of research.

Others have concluded that women are more likely to propagate error. If we review church history, however, we might come to a completely different evaluation. From which gender have more heretical practices and doctrinal error originated? Immediately our response would have to be men if we consider the Crusades, Salem witch trials, the Inquisition, indulgences, torture and gruesome deaths for those who hold different doctrine, etc. These remind me of Jesus' statement, *"You do not know what manner of spirit you are of. For the Son of Man did not come to destroy men's lives but to save them."* (Luke 9:55-56; see also Mark 9:38-42)

By research standards, however, the question is not entirely without fault. We would also have to bear in mind that most leadership and scholarship in the church has been male, so of course the results would be skewed to favor more error on the part of men. The sample results would have to be adjusted to account for this. However, this fact does establish that men are capable of being deceived and propagating error, especially when personal gain is a factor.

Women Are Easily Deceived and Men Are Treacherous Lawbreakers?

> *Also **it was not Adam who was deceived, but the woman** who, on being deceived, became involved in the transgression.* 1 Tim. 2:14, CJB

Much has been made of the verses where the serpent deceived Eve, using this as a *part-to-whole* argument (a common logic fallacy). This approach substantiates views that reason all women are therefore unfit for leadership because of their inborn nature to be easily deceived.

Note in the passage that follows, Paul is addressing the Corinthian church, which of course would include men. This establishes Paul's understanding that both men and women are in danger of being deceived.

> *But I am afraid that,* **as the serpent deceived Eve** *by his craftiness,* **your minds will be led astray** *from the simplicity and purity of devotion to Christ.* 2 Cor. 11:3, NASB

Using this same part-to-whole fallacious reasoning, one could argue that men are unfit for leadership because of their predisposed nature to break the law, hide their sin, and act treacherously.

> *Have I* **covered my transgressions like Adam**...? Job 31:33, NASB

> *But* **like Adam** *they have* **transgressed** *the covenant; There they have* **dealt treacherously** *against Me.* Hos. 6:7, NASB

In the next passage, Paul taught that the death sentence for the human race was attributed to Adam's actions, which were deemed treacherous (traitorous, rebellious), not Eve's, whose actions resulted from being tricked. Notice in the Complete Jewish Bible's translation of 1 Timothy 2:14 (previous), the translator correctly interpreted *en parabasei gegonen* as 'became involved in the transgression.' As an unwitting dupe, Eve became party to the crime masterminded by Satan. The transgression was Adam's, as these passages point out:

> *[S]in entered the world* **through one man... death reigned from Adam** *until Moses, even over those who had not sinned in the likeness of* **the offense of Adam**. Rom. 5:12a,14a, NASB

> *[I]n **Adam all die**, so also in Christ all will be made alive.* 1 Cor. 15:22, NASB

Is it proper to compartmentalize the errors of the first man and woman, hastily concluding that women are easily deceived and men are inherently treacherous? Don't we have several examples in the Word of men and women each demonstrating these traits?

The Bible establishes that men are not alone in their inclination to be treacherous. We have to concede there are examples of treacherous women in the Bible, most notably Jezebel (1 Kings 18:4,19; 19:1-2; 21:5-16,25; 2 Kings 9:30-37). The second most nefarious woman, in my opinion, is Athaliah, granddaughter of Omri (see 2 Kings 11; 2 Chron. 22:10-23:21). She killed all the royal offspring when her son, King Ahaziah of Judah, died. She did this so she could usurp the throne. Delilah must be included as well for betraying Samson for gain (Jdg. 16:4-21).

We also discover there are numerous biblical examples of men who were deceived. Samson is an obvious example of a man who was deceived by the treacherous Delilah (see previous). Abimelech was deceived by Abraham (Gen. 20). Isaac was deceived by Rebekah and Jacob (Gen. 27). Jacob was deceived by Laban (Gen. 29:25). Judah was deceived by Tamar (Gen. 38:12-26). Joshua was deceived by the Gibeonites (Josh. 9:22). King Hezekiah showed naïveté when the Babylonian envoys came to visit. He showed them the vast treasures of his kingdom, which were later taken from Israel by that nation (2 Kings 20:12-18).

From this evidence, we must conclude that women and men are both capable of being deceived and acting treacherously. Every individual has weaknesses, character flaws, and insufficient knowledge that prevent them from recognizing every trap the enemy has set for them.

Name Calling

We are quick to brand outspoken women with the moniker 'Jezebel,' but there are more examples of men than women in the Bible that we are warned not to emulate. For example:

> *Woe to them! For they have gone **the way of Cain**, and for pay they have rushed headlong into the **error of Balaam**, and perished in the **rebellion of Korah**.* Jude 1:11, NASB

The way of Cain evolves when our pride is injured because we didn't get the same recognition another received—praise we felt we deserved for our hard work. Cain let anger and jealousy escalate to a murderous rage. Balaam sought a secure and honorable position with monetary and other benefits over devotion to truth. Korah rebelled against God-ordained leadership by appealing to the argument that 'we are all holy' and therefore don't have to submit to leaders with whom we disagree.

God rejected King Saul because of his disobedience rooted in the fear of man and his own reasoning (1 Sam. 13:7-14). Absalom, the son who rebelled against David, provides a picture of selfish ambition and vainglory (2 Sam. 15). Are we to conclude only men are capable of these types of corruption because the names associated are all male?

This is only a brief look at scriptural examples given to teach us the inclination of both men and women to sin, be deceived, and act treacherously. Nonetheless, it gives adequate evidence that our practice of labeling certain frailties as male or female finds no support in the Word.

In summary, current medical research shows that men and women have roughly the same average IQ. Men and women have their emotional variances, one resulting in more prison sentences and the other contributing to the general annoyance of humanity. So do we have a clear-cut winner that will hands-down make a better leader?

But do we really need to appeal to intellectual, physical, or psychological reasons to convince ourselves that women are by nature inferior, supplying the fuel we need to confirm her need to submit to male authority? Has anyone stepped forward to imply that Jesus subordinated Himself to the Father's will because He was somehow 'less than' in His deity before the Father? If anyone has, I am certain he or she was immediately branded a heretic.

We are compelled to conclude that any alleged natural differences we discover between men and women do not furnish legitimacy for our views. We turn to the only plumb line we have—the Word of God.

Original Intent

Here is the first verse in Scripture indicating God's original intent in creating men and women:

> God created **man in His own image**, in the image of God He created him; **male and female** He created them. God blessed them; and God said to them, "**Be fruitful and multiply, and fill the earth, and subdue it; and rule** over the fish of the sea and

over the birds of the sky and over every living thing that moves on the earth." Gen. 1:27-28, NASB

Both are created in God's image, and therefore God's original purpose was to have a unified team of men and women created with God's likeness impressed on their spirits for ruling and reigning over the earth. He did not make them equal in reproductive function, but complementary to reinforce the spiritual truth that they need one another. A woman with child would need to rely on a man's strength in her vulnerable state. In turn, men are born of women. Just as procreation requires male and female, ruling and reigning would also require both male and female, which we will explore later in our discussion.

Are all men and women created equal? There is no such thing as true equality in the strictest sense of the word. Some are destined for leadership (Gen. 41:41; Ex. 3:10; 1 Sam. 16:1,8-13), some are given wealth (Deut. 8:18), others special skill (Ex. 31:1-6), some exceptional strength (Samson; Jdg. 14-16), some striking beauty (Gen. 29:17; Esth. 2:7), some discernment and wisdom (Gen. 41:39; 1 Kings 4:29), still others intelligence (1 Sam. 25:3; Dan. 1:4) or faith (James 2:5). Even the gifts of the Spirit are not given *equally*, but as the Spirit wills (1 Cor. 12:11).

God did not level the playing field by giving each person the same tools to work with. He did allow each of us to lack in some degree all the tools necessary for accomplishing His purposes so that we would see how we need God and each other. This is one reason God allowed Adam to work the day he was created, naming all the animals with God at His side. He wanted Adam to arrive at the conclusion that it was neither good nor advantageous for him to work alone. He needed a helper that would fill the void he experienced on day one.

God is after our hearts. The Lord wants to shape our character by establishing *His* character in us through the Word and Spirit in the environment we are placed. He does this through the assets we have been given as well as through the frustration we experience in the areas where we lack the skill, understanding, or resources we need.

Despite the inequality of ability and gifts, we are instructed to submit ourselves to one another (Eph. 5:21), not taking power over one another as the worldly do (Matt. 20:25-28; Luke 22:24-30; 1 Pet. 5:2-

3), but being humble toward one another and not thinking of ourselves too highly by honoring others above ourselves (1 Pet. 5:5; Rom. 12:3; Rom. 12:10). In the community of believers, vulnerability is a key component of humility and promotes a safe harbor where every believer can come as they are without adding the pretense of having it all together. It is a given that each believer has issues, baggage, and a need for community. No one has everything required to fulfill his or her personal mandate without the help of the community of believers.

Bear in mind also that each believer requires their own unique balance of time alone with God and time serving and experiencing fellowship with other believers. Each will require more of one and less of the other to such varying degrees that we cannot reduce the believer's walk to a proven formula of 'this much community' and 'this much time alone with God.' Let the Holy Spirit be the Guide in this regard. The church doesn't have to control everything.

As for fellowship within the believing community, let everything we do and say be undergirded with love so the church can experience peace and unity. Then the world will know we are different. In this way, we also honor the name of Christ who reconciled us to God by His blood. The following is a portion of what Jesus prayed before He went to the cross:

> *My prayer is... also for those who will believe in me through their message,* ***that all of them may be one,*** *Father, just as you are in me and I am in you. May they also be in us* ***so that the world may believe that you have sent me****. I have given them the glory that you gave me,* ***that they may be one*** *as we are one—I in them and you in me—****so that they may be brought to complete unity****. Then the* ***world will know that you sent me*** *and have* <u>***loved them even as you have loved me***</u>*.* John 17:20-23, NIV

Spirit of Partiality

In keeping with this theme of unity, we are admonished not to create division by showing favoritism or a 'spirit of partiality' (1 Tim. 5:21), a trait contrary to the nature of God whose image we carry (cf. Acts 10:34; Rom. 2:11; Gal. 2:6; Eph. 6:9; James 2:1,9). Partiality becomes justified only in the minds of those in the privileged class who benefit from its continuation. They become oblivious to the division and injustice caused by partisan policies.

A spirit of partiality hinders *koinonia* (Grk. 2842, typically translated fellowship, sharing, communion, community), which is found only in Christ in the new covenant. *Koinonia* is based on love, unity in the Spirit, and mutual sharing for the welfare of others. Believers were meant to share a strong bond of affection and like-mindedness that can only be experienced when the Lord is in their midst. When we allow each believer to function in his/her calling with the spiritual gifts he/she has been given, placing no restrictions on what the Spirit is allowed to do, *koinonia* can flourish.

When Paul made the following statement, he was not only speaking of no distinction pertaining to salvation. As the body of Christ, Paul emphasized that things must be this way because we are *one in Christ*.

> There is neither Jew nor Greek, there is neither slave nor free, there is neither male nor female; **for you are all one in Christ Jesus**. Gal. 3:28, NKJV

Jesus is our Husband and every believer, whether male or female, makes up His bride. The bride answers to Jesus, the Word made flesh. There is no hierarchy of brideship. Jews, Gentiles, slave, free, men, women—each takes the position of a betrothed wife and reserves her reverence (Grk. 5399 *phobeo*, typically translated 'fear' in various applications) for Christ. The respect and honor we have for God-ordained leadership in the church is not to be equated with the reverence we have for God (cf. Matt. 10:28).

Peter summed this up by stating we are to show the proper respect (Grk. 5091 *timao*) to everyone, love (Grk. 25 *agapao*) the family of believers, fear (*phobeo*) God, and honor (*timao*) our secular rulers (1 Pet. 2:17). Paul spoke of the fear (*phobeo*) men who break the law have for the power of secular rulers, because rulers are God's agents for justice on the earth. Since they function as God's agents, reverence (*phobeo*) is due them (Rom. 13:1-7). As a microcosm of governmental rulers and their subjects, both Peter and Paul remind slaves to reverence (*phobeo*) their earthly masters (1 Pet. 2:18; Eph. 6:5).

In the church, however, there is to be no reverential fear between believers, only mutual love and respect (Rom. 12:10). Our English translations do not always clearly make this distinction. Paying close attention to how we interpret the Word helps us function as the bride of Christ in unity. Jesus warned His disciples:

> *Pay close attention to what you hear. The closer you listen, the more understanding you will be given—and you will receive even more.* Mark 4:24, NLT

As believers, we are called to be free in Christ to serve in the grace we have been given. The indulgences of the flesh Paul addresses in his letter to the Galatians include discord, dissensions, factions, and envy (Gal. 5:20-21). Paul taught believers to serve one another humbly in love, rather than destroy one another through their words and practice (Gal. 5:13-15). Loving fellow believers and treating them the way we want to be treated demonstrates our love for God.

Paul's fervent desire is that believers would operate in unity and become mature. There are to be no divisions by race, gender, age, intellect, or socioeconomic status.

> *I appeal to you, brothers and sisters, in the name of our Lord Jesus Christ, that all of you **agree with one another** in what you say and that there be **no divisions among you**, but that you be **perfectly united in mind and thought**.* 1 Cor. 1:10, NIV

Our Identity Is in Christ

> *For you have died, and your life is hidden with Christ in God.* Col. 3:3, ESV

Every believer has a new identity in Christ, for the old has passed away (2 Cor. 5:17). Whatever role our culture or society has assigned to us must now be interpreted through the lens of the cross and God's original intent for humanity. These are the thoughts Paul wanted Onesimus' owner to understand (see the book of Philemon).

We cannot allow bruised feelings on one side or the other with regard to identity issues to dictate whether we have taken the proper stance on scriptural truth. The following real life examples illustrate why it is an invalid argument to say that just because our identity is rocked by new information or circumstances, we must uphold the old order to preserve the identity of those who are floundering (the details and names have been changed in these illustrations).

> Betsy enjoyed great popularity in her teens and twenties. Athletic, attractive, and engaging, she was accustomed to getting special attention and favors because of her ability, looks, and charm. This changed in an instant when she suffered a crushed femur and facial lacerations in a car accident. The leg injury left her with a limp, preventing her from her former sports participation. The lacerations left her beautiful face marred. Over the recovery phase and beyond, she noticed people no longer regarded her the way they had before. The special attention and favors came to an abrupt halt. Because her identity had been wrapped up in the privilege and special treatment she had previously received based on her beauty and charm, she went through a period of depression and self-doubt. The stress of this new identity exacerbated her depression and she became reclusive and unproductive for several years.

> Marie was the daughter of a very popular junior high school principal. She grew up in the associated elementary school and was accustomed to various privileges in the school office because of her mother's position. When her mom took another position at a larger rival school, Marie moved up to attend the junior high where her mom used to work. Under the new leadership, Marie soon fell out of the 'inner circle' and was no longer afforded the privileges she previously enjoyed. She suddenly realized the new principal thought of her with no more favor than he did the other students. This hurt her deeply and nearly caused her to leave this school.

In both examples, the young women enjoyed privileges based on beauty, charm, and ability in one case, and based on familial association in the other. Their privileges had to do with perceived personal worth based on external factors and not something internal. When the bases for their special treatment changed or were removed, they suffered loss causing them mental anguish and psychological suffering. They had to face the rude awakening that comes when someone who is accustomed to privilege suddenly has it taken away without remedy. The sudden realization of having the same standing as everyone else can cause a massive downward spiral in how we view ourselves and the future if we had previously convinced ourselves that our favored status was deserved or intrinsic.

Can we at least consider that privilege based on gender can have similar consequences? Some in the church are blaming feminists for challenging traditional masculine privilege and superiority with the men's subsequent confusion and inability to understand their role in our changing culture. But perhaps the problem is that some men are struggling to find their moorings once the gender-based privilege they expected and enjoyed is suddenly recalibrated. Finding out women are just as smart and excel in areas formerly boasting all male membership may have jostled the unstable and illegitimate base on which some men had been conditioned to rely. When the basis for the authority we assumed was ours is challenged, true motives and heart posture are revealed.

In history, we observed this kind of recalibration when the status quo regarding slavery was challenged. Those who had elevated themselves as masters were forced by law to reconsider their views. Many refused to change, fueling the racial segregation laws after the Civil War. Africans were given 'equal but separate' status in an attempt to *lawfully* maintain the order to which the South was accustomed. The inferior conditions relegated to the separate but equal Africans led to great disparity in employment, education, voting, and social consideration.

Is anyone hearing an echo? Some in the church will concede that women are equal before God with regard to salvation, but in everything else they are separate. Just as the freed African slaves painfully discovered, this separate status reflects anything but equality.

As His children, God desires that we give greater weight to His Word than our customs or feelings. Striving to maintain the order we are accustomed to prevents us from walking in truth or discernment. Earthly distinctions cloud our ability to stay in step with the Holy Spirit.

Set your minds on things above, not on earthly things. Col. 3:2, NIV

Our worth and identity are found in Christ (not looks, career, wealth, age, success, gender, etc.), and God gives gifts and callings as He sees fit. The Lord will often offend our minds and ideology to expose what is in our hearts. Jesus did this with the Pharisees. He purposely healed on the Sabbath to provoke dialogue with them to reveal the hypocrisy of their legalism as well as their shallow and shortsighted interpretation and view of Scripture.

God's Strength Overcomes Every Weakness

Paul remarked that he worked harder than all the apostles did, however not in his own strength but in the strength provided by the grace of God (1 Cor. 15:10). He also told the church at Philippi that we 'can do all things through Christ's strength' (Php. 4:13). Peter exhorted believers to serve with the strength God provides so that people will praise God and not us (1 Pet. 4:11). Jeremiah recorded the Lord's statement that the wise, the strong, and the wealthy are not to boast about their privileged position. The only boast worth making is that we know and understand the Lord, who delights in mercy, justice, and righteousness (Jer. 9:23-24).

Doesn't this demonstrate that any perceived advantage of intellect, natural talent, or strength that seeks to validate the selection of a particular people group actually invalidates the biblical basis for authority, namely, that God endows whomever He wills, without regard to or in spite of natural ability, societal status, race, age, or gender? Paul warned us not to put any confidence in our flesh (Php. 3:3).

God chose the weak and insignificant of the world so that no one could boast in His presence, and that he who does boast, boasts only in the Lord (Jer. 9:23-24; 1 Cor. 1:26-31; 2 Cor. 10:17). Is there another group of adults considered more weak and insignificant in our society than housewives and mothers?

When a pastor dutifully gives the yearly recognition of moms on Mother's Day, and then a short time later passionately introduces an 'up and comer' who is *really* accomplishing something impressive in the church or secular arena, the obligatory nod to the moms on Mother's Day can feel a bit like paternalistic condescension and duty. The church mirrors the thinking of the world when it ascribes greater worth to academically lettered intellect, impressive financial portfolios, and measureable success (dramatic rankings, numbers, impact, size, etc.) rather than God's view of success—to love mercy, to do justly, and to walk in humility (Mic. 6:8).

I include myself in this because it is very difficult not to be impressed by those with significant accomplishments both inside and outside the church. As a whole, our society does not value faithfulness to the Lord in obscure and mundane callings... but the Lord does! He records every movement of our hearts toward Him, every burning-heart conversation we have about Him, and every compassionate act of obedience we offer the needy and hurting people we meet, no matter how seemingly insignificant—even a cold cup of water (Mk. 9:41).

The church in America is far more impressed with the decisive, risk-taking extrovert who speaks with magnetism, exudes confidence in every situation, leaves a trail of accomplishments that makes the eyes bulge, and possesses a larger-than-life persona. These leaders excite us with their enthusiasm and encouragement to step out in vision and faith to 'have it all.' Sadly, this type of focus can become an issue when we place the emphasis on the weak, broken vessel rather than on the One who displays His power, grace, and mercy **through** that vessel.

On the other hand, we often view the devoted student of the Word who prefers to seek the Lord in a quiet place of retreat from the world as reclusive and spiritually tenuous. One is admired and sought after by the Western mindset, and the other largely ignored and even disapproved for shunning the religious activity of the church in favor of pursuing the oneness he or she seeks to have with God. But in Christ we overcome the thinking of the world:

> ***Do not conform to the pattern of this world,*** *but be **transformed by the renewing of your mind**. Then you will be able to test and approve what God's will is...* ***God chose the lowly*** *things of this world and the despised things...* ***so that no one may boast*** *before him... So from now on we* ***regard no one from a worldly point of view***. Rom. 12:2a; 1 Cor. 1:28a,29a; 2 Cor. 5:16, NIV

Chapter 5

A Wife of Noble Character

> *A wife of noble character who can find? She is worth far more than rubies.* Prov. 31:10, NIV

Before we get into our discussion of a woman's worth, we will take a brief look at Paul's desire for women to be free. Paul stated he believed women would be happier and have greater freedom to serve the Lord if they chose to remain single rather than be subject to the customary rulership of a husband. I believe he based this on his thorough knowledge of Scripture as well as personal observation.

> *Now to the unmarried and the widows I say: It is good for them to stay unmarried, as I do... those who marry will face many troubles in this life, and I want to spare you this.* 1 Cor. 7:8,28b, NIV

> *In my judgment, she is happier if she stays as she is—and I think that I too have the Spirit of God.* 1 Cor. 7:40, NIV

Prophetic Forewarning

We find the first mention of a husband ruling over his wife in Genesis 3 at the time God pronounced the curses after the Fall:

> *To the woman he said, "I will greatly increase your pain in childbirth. You will bring forth children in pain. Your desire will be toward your husband, **but he will rule over you.**"* Gen. 3:16, CJB

Translators are divided as to whether the word 'desire' should have been translated 'desire to control.' This word appears only here in this form (*t'shuqatek*; from Heb. 8669 *t'shuqah*: to stretch out after, a longing, a yearning; from the Heb. root 7788 *shuwr*, with the basic idea of turning; a similar form, *t'shuqatow*, is seen in Gen. 4:7 and Songs 7:10). The essential meaning seems to be 'yearning after' without reading into it the desire to control another—just the natural physical desire of a wife for her husband despite the pain of childbearing (see CEV).

After God pronounces the curse of pain in childbearing, some translators treat the second half of this statement as a prophetic warning, that is, 'you will desire your husband, but he will dominate you.' The following translations hint at this view:

- In spite of this (pain in childbearing), you will still have desire for your husband, yet you will be subject to him. GNT
- You'll want to please your husband, but he'll lord it over you. THE MESSAGE
- You will greatly desire your husband, but he will rule over you. NCV
- You will desire your husband; *but rather than a companion,* he will be the dominant partner. VOICE

[Note: Compare Deut. 17:14-20 and 28:36-37 with 1 Sam. 8:5-22 as a similar example of God's prophetic warning that Israel would ask for a king, rejecting God as their leader.]

I believe Paul may have based his advice to the single women in Corinth on this interpretation of Genesis 3:16b as a prophetic warning. This is supported by his statement, 'I believe I have the Spirit of God on this matter' when he spoke of women being happier if they remained single. Having the mind of Christ on any issue would entail some scriptural basis for the reasoning or decision. However, in marriages where husband and wife have mutual love and respect for one another and value each other's opinions, work, and abilities, satisfaction and companionship can flourish. They can find peace and contentment working together for the cause of Christ.

For those who argue that women yearn to be led, we have to question where they got their information. I have met many women with no such inclination. In fact, many women have great vision and creativity as well as the skill and desire to lead.

We may have to consider that we have confused this idea with: 1.) a specific temperament, which is not gender specific (there are also more men who are followers than there are male leaders), 2.) a learned cultural behavior, and/or 3.) a woman's desire for a father figure. A genuine father figure always looks out for the best interests of his daughter, gives her wise counsel so her life will be spent pursuing the purpose she was meant to fulfill, and protects her even at the cost of his own life. While Paul urged husbands to love their wives sacrificially (Eph. 5:25-33), they are no substitute for the special relationship a woman has with her heavenly Father.

Eve

Before the fall, Adam and Eve were given this charge (singular: not two individual charges): 'To rule over the earth and subdue it, and to be fruitful and multiply and fill the earth' (Gen. 1:26-28). Some have tried to force this statement into compartments, Adam ruling and Eve multiplying. Wow. For both mandates it takes two. Even if we are talking about the family unit alone, recall that the book of Proverbs counsels us that there is safety in a multitude of counselors (Prov. 11:14).

Eve was created to stand by Adam's side as a suitable helper (Heb. 5828 *ezer*: to help, helper) to rule with him over the earth. This Hebrew word is also used of the help God gives to men, e.g., Psalm 33:20, "*We put our hope in the LORD. He is our help and our shield.*" A case could be made that the needier person is the one who requires the help of the one more qualified, such as God helping man, or parents helping children. Since no helper was made for Eve, we might conclude that she was created as the generally more capable even though the man was endowed with greater physical strength.

However, I think the primary illustration here is that man will not find the type of help and companionship he needs from animals but from another like him—made in the image of God. Though Adam was in continual fellowship with God, he had been created to need fellowship and help from others like him. This is why Adam was overjoyed when he met Eve and declared her to be 'of him' (Gen. 2:23). Paul similarly enjoins men to love their wives as much as they love themselves, for they are one.

[As an aside, I muse about their first meeting. I imagine Adam, upon seeing Eve for the first time, saying with Smeagol-like glee, "For Meeeeeeeee...!" I picture Eve saying, "Wow, this is great! And I love being here with you, Adam!" Pausing to survey the landscape, she then says, "Let's get started by getting those baboons away from the bananas so the smaller monkeys can have some. And we've got to move the buffalo along - they're trampling the prairie dogs' homes." Adam responds by saying, "For Meeeeeeeee...!"]

The companionship and mutual aid the two would experience are pictured in the creation of Eve from Adam's rib, not his head, front, back, or feet. This placed Eve at his side—not at his head or in front to rule or lead him, nor under his feet or behind him to be ruled by him or to be in his shadow. She was to be in a position where she would be the most help to him—as a partner.

Husbands and Wives: A Picture of Christ and the Church

> *"For this reason a man will leave his father and mother and be united to his wife, and the two will become one flesh." This is a profound mystery—but I am talking about Christ and the church.* Eph. 5:31-32, NIV

This picture points to Jesus leaving His heavenly throne to claim and become one with His earthly bride, the church. This fulfills God's original intention for humanity to take dominion over the earth. Christ, the God-man, and His bride (the church) will rule and reign over the earth together in the prophesied millennial kingdom.

In Ephesians 5:21-33, Paul speaks of Christ sanctifying the church by His Word through the Spirit. This is paralleled with the husband seeking his wife's highest good, not just his own. He is to take care of his wife's needs and cherish her as he would himself.

As for the teaching that God made husbands the priest of the home, I could find no specific Scripture reference though I can understand how some see this implied. One of the priest's duties is to stand as an intermediary between God and man. In the new covenant, Christ alone is the mediator between God and the individual believer (1 Tim. 2:5). Believers are a priesthood to minister to the Lord and carry out their duties relative to their callings, including praying for one another. Every believer takes on characteristics of a priest. Because leadership in the church involves discipling and mentoring, those who oversee other believers' spiritual growth must have sufficient maturity and ability to teach, but they do not take on Jesus' role as mediator. Intercession may include pleading another's cause, but Jesus alone is our High Priest.

In this passage to husbands and wives, Paul exhorted men to love their wives with no reciprocal command for wives to love their husbands. The general directive for believers to love one another reminds us that wives are to love their husbands as well since they are also brothers in the Lord (John 13:34; Rom. 12:10; 1 Pet. 3:8; etc.).

Paul used the word *agapao* (Grk. 25, the verb form of 26, *agape*) in his exhortation to husbands. This is not a love based merely on feelings but on directing the will or heart to do what is best for another person based on the person's needs. Sacrificial love becomes the goal for every husband. Believing husbands cannot reduce their love to society's current definition, which is based primarily on hormonally based feelings and what is pleasing to the eye. Many broken marriages could be saved if Paul's directive was honored and practiced.

Wives, on the other hand, are told to respect their husbands, something that can be difficult to do if a husband only looks after his own best interests. While husbands are given no reciprocal command to respect their wives, it is absurd to walk away from this passage with the thought that men therefore do not need to respect their wives. In fact, many men naturally respect their wives as a consequence of observing the way she sacrifices her time and energy for the welfare of each family member. I have known several men who acknowledged their respect for their wives by a statement similar to, 'I don't know how she does it.'

Peter admonishes husbands to remember that their wives are also joint heirs. Even though marriage is a picture of Christ and the church, husbands must also keep in mind that their wives are their equals in Christ as part of His body. They are to respect (Grk. 5091 *timao*) their wives as they do every other believer (1 Pet. 3:7). Paul told believers to honor and respect one another more highly than themselves using a related word, *time* (Grk. 5092; Rom. 12:10). Mutual respect naturally occurs between two believers if the Holy Spirit is in their midst, and how much more should this be so if those believers are husband and wife.

The particular word Paul used in his instructions to wives, however, was *phobeo* (Grk. 5399). Its use is limited to the type of reverence given to a leader or master. Although *phobeo* is more often translated 'fear' or 'to be afraid,' the use here speaks more of reverence. We can infer this meaning because John the apostle stated that perfect love casts out fear:

> *There is no fear (**phobos**) in love. But perfect love drives out fear, because fear has to do with punishment. The one who fears (**phobeo**) is not made perfect in love.* 1 John 4:18, NIV

If we look at the literary structure of this portion of Paul's instructions, we note that the beginning and conclusion are related. The structure Paul employed is typical of a literary device known as a chiasmus (discussed in more depth in chapter ten). Paul began this chiasmus with the directive for wives to submit to their husbands as a picture of the submission the church gives to Christ (Eph. 5:21-23). He finishes the discussion by reminding wives to reverence their husbands as the designated leader (v. 33).

Types and Shadows Are Not the Same as Moral Laws

As in all flawed human relations, the submission a wife gives to her husband is dependent on the righteous and selfless manner of the husband's dealings. No one is to submit to unrighteousness (cf. Ex. 1:15-21). Failed marriages cannot be blamed on a wife who will not submit to unreasonable, unrighteous demands. When Paul wrote that wives were to submit to their husbands in all things, he did not precisely mean obedience but rather a posture of the heart. If Paul had obedience in mind, he would have used the word *hupakouo* (Grk. 5219) rather than *hupotasso* (Grk. 5293).

If a husband truly loves his wife as Christ loves the church, he would not expect his wife to submit in such a manner anyway. He would exhibit patience when a wife struggles to take a position of submission to another human being that is just as flawed as she. Remember, this is *a picture* of Christ and the church—an imperfect type and shadow subject to the weightier matters of the law, as Jesus tried to teach the Pharisees when they castigated Him for His treatment of the Sabbath. Has not Christ shown great patience with His wayward bride, the church?

The ceremonial law embodies many types and shadows of God's kingdom and His plan of redemption. As far as the *ceremonial* law is concerned (not the *moral* law), Jesus demonstrated its dynamic nature because its stipulations could be set aside to attend to the weightier matters of the law (compassion, justice, faithfulness, mercy). We also have the parable of the Good Samaritan, indicting the priest and Levite who did not want to violate the ceremonial law by becoming unclean through touching a bloodied, half-dead man. Likewise, the type and shadow of the husband-wife relationship as a picture of Christ and the church can be set aside to maintain the weightier matters.

Remember, the marriage relationship is meant to be a type and shadow of Christ and the church, not a brittle structure dependent on wooden compliance to principles that are meant to demonstrate a spiritual truth. It is interesting to note that Jesus *tightened* the Jewish understanding of the moral code (murder, theft, adultery, etc.), to which the populace had shown great laxity, and *relaxed* the legalistic, exacting, exaggerated reverence of the ceremonial law prevalent in that day. Ceremonial laws exist to demonstrate spiritual truths and are not an end in themselves, which they had become for many in Israel.

As far as the moral code was concerned, Jesus wanted the people to take stock of their own motivations and thoughts, not only their actions. He likened unchecked anger to murder and lustful thinking to actual adultery. He called them to a higher level of obedience to the moral laws. Regarding the ceremonial (religious practice) laws, however, the Pharisees were the opposite of lax, demonstrating an unholy allegiance and legalism that sought perfection in minutiae. Jesus rebuked this type of blind compliance in the exacting Pharisees, particularly with regard to their views of the Sabbath, fasting, and tithing. They were oblivious to the dynamic nature of the ceremonial law, which both Jesus and Paul argued could be set aside for the general welfare of others.

The ceremonial laws were meant to point the believer to spiritual truths about God's kingdom and plan of redemption. These laws were not intended to become an end in themselves—a spiritual scorecard to determine the spiritual worth of a believer's walk with God. Remember Paul's use of the laws on proper treatment of oxen when they tread the grain? He stated this was a principle meant to teach us that we are to physically support the needs of leaders who work for our benefit. 'God isn't concerned about oxen, is He? Certainly He says this for us, doesn't He? Yes, this was written for us' (1 Cor. 9-10). The actual law itself is not the main point—the spiritual truth is.

In a marriage, the primary truth demonstrated is the submission the church gives Christ. God is not primarily concerned about gender, is He? Wasn't this written to teach us about Christ and His bride, the church?

Paul wrote his directive for husbands and wives in the context of mutual submission (Eph. 5:21), the wife to the husband and the husband to the wife (see 1 Cor. 7:4; cf. Gen. 21:12). Headship as described here is not rulership, but rather servant leadership based on love and respect. With Christ as the example of selfless service and sacrifice for His bride, the bar is very high indeed. What woman wouldn't respect a man like that?

The husband and wife are meant to be a picture of Jesus and His bride. Jesus served the disciples and sacrificed His life for His bride because of His great love. He even invites those who overcome the world in this age to *share His authority and throne* to judge, rule, and reign with Him (1 Cor. 6:2-3; Rev. 2:26-28; 3:21; 20:4). Husbands who seek to control their wives' every movement and decision must examine themselves to see if they are moving in the spirit of Christ. Would they be willing to share their authority and throne with their wives?

Which couples last longer and are more satisfied with their relationship: those where husband and wife are mutually respected, trusted, and loved, as in a friendship, or those where one continually demeans the other as 'less than'? Dominating another individual, whether a husband doing so to a wife or a wife to a husband, is a subtle form of pride that will kill a marriage. Neither is this type of scornful, degrading, abusive, vainglorious control a picture of Christ and the church.

Men, It Is Biblical to Listen to Your Wives

Recall that God told Abraham to 'listen to his wife and do whatever she tells you' (Gen. 21:12). While there were terrible results when Adam listened to Eve (Gen. 3:6-19) and when Ahab listened to Jezebel (1 Kings 21:1-24), think of other examples where there were disastrous results when wives listened to their husbands. When Sarah listened to Abraham and Rebekah listened to Isaac to lie about being married to them, they jeopardized the covenant promise God made to them (Gen. 20; 26:6-11). When Ananias kept part of the proceeds from the sale price of his property, his wife stood by her husband's decision and both died as a result (Acts 5:1-10). When the self-preserving Levite donated his concubine-wife to the town rapists, she died as a result of the abuse she endured all night long (Jdg. 19:22-30). Even though he knew the torture she suffered through the long dark hours of the night, the Levite hardened his heart to save his own skin.

God has demonstrated that He will give divine revelation to wives that He does not share with husbands. The Angel of the Lord appeared to Manoah's wife to bring the news that she would bear a son who would be Israel's deliverer (Jdg. 13:2-7). The Lord told Rebekah, not Isaac, the prophecy that the younger son, Jacob, would inherit the blessing (Gen. 25:22-23). Jesus' mother, Mary, is another example of a woman who received the word of the Lord regarding the Messiah she would bear long before her bewildered husband-to-be knew what was taking place.

In Josiah's day, the Lord did not entrust His message for Israel to the king, the king's men or advisors, the priests, or the keeper of the wardrobe, Shalum. The message was given to Shalum's wife, Huldah. The king was not reluctant or ashamed to seek Huldah to get that prophetic message, nor did he lack zeal in his efforts to honor the Word of the Lord she delivered. Josiah took action accordingly (2 Chron. 34:19-33). He demonstrated humility and the fear of the Lord. Letting God be God requires that we guard our minds from unbiblical, narrow paradigms through which we will recognize God's work and will.

The Law of Jealousy

The Mosaic law provides other types and shadows that help us understand God and His ways, similar to our discussion of the house with mold on its walls. In Numbers, we find a procedure for determining a wife's unfaithfulness but nowhere do we find one to address a husband's suspected infidelity (see Num. 5:11-31). Some have assumed this means husbands can take whatever liberties they please in this arena. Others, similar to the Greek philosophers and early church fathers, decided that infidelity was a decidedly female issue because of her presumed inability to control her desires and emotional nature. [Note: This is a separate issue from catching someone in the act of adultery.]

But is God really saying that only women are capable of being unfaithful? The history of husbands' infidelity to their wives is well documented, if not legendary, demanding we look for another conclusion. What lies hidden more deeply in this passage for us to discover? Consider the following passage as a springboard for understanding:

> For I am jealous for you with a godly jealousy; for **I betrothed you to one husband,** so that to Christ I might present you as a pure virgin. 2 Cor. 11:2, NASB

Paul describes the church as betrothed to one husband. We cannot align our thoughts, desires, and affections with the world and its ways without arousing God's jealousy. The ways of the world are not so narrowly defined as theft, immorality, murder, etc., but also dissensions, factions, lording over another, and the like (see Matt. 20:25-28; cf. 1 Cor. 11:22).

In contrast to humanity, God describes Himself as ever faithful even if we are not because He cannot deny His own nature:

> **If we are unfaithful, he remains faithful,** for he cannot deny who he is. 2 Tim. 2:13, NLT

As our Husband, God is never described as unfaithful, a trait contrary to His very nature. With this information, how might we interpret the Mosaic law regarding a wife's suspected unfaithfulness? It seems obvious that God is drawing a parallel between Himself and His people. This provides the reason why no reciprocal law for the unfaithful husband exists—God, our only Husband, could never be unfaithful.

Just before He addresses the procedure for testing a wife's faithfulness, God instructs the Israelites in making restitution to someone they have wronged, which is a sign they have been unfaithful *to the Lord*. The Lord introduces the concept of a wife's suspected unfaithfulness by connecting it with the act of being unfaithful to the Lord. We have to consider that God is addressing humanity's unfaithfulness to its Creator by giving a spiritual principle about a wife's (believer's) unfaithfulness to her husband (the Lord).

> The LORD said to Moses, "Say to the Israelites: 'Any man or woman who wrongs another in any way **and so is unfaithful to the LORD** is guilty and must confess the sin they have committed.'" Num. 5:5-7, NIV

Doing wrong to another person displays unfaithfulness *to the Lord*. David understood this principle, evidenced by the focus of his repentance when his sin against Uriah was revealed: 'Against You and You alone have I sinned…' (Psalm 51:4).

In the procedure for testing a wife's faithfulness, which can be viewed as a believer who may have wronged another person, the priest gives her 'the water of bitterness' to drink. If she is guilty, she will miscarry and be barren and under a curse. This edict does not concern only females. When God disciplined national Israel for her unfaithfulness, giving them 'bitter water' as a metaphor for affliction, they conceded that though being with child, they had given birth only to wind:

> **We were with child**, we writhed in labor, but **we gave birth to wind**. We have not brought salvation to the earth, and the people of the world have not come to life. Isa. 26:18, NIV

John recorded in Revelation that wormwood would be sent to the earth to make the water bitter (Rev. 8:11). Many would drink this water and die. This is the bitter water of jealousy sent to indict the unfaithful of God's people.

> For jealousy arouses a husband's fury, and he will show no mercy when he takes revenge. Prov. 6:34, NIV

To interpret the passage on a wife's unfaithfulness as pertaining to women alone is shallow and shortsighted. It ignores recurring themes God makes throughout Scripture, namely that: 1.) He alone is faithful, 2.) we provoke Him to jealousy by having relations with or even flirting with the world, 3.) we invite His judgment when we wrong another person, and 4.) He will send the waters of bitterness (affliction) for His people to drink to test their faithfulness. The result for being unfaithful to the Lord, which includes wrong done to another person, is miscarriage and barrenness. Is the church at large experiencing this barrenness? Judgment comes first to the house of God (1 Pet. 4:17).

If we do not seek out the treasure hidden in God's Word, we open ourselves to the same rebuke the disciples received when they did not understand Jesus' warning to beware of the 'leaven of the Pharisees.' He said this because the Pharisees ignored the weightier matters of the ceremonial law, which are love, faithfulness, justice, and mercy (Matt. 23:23; Luke 11:42). Jesus attributed the disciples' lack of insight to a lack of faith, lack of understanding what He had demonstrated in His miracles, and a heart hardened to the truth (Matt. 16:8-12; Mark 8:14-21). The remedy for this blindness is found in Christ. Paul stated that as we behold Christ, whom John called 'The Word,' we would be changed and have the veils removed from our understanding (John 12:46; 1 Cor. 13:12; 2 Cor. 3:14-18; cf. 2 Cor. 4:3-4a).

> *How is it you don't understand that I was not talking to you about bread?* Matt. 16:11, NIV

Lord, remove the veils from our minds and hearts to reveal our wrongdoing to each other and our unfaithfulness to You and Your Word. Amen.

Proverbs 31: The Wife of Noble Character

> *A wife of noble (**chayil**) character who can find? She is worth far more than rubies. Her husband has full confidence (**batach**) in her and lacks nothing of value. She brings him good, not harm, all the days of her life.* Prov. 31:10-12, NIV

King Lemuel's mother *taught* this to her son (Prov. 31:1). Most boys would not be interested in nor would they remember a discussion about choosing the right wife if this was taught prematurely. This instruction must have been taught with the proper timing, perhaps in the young man's late teens or early twenties.

God desires that His people act with a noble heart. The Bereans were noted to have a more noble heart because of their attention to God's Word (Acts 17:11). Paul wrote that if we cleanse ourselves from the ways and thinking of the world, we will be vessels for noble use (2 Tim. 2:21). Jesus taught that those who possess a noble heart receive the Word, retain it, and by persevering grow to maturity (Luke 8:15). We are to direct our minds to contemplate noble themes (Php. 4:8).

> *I say of the holy people who are in the land, "They are the noble ones in whom is all my delight." Psalm 16:3, NIV*
>
> *But the noble make noble plans, and by noble deeds they stand. Isa. 32:8, NIV*

The ideal wife is described as *chayil* (Heb. 2428) and priceless. The word *chayil* conveys the might, strength, power, and valor of warriors as well as the noble and capable traits of virtuous character. *Chayil* is often used in the context of the military. It is used poetically in this poem and elsewhere as emblematic of God's image stamped on the bearer. We might also look at this poem as a type and shadow of the manner of bride the Spirit of God labors to fashion in the church to prepare her for Jesus' return. Said differently, both men and women need to study this poem as a depiction of how they should focus their energy in this age as Jesus' bride.

The Hebrew word *batach* (Heb. 982) in verse 11 has been translated 'full confidence.' Because the nuance carries the sense of being carefree because of this confidence, we note that the woman described is a very capable woman entrusted with all the affairs of the house, including financial matters. The bride of Christ will similarly realize the trust Christ has in her when He assigns each overcomer his or her sphere of governance in His future kingdom (cf. Luke 19:16-19).

Many of us have heard teaching that demands real men perform the addition and subtraction in the checkbook. Some men fear that letting their wives balance the checkbook will cause them to lose God's favor and bring them to ruin. Some believe women only want their husbands' money to spend on themselves (sadly, some have done this). But when a godly wife helps and encourages her husband in his work, cares for him when he's sick, prepares meals from a colorful variety of fruits and vegetables alongside lean meats so he can be healthy, collects his dirty clothes scattered about, and announces that the money she has been transferring to savings is enough for him to buy the garden tractor he's had his eye on, he should realize she is for him, not against him.

The husband's security is based on this woman's stellar character. She pursues her husband's and family's good and not harm. She serves her family to the best of her ability with the resources and talent she has been given. This does not mean she never makes a mistake, but it does mean her motives are not self-centered. She pursues her objectives with godly wisdom and attention to detail.

The body of this acrostic poem can be categorized as eight areas of activity in which this exemplary wife focuses her time and energy. This is not a checklist for a husband to judge his wife. It expresses the far-reaching vision by which a woman of valor plans her work and on which she focuses her time and the family resources.

If wives take hold of the vision that their role prophetically speaks of the bride being prepared for Christ, they could theoretically (though probably not perfectly) rise above the day-to-day frustration that can accompany the challenges this role poses in order to maintain focus on the noble tasks to which they have been called. If men could internalize deeper understanding of this poem as their own personal duty to Christ as His bride, the church would be propelled to maturity at an entirely new level.

Prophetically speaking, the tasks involved parallel the preparation with which believers must concern themselves if the church is to come to maturity and unity. This requires apostolic vision and oversight with the ability to teach, discern, evaluate, and plan. It requires perseverance, endurance, selflessness, and humility. It means pouring yourself out like a drink offering for another's spiritual benefit, just as Jesus and the apostles displayed in their lives while fulfilling their tasks to equip the next generation. With this in mind, consider the following eight areas as the work not only of wives, but also of the bride of Christ in this age, which of course includes men.

Work: She works diligently, eagerly, and vigorously at whatever tasks are at hand and with all the skill, ability, and training she has received. She makes financial decisions for the well-being of her family and does not waste money lavishing comfort on herself. She evaluates her investments and time to see that they are profitable (note: this is not merely about money, but about the investments of wisdom, righteousness, and ethical practice that she seeks to impart to her children). She does not indulge herself in lazing about or idle pursuits. For contemporary use, this would mean that no matter what socioeconomic status this woman has been allotted, she makes the most of what she has and the opportunities presented to further the interests and needs of her family. (vv. 13,15,16,17,18,24)

> *Therefore, my dear brothers and sisters, stand firm. Let nothing move you. Always give yourselves fully to the work of the Lord, because you know that your labor in the Lord is not in vain.* 1 Cor. 15:58, NIV

Family: She makes sure her family is well fed with food that will benefit their health. She trains her children to take responsibility and to be productive by giving them tasks they are accountable for each day. In addition to their ongoing education, she provides opportunities for her children to be enriched through learning practical skills they can use for the future. They grow up and bless her for looking after their training, welfare, and future success. (vv. 14,15,28)

> *Who then is the faithful and wise servant, whom his master has set over his household, to give them their food at the proper time? Blessed is that servant whom his master will find so doing when he comes. Truly, I say to you, he will set him over all his possessions.* Matt. 24:45-47, NIV

The poor: She takes notice of and has compassion for the poor and needy in practical ways. (v. 20)

> *Those who give to the poor will lack nothing.* Prov. 28:27, NIV

> *Whoever is generous to the poor lends to the Lord, and he will repay him for his deed.* Prov. 19:7, ESV

> *Whoever oppresses the poor shows contempt for their Maker, but whoever is kind to the needy honors God.* Prov. 14:31, NIV

Herself and her home: She makes her home inviting by the way she manages and cares for it. She also takes care of herself, for in addition to her work clothes, she also wears garments appropriate for dignitaries or ambassadors (2 Cor. 5:20). This description implies that she takes time to develop her spiritual life (the saints will be clothed in fine linen, Rev. 19:8). Similar to the description of church overseers, she faithfully and skillfully watches over herself, her family, and her home. (vv. 22,27)

> *Since an overseer **manages God's household**, he must be blameless—not overbearing, not quick-tempered, not given to*

> *drunkenness, not violent, not pursuing dishonest gain. Rather, he must be hospitable, one who loves what is good, who is self-controlled, upright, holy and disciplined. He must hold firmly to the trustworthy message as it has been taught, so that he can encourage others by sound doctrine and refute those who oppose it.* Titus 1:7-9, NIV

The Future: She stays one step ahead, being proactive in her pursuits to prepare wisely for the days ahead (Prov. 21:5a). Because she plans, prepares, and provides for the future, she is not anxious or fearful. This would include spending time in prayer and rightly placing her confidence in the Lord that He will guide her in and make opportunity for those preparations. There is no fear of lack because she has provided for the physical needs of her family (food and clothing) and trusts in the Lord. (vv. 21,25)

> *Let us hold fast the confession of our hope without wavering, for he who promised is faithful.* Heb. 10:23, ESV

> *Those who trust in themselves are fools, but those who walk in wisdom are kept safe... The plans of the diligent lead to profit.* Prov. 8:26; 21:5a, NIV

> *Oh, fear the LORD, you His saints! There is no want to those who fear Him. The young lions lack and suffer hunger; but those who seek the LORD shall not lack any good thing.* Psalm 34:9-10, NKJV

Teaching: She is not preoccupied with low matters (gossip, entertainment, the latest fashions, etc.) but speaks with courage and wisdom. She imparts that wisdom through faithful instruction. (v. 26)

> *My son, observe the commandment of your father and **do not forsake the teaching of your mother**.* Prov. 6:20, NASB

> *Let the word of Christ richly dwell within you, **with all wisdom teaching and admonishing one another** with psalms and hymns and spiritual songs, singing with thankfulness in your hearts to God.* Col. 3:16, NASB

> ***Teach what accords with sound doctrine**... in your teaching show integrity, dignity, and sound speech that cannot be condemned.* Titus 2:1b,7b-8a, ESV

Her Husband: She runs their home well; the children are orderly. This wife is productive, hospitable, and clothed with dignity and strength. Because of this, her husband is respected in the town where they live and takes part in governance and civil matters. The city gates were the place where civil matters were discussed and decided. These qualities are included in the NT requirements for deacons and overseers.

Her husband honors, blesses, and praises her. She helps him in whatever way she can so that his name is honored. Seeing the noble and selfless goals she sets and the diligent work she performs to pursue those goals, he says, 'You are amazing! Many women are virtuous, competent, and accomplished, but you have outdone them all.' This reveals his respect and admiration not only for her character, but also for the way she manages and works. (vv. 11,23,25,28-29)

> *A wife of noble character is her husband's crown... Houses and wealth are inherited from parents, but a prudent wife is from the Lord.* Prov. 12:4a; 19:14, NIV

As a portrayal of the bride of Christ, this poem provides a blueprint for the conduct the Lord expects of His bride. We have a long way to go. We don't have an orderly home. The name of Christ is dishonored because of the behavior of some professing Christians. Ghandi stated, "I like your Christ. I do not like your Christians. They are so unlike your Christ." The world is watching. Believers must concern themselves with their conduct to please God and bring honor to His name.

The poem concludes by reminding us that charm is deceptive and beauty fleeting. No matter what our culture tries to sell us, concentrating on these things more than character, intimacy with the Lord, and caring for our families will cause us to fail as women of God and as the bride of Christ.

Notice that her noble, virtuous *work* brings her public praise—a description only accomplished when undergirded by love alongside godly motives and character (note: this is not about perfection but rather heart posture). In the parables and in the letters to the seven churches, Jesus emphasized that He will judge us by what we have done. The righteousness of Christ secures our salvation and is freely given, but our faithfulness is determined by what we have accomplished with what He has given us in the environment we have been placed.

> *Charm is deceptive, and beauty is fleeting; but a woman who fears the* LORD *is to be praised.* **Honor her for all that her hands have done**, *and let her works bring her praise at the city gate.* Prov. 31:30-31, NIV

Closing Thoughts

In some marriages, husband and wife no longer enjoy each other's company but have resolved to continue the relationship because of their vows taken before the Lord. Neither lives to help or honor the other. This is far from the picture of Christ and the church that God intended married couples to model. As a parallel, many believers are in the same rut, neither enjoying their relationship with the Lord nor living to do what is pleasing to Him. It has become all about personal fulfillment and accomplishment, even for some in ministry.

In other situations, subtle forms of envy or jealousy crowd out love. I heard a message from Dr. David Jeremiah that exposed what can happen when a husband envies a wife who begins to develop her own talents and abilities. Fearing she may surpass him and be more successful, he does everything he can to demean her efforts and sabotage the opportunities that come her way. This harmful envy can cause her to shrivel inwardly and lose her identity and drive.

What a breath of fresh air the church would experience if husbands and wives determined to remain focused on higher matters, rather than spend their energies selfishly or trying to enforce perceived scriptural boundaries and prescribed divisions in practical matters of family life. Loving and honoring one another is the higher matter to which this relationship must aspire to attain. This is impossible for our natural self-centeredness, but by the Spirit we overcome worldly ways.

> *Love endures long and is patient and kind;* **love never is envious** *nor boils over with jealousy, is not boastful or vainglorious, does not display itself haughtily. It is not conceited (arrogant and inflated with pride); it is not rude (unmannerly) and does not act unbecomingly. Love (God's love in us)* **does not insist on its own rights or its own way**, *for it is* **not self-seeking**; *it is* **not touchy or fretful or resentful**; *it takes no account of the evil done to it [it pays no attention to a suffered wrong]* ('**keeps no record of wrongs**' *NIV). 1 Cor. 13:4-5, AMP*

Chapter 6

Wisdom Personified as a Woman

> ***Blessed are those who find wisdom***, *those who gain understanding, for she is more profitable than silver and yields better returns than gold.* ***She is more precious than rubies; nothing you desire can compare*** *with her.* ***Long life*** *is in her right hand; in her left hand are* ***riches and honor***. *Her ways are pleasant ways, and* ***all her paths are peace***. ***She is a tree of life*** *to those who take hold of her; those who hold her fast will be blessed.*
> Prov. 3:13-18, NIV

Wisdom is personified as a woman and described as 'more precious than rubies' (see also Job 28:18; Prov. 7:4; 8:11; 9:1-6; 14:33; Matt. 11:19; Luke 7:35, etc.). In Proverbs 31, a wife of noble character is also described as 'more precious than rubies' (v. 10) and speaking with wisdom (v. 26). The Word repeatedly links rubies with the worth of wisdom, women, and wives.

I would like you to consider the following passage in a new context, discussed shortly. Notice that John describes God as having the appearance of 'jasper and ruby' (other translations: carnelian, sardius, or red quartz—all red stones; e.g., cf. Ex. 28:17 ESV, HCSB, GW, etc.):

> *At once I was in the Spirit, and there before me was a throne in heaven with someone sitting on it. And* ***the one who sat there had the appearance of jasper and ruby***. *A rainbow that shone like an emerald encircled the throne.* Rev. 4:2-3, NIV

Jasper and Ruby

Every biblical description of God is meant to teach us something about His character. In this passage, John described our God as seated on His throne of authority, having the appearance of jasper (other translations: diamond) and ruby (other translations: carnelian or sardius stone). As a spiritual truth, I believe this concise portrayal displays God's manifold, strategic wisdom in creating men and women for the purpose of divinely delegated authority and balanced governance on the earth.

Since we have already mentioned the use of rubies to describe the worth of wives in chapter five, I want to begin this discussion by delving a little further into this aspect of God's image. Wisdom is also connected with rubies as noted in the opening passage. This is in keeping with wisdom's personification as a woman. Since the worth of both is consistently connected to rubies, the pattern suggests that this aspect of God's character—wisdom—can be found in His image as imparted to and represented by women. Do we have further support from the Word that God created women as a picture of His wisdom?

Just as the Lord endowed men with natural strength, He created women with a natural beauty men do not possess. The Hebrew word *yophi* (Heb. 3308), typically translated beauty, comes from the primary root *yaphah* (Heb. 3302), which properly means to be bright. The connection becomes apparent if we recall that the Man dressed in linen told Daniel that 'the wise will shine *brightly* as the heavens' (Dan. 12:3). Rubies and beauty, with its inherent meaning to be bright, are both biblical descriptions of wisdom as well as women.

In Scripture, beauty (to be bright) not only refers to the physical appearance of women (e.g., Esth. 2:7), but it also refers to God and wisdom in government. In reference to God, the sons of Korah wrote prophetically of Jesus, describing Him as unequaled in beauty (Psalm 45:2). David spoke of his desire to behold the beauty (Heb. 5278 *noam*: grace, beauty, splendor) of the Lord (Psalm 27:4). We witness the aspect of brightness as Asaph prayed that God would shine His face on Israel (Psalm 80). In Psalm 119:135, we note the connection between God shining His face on His people (a picture of His beauty) and learning God's Word (acquiring wisdom). John described Jesus' face as 'shining as the sun in all its splendor' (Rev. 1:16). Each describes the beauty of the Lord with the brightness of His splendor.

Beauty also describes God's heavenly government: 'Out of Zion, the perfection of beauty, God will shine forth' (Psalm 50:2). Isaiah spoke of 'seeing the King in His beauty,' referring to Jesus' future righteous government (Isa. 33:17). Prophetic passages lament corruption of governmental beauty caused by abandoning divine wisdom (Jer. 4:30; Lam. 2:15; Ezk. 6:14-15; 27:3-11; 28:11-12,17; 31:7-8; Zech. 9:17). Wisdom is essential for government to be beautiful rather than corrupt.

The desire beauty provokes is intentional as a picture of the desirable nature of wisdom. As far as the pure and holy desires instilled in men by the Spirit of God, the physical desire for a woman's beauty parallels the spiritual desire to acquire wisdom. Women were meant to be the embodiment of wisdom, evidenced by the beauty she was created to display for men to desire. Solomon desired wisdom above all else when he was crowned king. This greatly pleased the Lord. Solomon's desire for and acquisition of many wives demonstrates what happens when this desire becomes corrupted by insatiable appetite for the creation that was meant to *illustrate* as a type and shadow the beauty of God's wisdom. The longings God has instilled in every person can become corrupted when we seek to fulfill those longings in carnal or worldly ways.

Beauty pursued as only a physical attribute is a corruption of God's intention. Solomon warns of the trap this kind of seductive beauty holds for the unwary—a snare that leads to ruin and death (Prov. 5-7). Solomon immediately contrasts the physical beauty of the wayward woman with the spiritual beauty of wisdom (Prov. 8:1-9:12). He concludes this section of Proverbs with a warning about the foolish woman who desires to corrupt the simple into pursuing the cheap and fleeting substitute of physical pleasure for the prudence of staying on the narrow path of life that leads to wisdom (Prov. 9:13-18).

We now understand that beauty and the nuance of shining or being bright are connected in the Word with women, wisdom, God, and government. This sums up the ruby aspect of God's appearance.

Rebbetzin Tziporah Heller, full-time lecturer at Neve Yerushalayim College in Jerusalem, gives further support for the connection between women and wisdom. In her January 2000 article, "Men & Women: Jewish View of Gender Differences," Heller highlights the grammatical oddity of Genesis 1:27-28, "God created the man in His image; in the image of God He created **him**, male and female He created **them**. And God blessed **them**." Jewish oral tradition explains this by drawing from the knowledge that God is neither male nor female, and the first human created in His image was complete. To prevent self-sufficiency outside of relationship with God, the Lord brought two from the one—male and female who would carry different but complementary aspects of His image, and God blessed **them**. This would "create a healthy situation of dependence, yearning, and mutual giving. Human beings are not meant to be alone because then they would have no one to give to, no one to grow with, and nothing to strive for. To actualize oneself spiritually, a human being cannot be alone."

Heller then confirms the connection between women and wisdom:

> The Torah also describes the process of Eve's creation using the word *vayiven*, "God built." This word shares the same Hebrew root as *binah*, meaning "insight" or understanding. This suggests, as it says in the Talmud, that women were created with an extra dose of wisdom and understanding.
>
> *Binah* is much greater than "women's intuition"—it means the ability to enter something and understand it from the inside—what has been called "inner reasoning." Men tend to have more of what is called *da'at*, an understanding which comes from the outside, a type of understanding which tends to be more connected to facts and figures.
>
> Society loses an enormous asset when only one of these intellectual aspects is valued. Just as two eyes make our view of things more accurate, seeing things from the two different male and female perspectives makes our understanding of life more complete.[20]

So now we contemplate jasper's meaning. I believe the Word supports interpreting jasper as 'strength' as well as 'righteousness and justice.' In his description of the New Jerusalem (Rev. 21:9-27), John states that the first foundation and the walls are made of jasper (vv. 18-19). Both uses imply selection of the material for its strength for building a stable structure. Walls also speak of protection (e.g., Ezra 9:9; Isa. 26:1).

The Word further describes the foundation of God's throne as being one of righteousness and justice (Psalm 89:14; 97:2). Men were created with physical strength as a picture of jasper. Paul stated men reflect God's glory, which implies His power (cf. Deut. 33:17; Isa. 16:14; 21:16; Dan. 11:39; Mark 13:26). This is also paralleled with the New Jerusalem, which 'shone with the glory of God, and its brilliance was like that of a very precious jewel, like a jasper' (Rev. 21:11).

These two aspects of God's character, 1.) **strength** (might and protection) as a picture of righteousness and justice (represented by jasper for the walls and foundation), and 2.) **beauty** (light) as a picture of wisdom and good government (represented by rubies and personified as a woman), give us greater understanding of God's image given to humanity for the original mandate to rule over the earth. This remains God's purpose for the crown of His creation.

> *The LORD made the heavens. Splendor and majesty are before Him, **strength and beauty** are in His sanctuary.* Psalm 96:6, NASB

Righteousness and justice go hand-in-hand with wisdom. The Word also reminds us that God laid the foundations of the world (righteousness and justice) in wisdom (see also Prov. 8:27-31; Jer. 10:12; 51:15):

> **By wisdom the Lord laid the earth's foundations,** *by understanding he set the heavens in place.* Prov. 3:19, NIV

When God created man, He did so with the express purpose of establishing righteous and just rule on the earth. The foundations of the earth, God's footstool (Isa. 66:1), are righteousness and justice, and they were laid in wisdom. God created man and woman in His image to rule over creation and, more specifically, to reflect these traits as His representatives on the earth.

The man would represent God's strength and might (jasper) as the picture of a strong foundation of righteousness and justice expressed through his greater physical strength. Men would also offer protection for the physically smaller and weaker women. The woman would represent God's beauty as an illustration of wisdom, of far greater worth than rubies, expressed in her role as a 'suitable helper' with 'wisdom and faithful instruction on her tongue.' Both are necessary to rule.

'All the paths of wisdom are peace,' (Prov. 3:17). The current global lack of peace is the result of the Fall and our inattention to God's wisdom. Wisdom, righteousness, and justice are inseparable for ruling as God intended. We will fail in our efforts to fulfill God's mandate to govern if we isolate any of these away from the others and place our confidence in our own reason and design rather than God's.

> *I [Wisdom] walk in the way of righteousness... in the midst of the paths of justice, that I may cause those who love me **to inherit [true] riches...*** Prov. 8:20-21, AMP

Fathers and Mothers Are Both Needed

> *My son, heed the discipline* (**musar**) *of your father, and do not abandon the teaching* (**torah**) *of your mother.* Prov. 1:8, CJB

Notice Solomon's use of *musar* (Heb. 4148) for the father's role, and *torah* (Heb. 8451) for the mother's. *Musar* typically carries the meaning of discipline or chastening, most often in the form of oral instruction but also including corporal means, with the goal being self-control and instruction in what is right. Inherently, this entails training in righteousness and execution of justice for wrongdoing.

Torah comes from the word *yarah* (Heb. 3384), which means instruction in doctrine, building precept upon precept. *Torah* is often translated 'law' and associated with gaining wisdom (Psalm 19:7). Zodhiates explained that torah "was not to be perceived as restrictions, but the very means by which one could reach a spiritual ideal."[21] Confirming what we previously discussed, we see the woman's role depicted as imparting wisdom through teaching God's Word.

Recall also that Eve was tempted by the serpent to gain wisdom ahead of God's timing (Gen. 3:6), just as the adversary tempted Jesus to take His rightful rule over the earth outside of God's timing and plan (Matt. 4:8-9). Our enemy will often try to preempt God's timing by coaxing us into presumptive action in the arena of our callings. For example, David walked in humility and demonstrated great patience by inquiring of the Lord rather than acting presumptuously to take the throne ahead of time. He did this after he had been anointed and knew God had chosen him to be king (1 Sam. 16:1-13; 24:4-22; 26:5-25).

Similarly, as this study suggests, women were created in God's image as a type and shadow of His wisdom. Satan recognized this in Eve and exploited her God-given desire for wisdom. She did not have the experience to recognize his tactic and was deceived. It is a cruel irony that the one created as the type and shadow of wisdom would be deceived, and the one created to embody righteousness and justice would transgress God's law, as discussed in chapter four.

Two Pillars

When Solomon built the temple, he set two pillars in front and named them *Jachin* and *Boaz* (1 Kings 7:21; 2 Chron. 3:17). One meant 'He will establish' and the other 'in Him is strength.' The Lord *established* the earth by wisdom and in His *strength* laid the foundations of righteousness and justice. Solomon wrote that righteousness, justice, and the proper course can only be discerned through wisdom (Prov. 2:9). Once again, we see the pattern of interdependence between strength and beauty—jasper and ruby—for wise governance.

> [T]he pillars of the earth are the Lord's, and on them he has set the world. 1 Sam. 2:8b, ESV

Part of the church has rejected God's wisdom by presuming that only one pillar is needed. We often joke about men who don't ask for directions when they are lost. Some feel that accepting advice equals admitting weakness. Correction injures our pride. However, the Lord does not find it amusing when we fail to listen to counsel or wisdom, reminding us that only fools despise wisdom and instruction (Prov. 1:7; 23:9). God commends those who listen to wise counsel (Prov. 12:8).

> **Do not forsake wisdom,** and she will **protect** you; **love her,** and she will **watch over** you. Prov. 4:6, NIV

In the next passage, we find an object lesson where strength finds its success only when coupled with wisdom. The one swinging the axe finds he must exert more strength unless he possesses the wisdom to take time to sharpen the blade.

> **If the axe is dull** and he does not sharpen its edge, then he must **exert more strength. Wisdom has the advantage of giving success.** Ecc. 10:10, NASB

The old Irish legend of the larger and smaller lumberjacks in a contest to fell trees provides an excellent illustration with the same lesson. In this contest, the stronger lumberjack with the larger axe confidently felled tree after tree, knowing that his superior size and strength would propel him to victory. Although his strokes were not as accurate, by brute force and endurance he would succeed.

The smaller lumberjack, however, had to make every stroke count and therefore accuracy was needed. He also took time every hour to sharpen his axe. The onlookers thought this was a terrible strategy because while he sat to sharpen his blade, the huge man trudged on with much sweat, felling tree after tree.

At the end of the allotted time, it came as a surprise to everyone except the smaller lumberjack that the larger and stronger lumberjack had lost. Taking the time to sharpen his blade—to use wisdom—allowed the smaller, less impressive lumberjack to win.

Leveling the Playing Field

> *Wisdom and strength <u>belong</u> **to God**.* Job 12:13a, HCSB

This verse reminds us that the qualities required to rule the earth are not inherent in our nature but in God's. Men and women only represent those qualities. We cannot take our object lesson to make a rule that women have more wisdom and men more righteousness and justice. Men and women are emblems of these traits—types and shadows.

Many women have been judged for being empty-headed. But can we honestly say men are known for righteousness and justice? I think we would have to agree that corruption is seen at every level of the church, business, and government, each predominantly run by men. If wisdom is judged by the fruit it bears, the current state of the world reflects the wisdom we have used to establish government, economics, and the church.

Does this mean we are to blame men for all our problems? No, obviously the current state of affairs resulted not only from imbalance and ignoring divine wisdom, but also due to humanity's fallen nature and the adversary's activity. I think we can safely say that had women been in charge, the outcome may have been different, but it would still have been corrupt.

I am compelled to conclude that the traits of wisdom, righteousness, and justice are a picture pointing to God's plan for the human race: men and women working side-by-side with their respective gifts representing God's nature. Neither gender is given all the tools necessary to make this a unilateral endeavor (see Gen. 2:18). We need each other because the diversity of giftings makes it possible for us to reach the goal only when we work together. In addition, we get the coverage we need for those troublesome blind spots.

This is in keeping with God's nature to level the playing field, not by making things equal for everyone, but by imparting a particular strength to one and giving a complementary strength lacking in the first to someone else. For example, the Word tells us that some have been given worldly wealth, a wealth that fades and disappears (James 1:10; cf. Luke 16:9; Prov. 11:28; 27:24; James 5:1-2). To the poor, however, God gives faith and an exalted position (Psalm 12:5; 14:6; 107:9; 113:7; James 1:9; 2:5; Rev. 2:9; cf. Prov. 28:11; Matt. 13:22; Luke 1:48; 8:14; 12:21; 18:24; 2 Cor. 6:10; Rev. 3:17). The goal is equality.

> *Our desire is not that others might be relieved while you are hard pressed, but **that there might be equality**. At the present time your plenty will supply what they need, so that in turn their plenty will supply what you need. **The goal is equality, as it is written: "The one who gathered much did not have too much, and the one who gathered little did not have too little."*** 2 Cor. 8:13-15, NIV

God has chosen the poor to be rich in faith through greater personal reliance on God's Word and possessing the love of God that casts out fear incited by dire circumstances. The rich, as James described, have been humbled by God in that what they do to acquire wealth will wither away. Those who are rich should be humbled in their view of themselves because God has chosen them to receive *worldly* monetary wealth (temporary riches that fade) to support the poor. To others He has assigned the *spiritual* wealth of heaven (eternal riches that last) to enlighten and strengthen those that have not.

This explains the way God has chosen to humble the rich and honor the poor. Each is to use the gift of wealth he has been given, whether spiritual or monetary, for the edification and care of the believers and the poor among us. God's goal in doing so is to demonstrate that we need each other; that no one individual or group of individuals has everything necessary to run the show.

> *My goal is that they may be **encouraged in heart and united in love, so that they may have the full riches of complete understanding,** in order that they may know the mystery of God, namely, Christ.* Col. 2:2, NIV

Jesus: Our Wisdom, Righteousness, and Justice

Sadly, history reveals the regrettable course of humanity, namely that we prefer to work alone—one gender, race, nation, denomination, socioeconomic stratum, age group, intellectual caste, or academic clique exalting itself over another. This is rooted in pride and the reasoning of man. Isaiah spoke of the result:

> *Justice is turned back, and righteousness stands far away; for truth has stumbled in the street, and uprightness cannot enter.* Isa. 59:14, NASB

The Lord searched but could not find righteousness, justice, or truth on the earth. Isaiah wrote that God would return these to the earth by His own strength, prophesying the coming King (Isa. 59:15-16), the Messiah who would establish justice on the earth (Isa. 42:1-4). Jesus will reign with the spirit of wisdom, counsel, and might. He will be girded with righteousness to make just decisions for the earth (Isa. 11:1-5).

Through the Lord's righteousness and justice, He preserves both people and animals (Psalm 36:6; cf. Jonah 4:11). His righteousness and justice are an expression of His love (Psalm 33:5). Believers conformed to His character and walking in righteousness and justice will participate in His reign through exercising His wisdom, evidenced by the following passage that prophesies of rulers who will reign with Christ:

> *See, **a king will reign in righteousness** <u>and rulers will rule</u> with justice... Of the greatness of his government and **peace there will be no end**. He will reign on David's throne and over his kingdom, establishing and **upholding it with justice and righteousness** from that time on and forever. **The zeal of the Lord Almighty will accomplish this**.* Isa. 32:1; 9:7, NIV

Paul describes Jesus as our wisdom and our righteousness (1 Cor. 1:30). We had utterly failed to walk in humility or wisdom, resulting in a world mired in lies, unrighteousness, and injustice far from God's original intent. We are admonished many times in the Word to get wisdom at all cost (Prov. 4:7; 16:16; 19:8; 23:23; James 1:5). God's wisdom is characterized as pure, peace-loving, merciful, and impartial, among other qualities:

> ***Who is wise and understanding among you**? Let them show it by their good life, by deeds done in the **humility that comes from wisdom**... But **the wisdom that comes from heaven is first of all pure**; then **peace-loving**, considerate, **submissive**, full of mercy and good fruit, **impartial** and sincere.* James 3:13,17, NIV

Wisdom's Prerequisite: Humility and the Fear of the Lord

Returning to wisdom requires the fear of the Lord (Psalm 111:10a). Pride in race, nation, denomination, gender, age group/generation, wealth, strength, and/or our own abilities have brought us disgrace, as we were warned, and leads to partiality (Prov. 11:2). Humility comes before honor (Prov. 15:33), and only the humble receive grace for what has been set before them (James 4:6; 1 Pet. 5:5). Daniel also reminds us that wisdom and strength belong to God alone (Dan. 2:20). Jeremiah confirms that the only basis we have for boasting is that we know God:

> *This is what the LORD says: "**Let not the wise boast** of their wisdom or the **strong boast** of their strength or the **rich boast** of their riches, but let the one who boasts **boast about this: that they have the understanding to know me**, that I am the LORD, who exercises kindness, justice and righteousness on earth, for in these I delight," declares the LORD.* Jer. 9:23-24, NIV

Wisdom from God is the only means we have to 'understand what is right and just' (Prov. 2:9). God-ordained leadership will exhibit humility and the fear of the Lord, leading to wisdom, righteousness, and justice, a three-stranded cord that cannot be easily broken.

> *Moreover, an attacker may defeat someone who is alone, but two can resist him; and* **a three-stranded cord is not easily broken.** Ecc. 4:12, CJB

This three-stranded cord pictures the partnership of men and women in submission to God. They must work together with all their might as pillars for God's kingdom—strength through righteousness and justice and the beauty of wisdom to understand what true righteousness and justice entail. In order to function as intended, one pillar cannot be exalted above the other. Neither can one of the pillars be flimsier than the other. These pillars must have matching structural strength and integrity if the building they support is to maintain balance. God supplies the spiritual substance for both and created a partnership in His image to extend His character through those He created to rule over the earth.

Humility requires we understand that God alone possesses the wisdom, righteousness, and justice demanded for governance. Men were not created with the full package but were meant to personify the strength, righteousness, and justice inherent in that part of God's character represented by jasper. Since the man was not given everything, the woman was created alongside the man to personify God's character of beauty and wisdom represented by ruby. Together there is completeness for God's original mandate that those created in His image would govern the earth.

After Adam spent the day working by naming the animals, Moses recorded that no suitable helper was found for him. Despite walking in God's manifest presence, God decreed that it was not good for Adam to be alone; that neither work nor God's creation would fill this need.

Scriptural Parallels Between Wisdom and Women

Compare the following passages on both women and wisdom. Notice the similar language that furnishes additional support that women were created as a type and shadow of God's beauty as found in wisdom.

1. **Each is described as a crown**:

   A wife of noble character is her husband's crown. Prov. 12:4, NIV

   The crown of the wise is their wealth of Wisdom. Prov. 14:24, AMP

2. **Loving either demonstrates a man loves himself**:

   He who loves his wife loves himself. Eph. 5:28b, ESV

   He who gets wisdom loves his own soul. Prov. 19:8, NKJV

3. **Wise building is attributed to both**:

   Every wise woman builds up her home. Prov. 14:1, CJB

   By wisdom a house is built. Prov. 24:3, NIV

4. **Finding either is equated with obtaining God's favor**:

   *He who finds a wife finds a good thing and obtains favor from the L*ORD. Prov. 18:22, ESV

   For whoever finds me [Wisdom] finds life and draws forth and obtains favor from the Lord. Prov. 8:35, AMP

Wisdom is a 'tree of life to those who find her' (Prov. 3:18). Solomon added that 'those who **hold her fast** will be blessed.' When we remember that women personify wisdom, we can draw a parallel from this statement that reveals an aspect of God's hatred of divorce. Divorcing 'the wife of your youth' (Prov. 5:18) is the *opposite* of holding fast, displays unfaithfulness (Mal. 2:16), and symbolizes a departure from wisdom and life.

Abandoning wisdom leads to corruption. God's wisdom is seen as foolishness to the world, which reminds us that it is not based on man's ability to reason alone. Neither is strength, whether physical, military, or financial, the key to acting with righteousness and justice. Without wisdom from above, the power we wield is not beautiful but a corruption of the mandate given to humanity. I believe the Lord's directive to the church in this hour is:

> *Wisdom is the principal thing; **therefore get wisdom**. And in all your getting, **get understanding**.* Prov. 4:7, NKJV

Chapter 7

Scriptural Precedents

> *All Scripture is God-breathed and is valuable for teaching the truth, convicting of sin, correcting faults and training in right living; thus anyone who belongs to God may be fully equipped for every good work.* 2 Tim. 3:16-17, CJB

The Bible offers more than the regulatory law found in the Ten Commandments and Mosaic ceremonial and civil law. It also provides case law—examples of individual lives for believers to study. Understanding the principle of case law and the precedents provided is directly applicable to our study, as we will soon see.

"Law students principally study case law to understand the application of law to facts and learn the courts' subsequent interpretations of statutes."[22] Similar to a collection of court rulings, the Bible offers several precedents involving women who rose to notable positions of influence by the hand of God. A precedent is a binding legal ruling by which all lower courts must abide in similar cases. For our discussion, the decisions God made to include in His Word the stories of women in various roles furnish the legal justification and legitimacy of women exercising those roles. These stories range from those who were discipled at Jesus' feet to those who fulfilled more visible and prominent roles in leadership.

> In common law legal systems, a precedent or authority is a principle or rule established in a previous legal case that is either binding on or persuasive for a court or other tribunal when deciding subsequent cases with similar issues or facts. The general principle in common law legal systems is that similar cases should be decided so as to give similar and predictable outcomes, and the principle of precedent is the mechanism by which that goal is attained. Black's Law Dictionary defines "precedent" as a "rule of law established for the first time by a

court for a particular type of case and thereafter referred to in deciding similar cases."[23]

The use of precedents in a legal system provides a safeguard to make sure the regulatory law is interpreted properly and uniformly. It prevents abuse of the law based on faulty interpretation. Previous cases or examples in the Bible reveal God's judgment of how His own law should be interpreted.

The use of precedents "is built on the doctrine of *Stare Decisis* ("stand by decided matters"), which directs a court to look to past decisions for guidance on how to decide a case before it."[22] Decisions made by superior courts (for our discussion, God's heavenly court) are binding precedents that the court itself and all lower courts are obligated to follow. God's case law—the decisions He has provided in the Bible by the examples given—establishes binding precedent for lower courts (the church). Any matter in which the church renders a decision must be consistent with God's previous rulings. As believers subject to the Lord, we are duty-bound to respect God's established precedents as given in His Word.

"The use of precedent has been justified as providing predictability, stability, fairness, and efficiency in the law."

- **Predictability**: Precedent provides understanding of rights and obligations in particular circumstances, providing established legal outcome to evaluate the legality of a course of action.

- **Stability**: "Society can expect the law, which organizes social relationships in terms of rights and obligations, to remain relatively stable and coherent through the use of precedent. The need is great in society to rely on legal rules, even if persons disagree with particular ones."

- **Fairness**: The idea that similar cases should be treated the same is anchored in our belief that God considers everyone equal before the law. Similar cases cannot be treated differently unless there are "legally relevant and clearly justifiable reasons. Precedent promotes judicial restraint and limits a judge's ability to determine the outcome of a case in a way that he or she might choose if there were no precedent. This function of precedent gives it its moral force."

- **Efficiency**: "Reliance on the accumulation of legal rules helps guide judges in their resolution of legal disputes. If judges had to begin the law anew in each case, they would add more time to the adjudicative process and would duplicate their efforts."[22]

Biblical examples provide precedents that also establish a system of checks and balances. These precedents ensure that individual translations and transcriptions of the biblical text are properly validated by the precedents given. Stated differently, precedents help us discern whether we have introduced translator bias into a specific text incongruent with the precedents given. They also alert us to the possibility of transcription error. This is especially important because the original documents are no longer available. The Bible's internal system of checks and balances, provided by biblical *case* law (the real life examples of men and women God chose to include in the Bible), is meant to help interpreters and students of the Word to properly understand and interpret the *regulatory* law recorded in the Bible.

What precedents do we have of the God-ordained functions and roles of women in the Bible? In this chapter, we will explore examples of valiant and noble women provided in the Word. This will furnish us with adequate precedents for study in our quest to appreciate with greater clarity the roles God has ordained for women to fulfill in the public arena and church. This will also give us the necessary lens through which to understand and interpret the regulatory principles Paul established for church governance, especially as they pertain to women.

Some of the women we will study were single, some were married. We have no indication from the Word that the husbands of these *chayil* women felt threatened, neglected, diminished, or otherwise offended by their wives' higher stations. We also have no record that they needed to exert authority over their wives when these women exercised their gifts and callings publicly. To demand this must have been so is to read something into the text that is not there.

The 'Twelve' and the 'Seventy' Disciples (see Lk. 9:1; 10:1)

It seems a legitimate argument that if the Lord wanted women in leadership, He would have chosen at least one to be included among the twelve disciples. Using the same argument, we would also notice that Jesus chose no Gentiles or slaves. From this, we would have to conclude that the church must require all leadership to be free Jewish men, preferably fishermen, tax collectors, tent makers, or other tradesmen.

But what was Jesus establishing through His choices? If we remember that Jesus was establishing the prophesied new covenant, just as Moses established the old, the parallels become obvious. The old covenant was established with the twelve sons of Jacob and the seventy elders of Israel. Moses told the Israelites that God would raise up a prophet *like him*:

> *The Lord your God will raise up for you a **prophet like me** from among you, from your fellow Israelites. You must listen to him.*
> Deut. 18:15, NIV

Along with many other signs and prophetic fulfillments, the twelve and seventy disciples gave the people of Israel a direct and perfect parallel from which they could be convinced Jesus was 'the one' that had been promised—the long-awaited prophet just like Moses. The correlation is obvious and Israel should have recognized its importance. Moses instructed Israel to listen to the Prophet 'like him.' Sadly, they did not recognize Jesus despite all the proof and fulfillment of Scripture. In the final analysis, He wasn't what they expected or wanted.

Exemplary Women in the Word

The following discussion takes a brief look at the lives of exemplary women in the Bible called to fulfill various roles. These provide case law examples of God's inclusion of women in leadership and other functions. To dismiss them as exceptions to 'the rule' denies the reasons for which God included these stories: to establish His approval for women in these roles as well as implant an internal system of checks and balances into the biblical text.

This internal system promotes interpretation integrity and validity. In other words, it furnishes a safety check to keep translators and interpreters from imposing their own views on the regulatory passages. Precedents serve a protective function in that they can be used to expose translator or interpreter bias or carelessness.

Miriam

Miriam is recorded as a prophet (Ex. 15:20) and a leader to the nation of Israel during the critical period when God delivered the Hebrews out of Egypt.

> *I brought you up from the land of Egypt. I redeemed you from a life of slavery. I sent Moshe, Aharon and **Miryam to lead you**.* Mic. 6:4, CJB

Though she did not faultlessly fulfill her role (see Num. 12), we know from studying King David's life that imperfection does not invalidate a calling or even the overall success of a leader in God's eyes (see 2 Kings 16:2; Acts 13:22).

Deborah

Deborah was also a prophet and leader.

> **Then <u>the Lord chose leaders</u>** *called [raised up] ·judges [leaders; not courtroom judges, but* **leaders who guided the nation through difficult times,** *sometimes as military commanders],* **·who saved the Israelites** *from [to deliver them from the hand of] the ·robbers [raiders; plunderers].* Jdg. 2:16, EXB

> *Now D'vorah,* ***a woman and a prophet****, the wife of Lapidot, was judging Isra'el at that time.* Jdg. 4:4, CJB

Understanding that God Himself chose the judges (see the first passage) quickly nullifies any argument that God did not raise up Deborah. Some have argued that the absence of the specific language 'God raised up' next to her name in the biblical account implies that she took the honor upon herself. The recording of Judges 2:16 proves the Holy Spirit validated Deborah and every other judge in this book as God's selection for leader in Israel during this period.

I have read arguments stating that Deborah's selection as leader indicated there was no man available for God's work. This is a faithless statement and another example of reading into Scripture what is not there. The Lord is able to raise up anyone He wills, just as we learned in the lives of Abraham, Isaac, and Jacob (cf. Deut. 7:6-7). What about Balaam's donkey (Num. 22:28-30)? Consider also the cowering Gideon whom God made into a valiant war hero (Jdg. 6:11-7:25). God chooses whom He wills and empowers them to complete the task before them. It is not innate ability or any other factor of perceived or actual advantage or strength that makes us useful to God. It is our fear of the Lord and humility before God, knowing that unless His strength works through us, we will fall short of the goal.

Others argue that this was God's judgment, using a common translation of Isaiah 3:12 as support: *"O My people! Their oppressors are children, and women rule over them. O My people! Those who guide you lead you astray and confuse the direction of your paths."*

The Revised English Bible (REB) (Oxford University Press, 1992) consulted the Septuagint (later manuscripts have shown greater textual variance) and rendered this verse as, *"Moneylenders strip my people bare, and usurers lord it over them. My people, those who guide you are leading you astray and putting you on the path to ruin."* They are not alone in their translation (consult the following English versions: CEB, GNT, NET).

The Reformer's Notes to the Geneva Bible (as well as other commentators, e.g., Adam Clarke, Albert Barnes, etc.) agree that the word *nashim*, if translated 'women,' is not to be taken literally (see also English versions OJB, VOICE, TLB). This would contradict God's decision to raise up Deborah as a judge to bring deliverance to Israel. Israel was already under judgment for her faithlessness. Deborah was God's answer to their prayer for deliverance as were the other judges.

The verses immediately following the Isaiah passage make better cohesive sense when the Septuagint rendering is used. The Lord proceeds to judge those people indicted as poor rulers, and He singles out the elders and princes as the ones who were oppressing the people and robbing the poor (most likely through usury; see vv. 13-15).

Deborah's name comes from a Hebrew word (1682 *d'vorah*) that means orderly or systematic as seen in the life of a bee. It is derived from the root word, *davar* (1696). This root figuratively refers to speaking but also of subduing. It is commonly translated not only as to say or speak, but to command, exhort, consult, and answer. Deborah's name prophetically foreshadowed her functions as prophet, judge, and military leader.

She was married to Lappidoth who no doubt received honor because of his association with Deborah. There is no evidence that he relinquished his man card or needed years of therapy to find himself because the Lord chose his wife rather than him for the position of judge.

When a friend receives an honor or promotion, a true friend will be genuinely happy for their success and rejoice in their achievement. This is how husbands and wives especially need to direct their hearts toward each other. If we feel rejected, offended, jealous, dejected, or somehow less as a person when our spouse receives an honor and is suddenly thrust into the spotlight, leading us to question our very existence and role in society, we have to wonder what is at the center of our heart. Some may have deep-seated issues with rejection, but for others this reaction may be rooted in self-centeredness, vain ambition, and pride. We need the mind of Christ to be in agreement with the leaders God chooses to serve the family, church, and society as a whole.

Jael

Jael 'with the nail' is an example of a courageous hero in the OT. While it is a well-established fact that the average male strength is greater than that of the average female, Jael demonstrated that women are capable of cunning and bravery as well (read the story in Jdg. 4:17-24).

A woman performing courageous and valiant action is in keeping with the Proverbs 31 definition of women as *chayil*. Though Jael's actions may make believers today a little squeamish, they were fitting under the circumstances and for their time in history.

Abigail

Abigail, described as intelligent and beautiful, was married to a harsh and shrewd man, Nabal, who was unethical in his business dealings. Read 1 Samuel 25 if you are unfamiliar with the story.

The servants knew Nabal as a worthless man who would never listen to anyone. Abigail took charge of a very dire situation in order to prevent her husband and the other men in their household from being killed. She directed her servants to load up food and drink for David's men without her husband's consent or knowledge. When they met up with David, she stated, 'Please do not let my lord pay attention to this worthless man, Nabal, for as his name is, so is he. Nabal is his name and folly is with him.' She gave an accurate assessment of his character, but little she said could be construed as publicly honoring him except for the fact that she took drastic measures to save his life.

David *praised her wisdom,* saying, 'blessed be your discernment, and blessed be you, who have kept me this day from bloodshed and from avenging myself by my own hand.' Her actions saved all the men in their household, though the Lord Himself took Nabal's life shortly after Abigail revealed to him what she had done and the events that transpired.

Abigail is an excellent example of a woman who remained loyal to her husband despite his notorious and brutish ways and arrogance. The manner in which she dealt with this desperate situation demonstrated not only wisdom, but an obvious awareness of the weightier matters of the law (justice, mercy, faithfulness, compassion).

Huldah

Huldah was a prophet during the reign of Josiah. Her husband, Shallum, was keeper of the wardrobe. Yet it was not Shallum whom the priest (*cohen*) sought out when the King ordered him to consult the Lord—it was Huldah.

> **"Go; and consult ADONAI for me..."** So Hilkiyahu the cohen... **went to Huldah the prophet,** *the wife of Shalum... keeper of the wardrobe... and spoke with her.* **She told them, "ADONAI the God of Isra'el says to tell the man** who sent you to me..." So they brought word back to the king. 2 Kings 22:13a,14-15,20b, CJB

Her counsel was sought after because she had a reputation for hearing from the Lord, which implies she also walked in the fear of the Lord. This woman is described in Proverbs 31:26, 'She speaks with wisdom, and faithful instruction is on her tongue.' Part of being a prophet requires faithfully teaching the Word of God.

Anna

Anna, the elderly woman the Bible calls a prophet, daily prayed and fasted at the temple. She began proclaiming the arrival of the Messiah when Jesus' parents presented Him at the temple (Luke 2:36-38). The Word states that she *never left the temple* and *continually spoke* (*laleo*) of Jesus to any who were looking for prophecy to be fulfilled (contrast with the typical understanding of 1 Cor. 14:34-35).

Philip's Four Daughters

Philip's four daughters prophesied (Acts 21:9). The word used is *propheteuo* (Grk. 4395), from *prophetis* (Grk. 4396). This latter word is derived from the root word *phemi* (Grk. 5346): to speak, to say with the intent to enlighten the hearer. This word not only means to foretell things to come but to declare truths through the inspiration of the Holy Spirit. This includes revealing God's purposes and the meaning of divine mysteries. Zodhiates wrote, "It is clear that what really characterized the prophet was immediate communion with God, a divine communication of what the prophet had to declare... a showing forth of God's will... **Two things are necessary for a prophet**, an **insight granted by God** into the divine secrets or mysteries, and **a communication to others of those secrets**."[24]

Zodhiates explained that the prophets named alongside the apostles as the foundation of the church are to be understood as exclusively the NT prophets rather than the OT counterparts.[25] Does it make sense to anyone that these women prophets should remain silent, or if they do speak, they cannot teach (cf. Luke 8:16)? Is not teaching at the very core of enlightening another about the mysteries in God's Word? Why give the gift of prophecy to someone who is restricted from teaching or even speaking, or in some circles, can do so only if her husband or another male authority figure is present? Is it not splitting hairs to concede that a woman can prophesy but not teach? Are not God's authority and selection of an individual for a divine message or explanation of mysteries in the Bible of far greater worth and weight?

The great commission was not given to men only. Each believer must do his or her part in fulfilling Jesus' directive to disciple the nations.

> *But how are they to call on one in whom they have not believed? And how are they to believe in one of whom they have never heard? And **how are they to hear unless someone proclaims** (**kērussō**) the message? And how are they to proclaim the message unless they are sent (**apostellō**)? As it is written, "How timely are the feet of those who preach (**euangelizō**) good news!"* Rom. 10:14-15, MOUNCE (This is a reverse English-Greek interlinear translation; I have only included the Greek words pertinent for our study.)

Preaching and proclaiming (*kerusso*), being sent out (*apostello*), and evangelizing (*euangelizo*) are activities for all believers, and especially so for those who have prophetic gifting. Think of the many women missionaries the church has sent abroad, many on their own or leading their missionary teams. In China, where the church is experiencing profound growth, women frequently function as house church leaders.

Peter explained (by quoting Joel) why the one hundred twenty men and women were proclaiming the good news in other languages on Pentecost. The gift of prophecy is not restricted to men.

> *Even on my servants, **both men and women**, I will pour out my Sprit in those days, and **they will prophesy**.* Acts 2:18, NIV

Paul confirmed women's prophetic role in the church by giving parameters for orderly meetings when believers, both men and women, publicly pray and prophesy ('any woman who prays or prophesies,' 1 Cor. 11:5). The Amplified version includes a parenthetical after the word 'prophesies' in the Corinthians' passage to expand the Greek meaning of this word: "*teaches, refutes, reproves, admonishes, or comforts.*" Speaking and teaching are essential components of prophesying.

The Women at the Tomb

Taking all the gospel accounts into consideration, Mary, Mary Magdalene, Salome, Joanna, and 'the other women' were the first to see Jesus after His resurrection. Jesus sent the women as His messengers to the disciples to tell them they had seen Him and that Jesus rose just as He said He would (Matt. 28:1-10; Mark 16:1-13; Luke 24:1-12; John 20:1,11-18). This act demonstrated Jesus' higher opinion of women, because the Jewish oral law taught that the testimony of a woman could not be trusted. Jesus entrusted women with this good news despite the traditional cultural taboo of His day.

Marie N. Sabin, Ph.D., taught the Book of Mark at Bangor Theological Seminary. In her article, "Women Transformed: The Ending of Mark in the Beginning of Wisdom," Dr. Sabin contrasted the male disciples with the women in Mark's account. Dr. Sabin noted that Mark recorded episodes where Jesus reproached the disciples for their lack of faith but commended women for theirs.

Mark portrayed the disciples as slow to understand when Jesus sought to teach them about God's kingdom. The priests plot to murder Jesus, a disciple betrays Him, witnesses falsely testify against Him before the Sanhedrin (these were male because a woman's testimony would not be considered in a legal case), Pilate condemns, and soldiers scourge and mock—all men. The remaining disciples fell asleep when Jesus asked them to watch and pray with Him at Gethsemane. When the officials arrived to arrest Jesus, every disciple fled from His side (Mark 14:50). Peter later denied even knowing him (Mark 14:66-72).

Conversely, Dr. Sabin noted the positive light shed on the women Jesus encountered. Jesus praised the woman who gave only two mites at the temple offering box, marveling at her faith. Jesus also commended the woman with the issue of blood for her faith. He honored the Syrophoenician woman's faith when she sought deliverance for her daughter. He pointed out that husbands who abandoned their wives through divorce to marry another commit adultery (men typically justified their divorces 'for any and every reason' as taught by rabbinic tradition). Women followed Jesus and served Him, the true characteristics of disciples. A woman anointed Him, an act to be remembered for all ages. The women stayed with Jesus and watched as He suffered. They noted where He had been buried and made preparations to bring spices to the site when the Sabbath concluded. They were the first messengers sent out with the good news that Jesus was no longer dead.

In summary, Dr. Sabin noted that Jesus' disciples were called to follow Him and become servants. Jesus called them to prepare for His death and watch with Him in His distress as well as bear witness to the events. His male disciples failed on every account, but the women fulfilled each aspect of discipleship as recorded in Mark. The only notable exception was Joseph of Arimathea, who donated his own tomb and fresh linen for Jesus' burial.[26]

The gospel accounts give conclusive evidence that Jesus valued women as disciples and messengers despite the cultural distaste for and distrust of women in His day. Jesus broke ground by including them, especially as evidenced by entrusting them as the first messengers. Sending the women to testify as witnesses to the male disciples broke the cultural norm of that day since a woman's testimony was not honored. Even though the disciples did not believe the women, Jesus once again challenged the mindsets of His day by deliberately acting in a way contrary to an established paradigm He sought to correct. If the Son of God could entrust the most important revelation in human history to women, then the disciples (and the church) should as well.

[Note: It is an invalid argument that states only those messengers who will be received and trusted by the targeted audience should be sent in order that the message might be better received. This is based on the reason and wisdom of man. The OT records that the prophets God sent were largely ignored. These prophets were of various vocations, from priests to farmers. John the Baptist offended the minds of the ruling class and likewise was not received well by them. Do we think this surprised God? God still sends those who may offend our minds to reveal what is in our hearts. This is wisdom from above.]

Two Female Evangelists

The Samaritan woman at the well evangelized her town after Jesus broke tradition to speak with her. His conversation and prophetic insight into her life convinced her that He was the Messiah. She spread this news in her town and many believed. Jesus stayed two more days at their request, resulting in even more people who believed Jesus was the promised Messiah (John 4:7-39).

A little Israeli servant girl evangelized her Syrian master, Naaman, who suffered with leprosy. He had high standing and rank in the Syrian army. The young girl had faith that if her master would encounter God by visiting the prophet Elisha, he would be healed. Naaman went to Israel to meet with Elisha. God healed him and Naaman vowed to serve the God of Israel alone (2 Kings 5:1-44).

Aquila and His Wife Priscilla

Aquila and Priscilla are mentioned six or seven times in the New Testament (some versions omit their names in Acts 18:19). Priscilla is mentioned first in five of those passages (Acts 18:18,19,26; Rom. 16:3; 2 Tim. 4:19), implying Priscilla's greater authority and/or prominence. This is in contrast with the typical Greek custom of the day which introduced a married couple by stating the husband's name first.

In the following passage, Priscilla and Aquila took Apollos aside to give him a more accurate explanation of what he was preaching. By any definition of the word, this is a form of teaching.

> *Now a Jew named Apollos... an eloquent man, came to Ephesus; and he was mighty in the Scriptures. This man had been instructed in the way of the Lord; and being fervent in spirit,* **he was speaking and teaching accurately the things concerning Jesus**... *and he began to speak out boldly in the synagogue. But when Priscilla and Aquila heard him,* **they took him aside and explained** (ektithemi) *to him the way of God* **more accurately**. Acts 18:24-26, NASB

Some have argued that this wasn't really teaching because Luke used the word *ektithemi* (Grk. 1620; to expound) rather than a form of *didasko* (Grk. 1321; to teach). In Acts 11:1-18, Peter gave an orderly account explaining (*ektithemi*) how God was including the Gentiles in the new covenant. Peter established new covenant doctrine with his explanation. Likewise, Paul spoke to the local Jewish leaders in Rome, trying to convince them from the Scriptures that Jesus is the Messiah. Luke recorded that Paul expounded (*ektithemi*) from morning until evening (Acts 28:17-23). These examples clearly show that *ektithemi* encompasses the meaning 'teaching' in these contexts.

From the example of Priscilla and Aquila, some concede a woman can teach in the presence of her husband or another male leader. This displays ignorance of the reason for male headship in marriage—as a picture of Christ and the church. The value of male headship is not dependent on nor determined by any intrinsic superior quality resident in men, but rather on the type and shadow this relationship portrays. When it comes to calling and purpose in the church, headship is provided by Christ alone (not to be confused with God-ordained leadership).

This requirement to have the husband present also essentially nullifies Proverbs 31:11, which states that the husband has 'full confidence' (Hebrew, *batach*) in his wife. This word is used throughout the Psalms to define our complete reliance, confidence, and trust in God. It means to feel safe and to attach oneself to another with the sense of being careless, confident, and secure in someone or thing. Given the findings of recent research indicating that women are every bit as competent as men intellectually, a husband and wife could find this trust in one another if their relationship is rooted in Christ and based on mutual love, esteem, and true friendship.

> *More Men than Women Cited for Error in the Word*

Others will cite the Jezebel of the church at Thyatira as further support that women should not be allowed to teach (Rev. 2:20ff). Notice that the rebuke was not that the church allowed a woman to teach, but that the church tolerated her *false* teaching, a theme recurrent throughout the epistles. Remember also that Paul cited certain men, Hymenaeus and Philetus, as false teachers.

> *Their teaching will spread like gangrene. Among them are Hymenaeus and Philetus, who have departed from the truth.* 2 Tim. 2:17-18a, NIV

There are more men cited for error and false teaching than women in the Bible (cf. Mark 9:38-40; Luke 9:51-56; 18:15-17; Acts 8:9-24; 19:13-17; 1 Tim. 1:20; 2 Tim. 2:16-18; 4:14-15). Remember also that when Paul rebuked Peter for succumbing to intimidation from the Judaizers, even Barnabas had been carried away with the rest of the Jews in this *error* (Gal. 2:11-13). Jesus told the Sadducees, who had memorized the

Pentateuch as children and received broad instruction in the Word of God, that they erred because they *did not know* the Scriptures or the power of God (Matt. 22:23-33).

Knowing the words of the Bible without understanding their meaning or the wisdom the Lord desires to impart may place us in a position to receive a rebuke from the Spirit of God. Jesus said the following to the Pharisees who rebuked Jesus for allowing His disciples to pick and eat grain on the Sabbath. This act was contrary to the law as they interpreted it (Matt. 12:1-14):

> *If you had known what these words mean, 'I desire mercy, not sacrifice,' you would not have condemned the innocent.* Matt. 12:7, NIV

Has the church likewise condemned strong female believers who have 'presumed' to teach, evangelize, or take leadership roles without male headship, contrary to traditional interpretations of God's Word? Is this not the equivalent of condemning the innocent?

Our interpretation and practice of the instructions in God's Word must reflect His character, especially mercy and grace, acknowledging that we may be shortsighted in our interpretations, just as the disciples and apostles demonstrated. Wisdom and understanding come with humility (Prov. 11:2).

> ➤ *All Believers Must Mature So They Can Teach*

In the next passage, the author of Hebrews rebukes believers who have not acquired further knowledge than just the basics. They should have been teachers by now to help equip the influx of new believers. These believers are admonished to sharpen their discernment so they can distinguish good from evil, true from false.

> *We have much to say about this, but **it is hard to make it clear to you because you no longer try to understand**. In fact, though **by this time you ought to be teachers**, you need someone to teach you the elementary truths of God's word all over again... But **solid food is for the mature, who by constant use have trained themselves to distinguish good from evil**.* Heb. 5:11-14, NIV

Are we to believe Paul directed these verses to men alone? Are women to be ever learning but never quite arriving at an adequate knowledge of the truth? Women make up half the body of Christ (theoretically half—most studies show there are more women in the church than men). Do we really believe the author of Hebrews is admonishing only men? Furthermore, Paul singled out 'silly women' for their foolishness of always learning but never coming to the knowledge of the truth as an admonishment to change (2 Tim. 3:6-7). Jesus gave worldliness as a reason for not reaching maturity:

> *The seed that fell among thorns stands for those who hear, but as they go on their way they* **are choked by life's worries, riches and pleasures,** *and* **they do not mature**. Luke 8:14, NIV

Maturity is the goal for *all* believers and a recurring theme in the epistles. Paul preached 'so that we may present *everyone* fully mature in Christ' (Col. 1:28). James spoke of 'letting perseverance finish its work so that you may be mature and complete, not lacking anything' (James 1:4). The author of Hebrews lamented that some in the church were not trying to understand, needing to hear elementary truths repeatedly instead of eating the solid food for the mature, who are to teach.

This mirrors what Paul said about the 'silly women'—they never come to knowledge of the truth, a state he did not want to see in any believer. He wanted all believers to mature and be counted among those who teach others. Everyone is to show diligence in their labor for Christ, ministering to and teaching the newer believers so that they also can mature (Heb. 6:10-12). We have a ministry of multiplication (Acts 6:1a; 2 Cor. 9:10), not division. As maturing believers, the apostles considered growing in understanding essential so each would be competent to teach in his or her sphere of influence.

There are numerous Greek words with varying nuances for the act of teaching, several of which are derivatives of *didasko* (Grk. 1317-1322). Notice that the goal of instruction is that believers become mature, able to teach. These instructions are not directed to men alone. If we restrict women from teaching or even speaking based on our understanding of a few 'proof texts,' we essentially deny application of dozens of other apostolic directives in the NT as pertaining to women.

> *I myself am convinced, my brothers **and sisters**, that you yourselves are full of goodness, filled with knowledge and **competent to <u>instruct one another</u>**.* Rom. 15:14, NIV
>
> *Let the word of Christ dwell in you richly, **<u>teaching</u> and admonishing <u>one another</u> in all wisdom**, singing psalms and hymns and spiritual songs, with thankfulness in your hearts to God.* Col. 3:16, ESV
>
> ***The Lord's bond-servant** must not be quarrelsome, but be kind to all, **<u>able to teach</u>**, patient when wronged.* 2 Tim. 2:24, NASB
>
> *And the things you have heard me say in the presence of many witnesses **entrust to reliable people who will also be <u>qualified to teach</u> others.*** 2 Tim. 2:2, NIV
>
> *He is the one we proclaim, admonishing and **teaching everyone** with all wisdom, **so that we may <u>present everyone fully mature in Christ</u>**.* Col. 1:28, NIV

Ability to teach, then, is a mark of maturity for all believers who count themselves bondservants of Christ. To ignore these instructions or deny that they pertain to both men and women will not hold up in the court of heaven.

Jesus told us to pray for workers to be sent into the harvest. Many have come, but the paradigms of some church leaders blind them to the workers right in front of them—workers the Lord has sent (Matt. 23:37). Capable *chayil* women, whom the men must *batach* (fully trust) as they do other men, are in our midst to co-labor for the cause of Christ. A credential given by an approved institution of higher learning cannot be that in which we place our trust, but rather in the approval given by the Spirit of God (2 Cor. 3:1; 10:17-18; Acts 13:1-3).

Paul's Female Co-laborers

Junia and other women co-labored with Paul. Many debate the function these women filled, but we know for certain Paul considered them co-laborers. He valued and esteemed them as they proclaimed the Gospel and served the body of Christ.

> *Greet **Priscilla** and Aquila, **my fellow workers** in Christ Jesus.* Rom. 16:3, NKJV

> *Greet Andronicus and **Junia**, my fellow Jews who have been in prison with me. They are **outstanding among the apostles**, and they were in Christ before I was.* Rom. 16:7, NIV

> *I plead with **Euodia** and I plead with **Syntyche** to be of the same mind in the Lord. Yes, and I ask you, my true companion, **help these women since they have contended at my side in the cause of the gospel**, along with Clement and the rest of **my co-workers**, whose names are in the book of life.* Php. 4:2-3, NIV

In the following passages, Paul exhorts believers using gender-neutral language to submit to anyone who is laboring for the cause of Christ. He exhorts us to highly esteem these leaders, whether male or female.

> *I urge you, brothers and sisters, to **submit (hupotasso) to such people and to everyone who joins in the work** and labors at it.* 1 Cor. 16:15b-16, NIV

> *And we urge you, brethren, to **recognize those who labor** among you, and **are over you in the Lord** and admonish you, and to **esteem them very highly** in love for their work's sake. Be at peace among yourselves.* 1 Thes. 5:12-13, NKJV

Phoebe

Phoebe was a prominent woman in the church at Cenchreae. There is a bit of debate as to whether Phoebe was a deacon or not, some believing *diakonos* (Grk. 1249) should be translated servant, others more inclined with minister. If we examine another description of Phoebe in this passage, we draw a deeper understanding about her and Paul's estimation of her work.

> *I commend to you our sister Phoebe, a deacon (**diakonos**) of the church in Cenchreae. I ask you to receive her in the Lord in a way worthy of his people and to give her any help she may need from you, for she has been the benefactor (**prostatis**) of many people, including me.* Rom. 16:1-2, NASB

The Greek word *prostatis* (Grk. 4368) means a female guardian, protector, patroness. It is a feminine derivative of *prosteimi* (Grk. 4291b), which means to put before in rank, to set over, to preside, to rule; have charge over, manage, lead. Because both Jesus and Paul depicted leadership in the new covenant community as characterized by servanthood, Paul's description of Phoebe as a *diakonos* (servant, minister) that was a *prostatis* (leader, manager, in charge, guardian) precludes reducing her to merely an exceptionally hospitable and helpful person. There is little room for doubt that she served at the church at Cenchreae in some leadership capacity. Paul entrusted her with carrying his letter to the Roman church, and he wanted them to receive her as his co-laborer in a worthy manner with respect and esteem.

In Summary

We have taken a brief tour of twenty-two women who were leaders, prophets, teachers, and/or evangelists found in the Word. Esther must be included as well, for God raised her up to a prominent, influential position to be His voice to expose the genocidal plot against the Jews. Additionally, the stories of unnamed wise women (one from Tekoa, 2 Sam. 14:2; the other from Abel, 2 Sam. 20:15-22) are also included in the Word, once again attesting to the connection between women and wisdom.

The truly remarkable element in these examples is that they even exist considering the staunchly patriarchal climate. God intervened against the cultural norms to make sure we had adequate precedents by which we could correctly discern His intent in the regulatory laws and principles given in the Word.

These examples were recorded to 'teach, convict, correct, and train.' These exemplary women **teach** us that God has not excluded women from ministry, teaching, or leadership. These examples **convict** the present day church for ignoring women's gifting and contribution to God's work, as well as for dismissing scriptural examples as 'exceptions to the rule.' We need to take these examples to heart rather than ignore them so we can **correct** the course we have taken. And we need to **train** believers, men and women alike, that God can choose whomever He wills to place in whatever position He desires for the good of His kingdom and the salvation of the lost. To accept this, we need only to have a teachable heart and our veils removed to hear what the Spirit says to the church.

These examples are binding precedents given by the court of heaven. All lower courts, which implicitly means the church in our discussion, are bound to obey the Heavenly Judge's rulings on the inclusion of women in authority for whatever calling God has ordained in His wisdom. Every decision God made to send women to fulfill roles of authority, whether as leaders, teachers, evangelists, or prophets, amounts to a legally binding precedent that cannot be ignored on the basis of tradition, cultural views, or even conflicting 'proof texts' that some have used as their basis for ignoring these God-given precedents.

Moses made a statement that parallels the heart of God on this issue. When Joshua wanted Moses to stop two men in the midst of the camp from prophesying, Moses replied:

> *Are you jealous for my sake? I wish that all the LORD's people were prophets and that the LORD would put his Spirit on them!* Num. 11:29, NIV

The Lord answered Moses' prayer on the day of Pentecost. Are we like Joshua, trying to still the voices of those we reject as recipients of the grace of God for prophesying? Are we jealous for God's sake, attempting to be champions for the restrictions we believe are in His Word, sacrificing the remainder of Scripture where examples of women leading, teaching, prophesying, and serving the people of God clearly teach otherwise? Are we like the disciples, attempting to silence those who don't follow us or agree with the way we interpret Scripture (Mk. 9:38-40)? God wants all of His children to prophesy, and He is looking for willing and available workers to send into the harvest.

> *What then shall we say, **brothers and sisters**? When you come together, **each** of you has... a word of **instruction**, a revelation... Everything must be done so that the church may be built up... Two or three prophets should speak, and the others should weigh carefully what is said... For **you can all prophesy in turn so that everyone may be instructed and encouraged**.* 1 Cor. 14:26,29,31, NIV

Chapter 8

Moving Forward

> *The Lord gives the command; the women who proclaim the good tidings are a great host.* Psalm 68:11, NASB

Over half of our English Bible versions translate this passage with 'women' as the proclaimers of the good news. This provides further evidence that God intended women to be proactive participants on the front lines.

We know that God placed women in various leadership, prophetic, evangelistic, and teaching roles throughout biblical history in spite of the cultural taboos and patriarchal norms of the day. We know that women followed Jesus and were counted among His disciples. Women were the first to be sent to proclaim the good news of the resurrection.

We know that women received the same Holy Spirit at Pentecost and prophesied in other languages as Peter preached the fulfillment of Joel 2:28-29. We know that Paul described women as co-laborers for the cause of Christ, to whom believers were to submit, esteem, and serve, recognizing that the Lord had given them this authority for building up the church. Paul commended women in leadership roles and gave orderly procedures for accommodating the men and women who would publicly pray or prophesy in the NT churches.

Contrary to historical and early philosophical views and ideas about women, we know from current research that women have the same average intelligence as men. Their biological function is designed by God and not the result of inferior design. We also discovered that the bases for widely held beliefs about the supposed predisposition of women to be deceived is unfounded through a scriptural survey of the same trait demonstrated by men.

We know that the *ideal* godly wife as described in Proverbs 31 is a diligent, intelligent, decisive, resourceful, compassionate, wise, faithful, able, trustworthy woman of valor and suitable companion/helper to her husband, not a needy, brainless, indecisive, self-absorbed, domineering, manipulative, unstable, immoral, fearful weakling. She is the type and shadow of the church, Christ's bride. Her home runs well whether she works primarily outside or inside the home, each woman discerning the nature of the assignment the Lord has given her and laboring accordingly.

The Sum of God's Word Is Truth

It is vital that we remember the Psalmist's words that it is the *sum* of God's Word that gives us truth on any given biblical topic (Psalm 119:160). So how do we reconcile this collection of women functioning in roles of authority with some of Paul's teaching in his letters to the Corinthians and to Timothy?

Some have dismissed these exemplary women as exceptions to the rule so that the 'proof texts' in question can stand as they are translated. Explaining away clear examples in the Word so they can fit another passage is poor scholarship and displays contempt for God's decision to include women in leadership and other roles. God included these examples (case law) as checks and balances to make sure we properly interpret biblical directives (regulatory law). These examples are meant to keep us honest in our interpretations and views of other passages, safeguarding each generation from cultural and personal sway that would otherwise pervert God's original intent.

Digging deeply into the grammatical-historical context of each 'dissenting' passage brings us closer to solving a puzzle like this. When we do this, we have to be brutally honest with ourselves about our presuppositions and preunderstandings. For some, the dichotomy that exists in the mind that a wife can exercise authority in the public arena and still honor and respect her husband at home has proved a formidable obstacle. We need to stretch our minds beyond our pride and human reasoning, and in humility accept that God doesn't think as we do. The husband-wife relationship is a type and shadow of Christ and the Church. The weightier matters of the law take precedence over types and shadows, as Jesus taught and Paul practiced.

> ***The pride of your heart has deceived you...*** *Where there is strife, there is pride, but wisdom is found in those who take advice.* Oba. 1:3; Prov. 13:10, NIV

In the next two chapters, we will examine the two passages most widely used to subjugate and silence female believers, 1 Corinthians 14:34-36 and 1 Timothy 2:11-15. An exhaustive study of all pertinent passages would make this book too large for the average reader, and I want this to be accessible for those who only have time for a prioritized reading. As for the other verses, it is my hope that what I have written will inspire those who want to dig further to do so with the proper foundation and goal to arrive at the *sum* of God's truth, not a favored stance on this or any other scriptural matter.

As we transition to taking a magnifying glass to these two texts, keep in mind what we have discussed:

- sincere and otherwise faithful pastors can be off in their teaching on certain points; believers are not to blindly receive teaching without searching the Scriptures on their own
- each individual believer has preunderstandings that affect how they interpret certain texts
- misogyny (hatred, dislike, mistrust, and/or deeply rooted prejudice toward women) leads to a view of women that is based in fear, lust, or the need to dominate, preferring to treat women as objects rather than see them as co-heirs made in God's image whose identity is in Christ
- the husband-wife relationship is a type and shadow, not a brittle structure dependent on blind obedience with the same weight as the moral code; types and shadows can be set aside to remain faithful to love, faithfulness, mercy, and justice (refer to chapter 8 in *The Bondservant's Life*, J.B. Chandler, for further study on the dynamic nature of the Mosaic ceremonial law)
- God created women as the picture of His wisdom (beauty)
- Biblical case law provides binding precedents of women in leadership and other roles of authority

Misogynist undercurrents in part of the church have hindered our ability to recognize the spiritual gifts and contributions women are ready to make. More tragically, we train women to view themselves as objects, diverting their attention to beauty/outward adornment. The current degree of self-loathing in women as well as their fixation on attaining size 0 and youthful beauty indicates just how far their attention has been diverted from true purpose. Women, you are more than a number.

Personal Expectations

Jesus was not what the people of Israel expected or wanted, and they rejected Him. John the Baptist came without the finery the Pharisees had convinced themselves demonstrated the favor of God. Balaam paid no heed to the donkey that tried to save his life when the Lord stood to oppose Balaam because of the course he had taken. The nation of Israel rejected the prophets sent to them because those true prophets of the Lord didn't tell them what they wanted to hear.

Learning from their mistakes will keep us from missing God's direction and intervention. Personal expectations and preferences can sabotage our ability to move in true spiritual discernment. We cannot let our feelings or traditions nullify the Word of God (Mark 7:13). If we build our foundation in Christ by what feels right to us, a hybrid mixture of bits of biblical truth mixed with the fallen reasoning and traditions of men results. We are broken and sinful human beings whose thoughts are far from God's thoughts. We cannot trust our gut instincts because we cannot even discern our personal errors. Our hearts deceive us.

The only compass—plumb line—we have is the Word of God and the guidance and discernment of the Holy Spirit, not our personal agreement with or offense at what the Word of God teaches us. We cannot whitewash our traditions and read them into God's Word.

> *For the time will come when **people will not put up with sound doctrine**. Instead, **to suit their own desires**, they will gather around them a great number of **teachers to say what their itching ears want to hear.** They will **turn their ears away from the truth** and turn aside to myths.* 2 Tim. 4:3-4, NIV

The Climate of the First Century Church

On Pentecost, Luke recorded that three thousand people believed after hearing Peter's message (Acts 2:41). These were predominantly Jewish men and women celebrating the Feast of Weeks (Pentecost) in Jerusalem. The Gospel message spread quickly through the Jewish community (Acts 2:47; 4:4; 5:14; 8:12), and even a large number of priests (Acts 6:7) and some Pharisees (Acts 15:5) were added to the company of believers. When Paul took the message to the Gentiles, the church continued to expand (Acts 10:45; 11:20-21; 13:48; 14:1; 17:4,12).

Two of the primary challenges the new churches faced were:
1. believing Jews who wanted to impose the Jewish laws and traditions on the Gentile believers (e.g., Acts 15:5)
2. the pagan religious practices the new Gentile believers would have to relinquish if they were to follow Christ (e.g., 1 Cor. 12:2)

Luke recorded that 'thousands of Jews have believed, and all of them are zealous for the law' (Acts 21:20). Paul warned the Gentile converts to beware of the Judaizers who wanted to force them to become Jewish converts to the law of Moses and the Jewish traditions found in the oral law (e.g., Gal. 2:4; 3:18).

The Gentile believers, on the other hand, brought with them ingrained idolatrous practices (1 Cor. 5:11; 10:7,14; 12:2; 2 Cor. 6:14-16; Eph. 5:5,8; 1 Thes. 1:9). The Jerusalem council addressed both the Judaizers and the pagan Gentile practices, deciding that Gentile believers had no obligation to Mosaic law and Jewish traditions, but that their idolatrous practices had to cease, naming in particular the need to abstain from fornication, blood, and eating meat strangled or offered to idols.

These injunctions would make it possible for Jews and Gentiles to worship alongside one another without causing offense. Paul admonishes believers to pursue peace by destroying obstacles that hinder unity and/or cause the conscience of another believer to suffer (Rom. 14). These rulings, however, do not negate the moral code (laws against stealing, murder, adultery, etc.) etched on the conscience of every believer (Rom. 2:15; cf. 1 Tim. 4:2; Titus 1:15).

Jesus warned believers to beware of false teaching (Matt. 24:11,24) and the 'leaven of the Pharisees' (those traditions or 'laws' that were part of the Jewish oral tradition but not part of the Mosaic law; Matt. 16:12). We also find that Peter (2 Pet. 2:1), James (implied, James 3:1), John (1 John 4:1; 5:21; 2 John 1:7), and Jude (Jude 1:4) each warned the new believers about false teaching. Paul's vigilance in confronting nonessential religious practice and false teaching, whether the zealous Judaizers' extrabiblical traditions or the Gentiles' idolatrous practices and myths, undergirded the letters he wrote to the young churches and church leaders (e.g., Acts 20:29-30; Rom. 16:17; 2 Cor. 11:13ff; Gal. 3:1-3; Php. 3:2; 1 Tim. 1:3,6-7; 2 Tim. 2:17-18).

> *A little leaven **(a slight inclination to error, or a few false teachers)** leavens the whole lump [it perverts the whole conception of faith or **misleads the whole church**].* Gal. 5:9, AMP

The newly formed church contended also with the customs of the day, including widespread slavery and the influence of the Greek Philosophers. Roman and Greek societies held women in much lower regard than men, denying them many of the privileges we enjoy today, particularly education. Plato viewed women as inferior, stating, "It is only males who are created directly by the gods and are given souls... obviously it is only men who are complete human beings and can hope for ultimate fulfillment; the best a woman can hope for is to become a man."[27] Aristotle later wrote that women were "defective by nature" and lacked the intelligence with which men were naturally endowed. He believed men were by nature of a higher order and therefore must rule women. Roman households were completely under the father's rule.

Into this climate the neophyte community of believers in the new covenant appeared. There would be no distinctions between male and female, Jew and Gentile, circumcised and uncircumcised, barbarian, Scythian, slave and free (Gal. 3:28; Col. 3:11; Rom. 10:12).

Post Hoc Ergo Propter Hoc Arguments

> *For the time has come for **judgment to begin at the house of God**; and if it begins with us first, what will be the end of those who do not obey the gospel of God?* 1 Pet. 4:17, NKJV

Prophetic voices in the church agree that the church is about to go through significant upheaval along with the rest of the world. Many in the church will try to blame the emergence of women in leadership and teaching roles for the shaking the church will experience. Instead of viewing these women as the divinely timed co-laborers needed for 'such a time as this,' some will be tempted to ascribe blame to them for the state of the church.

This parallels the way the children of Israel reasoned when God finally disciplined them for centuries-long covenant breaches. The Mosaic law warned Israel that breaking God's covenant would result in being plundered by enemies and exiled (Lev. 26:14ff). The Lord prophetically told Moses that Israel would indeed break the covenant in the future by forsaking God and pursuing worthless idols (Deut. 31:15-22). But in the following story, we will see that the remnant that remained in the land after the exile did not base their response on God's Word, but rather on their own reasoning and the concurrent circumstances.

The prophesied exile took place in Jeremiah's day. Those who were not carried off to Babylon but remained in the land asked Jeremiah what they should do. When Jeremiah told the people that God wanted them to stay in the land because He would protect and bless them, the remnant balked. They had already reasoned in their minds that they would suffer or be killed if they stayed. They wanted to go to Egypt to be protected by the strength of Pharaoh despite being warned that this action would bring death, not life. The Lord warned them through Jeremiah that the sword and famine they feared would overtake them in Israel would, in fact, visit them if they went to Egypt (Jer. 42-43).

Blinded by their own reasoning and fear, these people not only left for Egypt, but they also returned to the worship of the queen of heaven, forsaking all the reforms that had recently occurred during King Josiah's reign. They reasoned that because their lives were still pleasant when they were worshipping the queen of heaven (they had plenty to eat and no war), then favorable circumstances would return if they resumed her worship (Jer. 44:16-18). Though Jeremiah reminded them of all the times the Lord warned them that worshipping false gods would bring destruction, not favor, they would not listen (Jer. 44:21-23).

> *Whom have you so dreaded and feared that you have not been true to me, and have neither remembered me nor taken this to heart?* ***Is it not because I have long been silent that you do not fear me?*** Isa. 57:11, NIV

This example gives evidence that by nature we make associations between what we are doing now and the circumstances we immediately experience. Oftentimes this association is valid, e.g., touching the hot stove causes a burn. In other instances, however, it is a *post hoc ergo propter hoc* argument, a common logic fallacy that means 'after this, therefore because of this.' For example, 'I fell out of bed this morning, and then it rained today. Therefore, if I fall out of bed, it will rain.'

The people in Jeremiah's day associated pleasant times with their worship of the queen of heaven rather than understanding God's patience and long-suffering. The Bible teaches that God is slow to anger and long-suffering in his dealings with humanity. For example, He waited patiently in the days of Noah while Noah built the ark (1 Pet. 3:20). The Lord was patient with the Amorites because their collective sins had not yet reached the tipping point (Gen. 15:16). Likewise, the church at Thyatira was given time to repent (Rev. 2:21).

The Bible is replete with examples of God refraining from exercising judgment for crimes committed. Here are only a few of the many verses that attest to God's nature of longsuffering. The point of His longsuffering is to give us time to turn from the course we have taken.

> *For my own name's sake I delay my wrath; for the sake of my praise I hold it back from you, so as not to destroy you completely.* Isa. 48:9, NIV

> *But He, being compassionate, forgave their iniquity and did not destroy them; and **often He restrained His anger and did not arouse all His wrath**.* Psalm 78:38, NASB

> *Or do you show contempt for the riches of his kindness, **forbearance and patience**, not realizing that **God's kindness is intended to lead you to repentance**?* Rom. 2:4, NIV

> *The Lord is not slow in keeping his promise, as some understand slowness. Instead **he is patient with you, not wanting anyone to perish, but everyone to come to repentance**... Bear in mind that our Lord's patience means salvation.* 2 Pet. 3:9,15a, NIV

The Preacher of Ecclesiastes observed that when the sentence for a crime is delayed, people often reason that what they are doing must not be wrong, or at least not bad enough to warrant God's judgment:

> *Because the sentence against an evil deed is not executed quickly, therefore the hearts of the sons of men among them are given fully to do evil.* Ecc. 8:11, NASB

Trials Bring Forth Purity

We will fall prey to the same trap the Israelites of Jeremiah's day succumbed to if we don't take to heart God's use of refinement to bring forth purity. Traditionally, olives were beaten (Heb. 3795 *kathiyth*:

beaten, i.e. pure) to bring forth pure oil (e.g., Ex. 27:20; Lev. 24:2). In the same way, believers are 'beaten' through trials and testing to bring forth the purity God desires in His children:

> When He has **tried me, I shall come forth as refined gold** [pure and luminous]. Job 23:10b, AMP

> For You, O God, have proved us; **You have tried us as silver is tried, refined, and purified.** Psalm 66:10, AMP

> Behold, **I have refined you,** but not as silver; **I have tested you in the furnace of affliction.** Isa. 48:10, NASB

> And some of those who are wise, prudent, and understanding shall be weakened and fall, [thus, then, the insincere among the people will lose courage and become deserters. **It will be a test] to refine, to purify, and to make those among [God's people] white, even to the time of the end,** because it is yet for the time [God] appointed. Dan. 11:35, AMP

> **Many will be purged, purified and refined,** but the wicked will act wickedly; and none of the wicked will understand, but **those who have insight will understand.** Dan. 12:10, NASB

> **Who may ascend into the hill of the LORD? And who may stand in His holy place? He who has clean hands and a pure heart.** Psalm 24:3-4a, NASB

Jesus will return for a pure bride (Eph. 5:27; 2 Pet. 3:14), and the apostles remind us that we are destined for trials *to refine and make pure* our faith (1 Thes. 3:3; James 1:2-3,12; 1 Pet. 4:12-13). The Lord's jealousy for His bride moves Him to do whatever it takes to bring forth purity in her. He works through the ministry gifts to not only teach and train, but to correct and rebuke as well. The Lord also works through family, friends, circumstances, and business or employment to discipline believers on the road to maturity—individually and corporately.

> For I am jealous for you with a godly jealousy; for I betrothed you to one husband, so **that to Christ I might present you as a pure virgin.** 2 Cor. 11:2, NASB

God is waiting patiently for the women to take their ordained places in the body of Christ so that the church will be better equipped to handle the trying days ahead and the harvest. Restoring women to places of authority is God's merciful gift to the church in this hour—reinforcements to help the bride stand firm and labor in the harvest.

Humility Is Crucial

> **Humble yourselves in the presence of the Lord,** and He will exalt you. James 4:10, NASB

We are furthered warned not to harden our hearts in pride during testing (Heb. 3:8). Walking before God in a posture of humility is a benchmark of maturity. The days ahead will cause the hearts of those not firmly and humbly rooted in their faith to melt with fear or turn back because of the rigor required. Restraining ourselves from ascribing blame to one group or another when we undergo God's refining fire is also a mark of maturity (Mal. 3:2). This requires patience, perseverance, discernment, and humility. Micah, Zephaniah, and Jesus remind us of the invaluable worth of humility before God:

> He has showed you, O man, what is good. And **what does the Lord require** of you but to **do justly**, and to **love kindness and mercy**, and **to humble yourself and walk humbly with your God**? Mic. 6:8, AMP

> **God blesses those who are humble,** for they will **inherit the whole earth**. Matt. 5:5, NLT

> **Seek the Lord, all you humble** of the land, you who do what he commands. Seek righteousness, **seek humility; perhaps you will be sheltered** on the day of the Lord's anger. Zeph. 2:3, NIV

Blaming others for the failures we experience shows a lack of discernment and/or pride that won't assume responsibility. When the Lord brings our faults to our attention in this age, it is because of His mercy and great grace. He wants us to take corrective action now rather than face the judgment to come when we can no longer right a wrong course we have taken. Believers must agree with God quickly when He reveals darkness in them, whether darkness due to sin, error, worldly ways, or taking a course other than the one ordained by God.

The mature church will be made pure through the trials she endures today. Believers are exhorted to walk in a spirit of humility and love, honoring the gifts God has given to each believer, using the true discernment provided by the Holy Spirit to exercise sound judgment in governance. Judgment will begin with the house of God, and the Lord is sending forth women in this hour to help the church overcome the fiery trials she is destined to undergo for purity. The goal is to be found faithful at Jesus' return, without spot or wrinkle.

Pure and Undefiled Religion

James 1:27 states, 'Religion God accepts as pure and undefiled is this: to look after needy orphans and widows and to keep oneself from being polluted by the world.' The Lord interrupts our schedules, comfort zones, and pocket books to test us in the area of taking care of the needy. Most of us are traveling too fast in the direction we have chosen for ourselves to give even a second glance at the person who needs our help.

We don't mind giving a few dollars for someone in need, or maybe an afternoon to help someone out. But many stiffen at the thought of having to rearrange their lifestyles to accommodate the needs of others, or empty their bank accounts for someone else's acute need. We say we will do anything for *Jesus*, even give to famous *ministries* in need (nice tax break, too), but we draw the line when our comfort zone is interrupted or if we have to sacrifice our plans for a *nameless individual*. Contrast this mindset with Jesus' promise to reward those who take care of the insignificant by worldly standards (see Matt. 10:42).

We will not be judged by our adherence and attention to religious ceremony and tradition. Believers will be judged by the degree to which they loved one another in practical ways, as Jesus and James explained (Mark 9:41; Matt. 25:34-40; James 2:17). Many believers are willing to go to church each week, practice religious rites, and pursue personal righteousness. But like the rich young ruler, they are not willing to give everything they have—to sacrifice their time, goals, wealth, and desires in this life—to follow and serve Christ.

If our Christian lifestyle does not involve sacrifice, how does it mirror Jesus' life? There is no other way to fulfill Jesus' mandate to pick up our cross (forego control of our lives) and follow Him than to sacrifice: 1.) control over our schedules, 2.) control of our money, time, and resources, and 3.) our personal dreams and aspirations.

Jesus examined the churches in Asia and judged them by their works. He indicted them for their lack of love and neglecting deeds that naturally flow out of love (Rev. 2:4-5); for putting stumbling blocks before others that cause them to sin (Rev. 2:14,20); for allowing false teaching and creating division (Rev. 2:15,20); for having a dead faith that is not committed to extending God's hand to others through sacrificial and charitable deeds (Rev. 3:2); and for demonstrating a lukewarm faith as a result of thinking too highly of oneself, which entails not discerning one's true condition (Rev. 3:17-19).

The judgment we receive from the Lord will be based on how well we expressed our love for God and man with the time, resources, ability, and gifts we were given. We demonstrate love for God by obedience to His voice in the calling He has ordained for us, attention to the Holy Spirit as He guides us in the race marked out for us, and commitment to God's truth as revealed in His Word. Our love for our fellowman is demonstrated by the way we allow the Lord to interrupt us along the way to care for the needy and poor, by abstaining from wrongdoing (includes putting stumbling blocks before others), and by considering the needs of others *before our own*.

The church today tends to judge a believer by whether or not they attend church every week (or multiple times in a week), whether or not they tithe, and the degree to which they support and participate in church programs. But God weighs the heart before He judges the actions. Even the right actions are defiled if our motives and heart posture are not rooted in humility and God's love.

The stumbling block placed before women by our traditions brings not only division, but hinders the Spirit of God from moving as He wills. When we take this seriously, we will move closer to corporate maturity. We will be judged based on our heart motives as well as the effort we exert to truly understand the heart of God on this or any other issue.

> ***Do nothing from factional motives*** *[through contentiousness, strife, selfishness, or for unworthy ends]* or ***prompted by conceit*** *and empty arrogance. Instead, in the* ***true spirit of humility*** *(lowliness of mind) let* ***each regard the others as better than and superior*** *to himself [thinking more highly of one another than you do of yourselves]*. Php. 2:3, AMP

Chapter 9

1 Corinthians 14:34-36

> *Women should remain silent in the churches. They are not allowed to speak, but must be in submission, as the law says. If they want to inquire about something, they should ask their own husbands at home; for it is disgraceful for a woman to speak in the church. Or did the word of God originate with you? Or are you the only people it has reached?* 1 Cor. 14:34-36, NIV

This passage strikes every female believer in the heart. Single women wonder how this affects them. Married women wonder why Paul thought only husbands would know the Word of God. Others wonder why Paul would give instructions to women on the proper procedure for praying and prophesying in the congregation (1 Cor. 11:5), and then prohibit them from speaking altogether in the same letter. Nearly everyone wonders why Paul made an appeal to the law, a practice he refutes elsewhere (Rom. 6:14; 7:4-6; Gal. 2:19; 3:2,5,11,13; 5:4).

> But **if you are led by the Spirit, you are not under the law**... *avoid foolish controversies* and... *arguments* and **quarrels about the law**, *because these are* **unprofitable and useless**. Gal. 5:18; Titus 3:9, NIV

We will first look at the historical climate of the city of Corinth and then tackle this passage by looking at the way Paul ordered the Greek construction of this letter to address the other issues the Corinthians faced. Paul's repetitive construction and teaching style will shed light on this passage, allowing it to be in unity with the whole of scriptural thought on this subject.

Historical Context

Paul established the church at Corinth and remained there for over a year teaching the new believers. He met Aquila and Priscilla there and initially spent every Sabbath teaching at the synagogue. The majority of the Jews, however, opposed his message. At this point Paul took the gospel message to the Gentiles. He began teaching at the house next door, which belonged to a believer named Titius Justus. Many Gentile Corinthians believed and were baptized, as was the leader of the synagogue, Crispus, and his whole household (see Acts 18).

The Climate at Corinth

Paul kept in touch with this church and apparently received a letter from them stating the concerns and issues that surfaced after Paul left (cf. 1 Cor. 1:11-12). We don't have that letter and can only extrapolate those issues from the letter Paul wrote to address their concerns.

Paul began his letter by greeting and blessing the church. He then states the purpose of his letter, revealing that the issues the Corinthians faced were causing division. Paul's emphasis in this letter is to expose the critical nature of their disagreements because these issues were causing disunity and factions. A fractured church contradicted the oneness believers are to experience in the Lord. Paul's urgency for church unity presents believers today with the priority we, too, should place on pursuing like-mindedness.

> *I appeal to you, brothers and sisters, in the name of our Lord Jesus Christ, that all of you* **agree with one another** *in what you say and* **that there be no divisions among you**, *but that you be* **perfectly united in mind and thought**. 1 Cor. 1:10, NIV

Context Is Important

When we are not directly impacted by the literal meaning or face value of a passage of Scripture as interpreted into English, or if it does not disturb our worldview, we typically exert little effort to scrutinize it more closely to make sure we understand the author's intended meaning. Dr. Nebeker summarized, "Cognitive interests, then, are motivated by a practical concern on the part of the interpreter: It is only when we are faced with a practical problem that we acquire sufficient knowledge to overcome it."[28]

For example, consider the following text. Since historically men have furnished most scholarship, the following passage likely was never taken out of context. However, under other circumstances it might have been.

> Mark my words! I, Paul, tell you that **if you let yourselves be circumcised, Christ will be of no value to you at all**. Again I declare to **every man who lets himself be circumcised** that he **is obligated to obey the whole law.** Gal. 5:2-3, NIV

If taken literally as a standalone truth, any man who has been circumcised would be denied salvation in Christ—it's right there in black and white. As a matter of fact, Paul emphatically declared it twice! If the church had developed doctrine around this one passage as a 'proof text' to which all contrasting passages must comply (similar to the way we have treated certain passages on women's roles in the church), a circumcised male believer would most likely protest.

He might argue that it's not his fault his mother circumcised him when he was born. He would struggle with the injustice this interpretation leaves in his mind and heart. Didn't Christ do away with the curse and freely invite whosoever? He would argue that there are many examples in Scripture of circumcised men that not only were saved, they were used mightily of the Lord. What would happen to his faith if the church told him that these were merely exceptions to the rule?

Using this passage as an isolated principle/proof text, as many have done with other passages, one could argue that any male who has been circumcised has no hope of being saved because Christ will be of no benefit to him. That is the literal, face value English interpretation of this passage. But we know this is not accurate. It would be considered a preposterous conclusion and an abuse of the text based on our knowledge of the point Paul is making in the entire passage.

Paul was speaking of reliance on circumcision, here equated with the law, to save. We need to examine ourselves on the more controversial passages in the Word to see if we have done this with other verses, especially if those verses present a challenge when trying to reconcile them with other seemingly contradictory passages and examples in the Bible.

Other believers see no need to take verses in context if they were commands given by Jesus—the words written in red in some Bibles. However, consider this verse:

> *Jesus sent out the twelve apostles with these instructions:* **"Don't go to the Gentiles or the Samaritans, but only to the people of Israel—God's lost sheep."** Matt. 10:5-6, NLT

If we took this verse as a literal principle for all time, we would summarize Jesus' command into two thoughts: Gentiles are not to be evangelized, and the lost sheep are narrowly defined as those from the house of Israel. But do these statements fit with the whole of Scripture? Interpreted literally at face value, these verses would change every paradigm we have of evangelism and the Great Commission.

The Wise Man Built His House upon the Rock

Knowing nuggets of God's truth plucked out of the Word without seeing the Word as an integrated whole can be compared to taking the solid foundation of God's Word (the Rock) and breaking it into *bits* of truth. These little pieces become sand if we do not consider all God has to say on a particular topic, or if we only pick the pieces that fit our personal worldview (see Matt. 7:24-27).

For example, if we take Jesus' words about prayer that we can ask for anything we want and, as long as we believe, we will have what we ask for (Matt. 21:22), we ignore the rest of Scripture which moderates unsanctified use of this verse. Under the inspiration of the Holy Spirit, James expounded on Jesus' statement, explaining we cannot ask with wrong motives and expect to receive what we ask for (James 4:3). John wrote that our confidence in prayer before the Lord comes from asking for what is in agreement with God's will (1 John 5:14).

If we do not consider the whole counsel of God on any particular subject, we may find ourselves standing on an unstable foundation that consists of only partial truth. The *sum* of God's Word gives us truth and a solid foundation. Jesus made it clear we are to build our spiritual house upon the Rock—the entirety of God's Word. Without examining the context in which a verse is situated, the intended meaning can be greatly altered. Standing on a piece of rock broken off and isolated from the whole may, at the very least, cause us to lose our balance. Guarding ourselves against this tendency is critical for stability.

So how does this help us understand why Paul included the verses in our current study? We will soon find out that, along with the grammatical construction of this letter, Paul's intended meaning is far from what many have believed about this passage's prohibition against women speaking in church.

Grammatical Construction

Throughout the letter, Paul confronts different trouble areas this congregation experienced. The methodical way in which Paul addressed key divisive issues plaguing Corinth was strikingly uniform. In several of the discussions in this letter, Paul employed a disjunctive particle (a word setting two thoughts in opposition to each other), the small Greek word ἤ (Grk. 2228 *é*, pronounced *ay*), between what the Corinthians have done or said and his rebuttal of their practice or teaching.

The Greek Word ἤ

É (ἤ) is often translated as 'or' when a list of thoughts are introduced (e.g., 'you must not associate with anyone who claims to be a believer but is sexually immoral **or** greedy, who is an idolater **or** slanderer, a drunkard **or** swindler...' 1 Cor. 5:11). It is also translated 'than' or 'rather than' when differentiating choices ('...better to marry **than** to burn...' 1 Cor. 7:9).

In other instances, it takes on a stronger emphasis when used to syntactically connect two opposing ideas with the intent to show the illegitimate nature of typically the first idea presented. In these cases, it is used as an exclamatory expression with an emotional feel of incredulity, dissociating what has been said with an appeal to reason, principle, etc. For example, the KJV interprets this use of ἤ as "What?" in the sense of 'are you listening to what you are saying?' or 'can't you see the error of thinking this way?' or in modern language, 'seriously?' (e.g., 1 Cor. 6:19).

I retrieved Paul's use of this particle from biblehub.com[29] but the idea was not my own. David Joel Hamilton pointed this out in his work, and he gave credit to Dr. Gilbert Bilezikian, Th.D., for the definitions discussed above.[30] Paul used this small word throughout this letter to refute the Corinthian's false ideology and practices that were causing division. With each use discussed below, Paul challenges the Corinthians to thoughtfully examine their policies and practice in light of the truth.

The following issues Paul addressed in his letter to the Corinthian church demonstrate his use of ἤ to question or object to their ways and thinking. In the following discussion, the expression in the parentheses is not a literal translation, but is meant to demonstrate the disjunctive function of ἤ in the narrative. Notice that each practice Paul addressed was a source of division in this church.

1. The Corinthians were taking sides on which leader each followed.

   Paul's response ('**PR**' hereafter): ἤ (What?) *Were you baptized in the name of Paul?* (1 Cor. 1:13)

2. These believers were suing each other in the secular courts.

   PR: ἤ (Really?) *Don't you know believers will judge the world?* (1 Cor. 6:2)

3. The Corinthians were cheating and wronging fellow believers.

   PR: ἤ (What were you thinking?) *Do you not know that wrongdoers will not inherit the kingdom of God? Do not be deceived...* (1 Cor. 6:9)

4. Some Corinthian believers taught that they had the right to do as they pleased with their physical bodies (gnostic heresy), including sexual immorality.

   PR: ἤ (Seriously?) *Do you not know that he who unites himself with a prostitute is one with her in body?* (1 Cor. 6:16) ... ἤ (What?) *Do you not know that your bodies are temples of the Holy Spirit, who is in you, whom you have received from God?* (v. 19)

5. The married among them were unsure about whether they should remain with an unbelieving spouse.

   PR: ἤ (Don't you see?) *How do you know, wife, whether you will save your husband? Or, how do you know, husband, whether you will save your wife?* (1 Cor. 7:16)

6. A dispute among the Corinthians re: Paul's authority and therefore his right to receive aid from them must have surfaced. Paul gave his argument in 1 Corinthians 9, appealing to the Word and what makes conventional sense:

   PR: ἤ (What?) *[I]s it only I and Barnabas who lack the right to not work for a living?* (v. 6)

   ἤ (Have you thought this through?) *Who tends a flock and does not drink the milk?* (v. 7) *Do I say this merely on human authority?* (v. 8a)

   ἤ (Is your thinking really so shallow?) *Doesn't the Law say the same thing?* (v. 8b) *Is it about oxen that God is concerned?* (v. 9)

   ἤ (Don't you understand?) *Surely he says this for us, doesn't he?* **Yes, this was written for us...** (v. 10)

7. Paul appeals to the Corinthian believers to flee idolatry by not participating at pagan tables where the food is offered to idols, which some of these believers must have continued to practice (1 Cor. 10:14-21; cf. Acts 15:19-20).

   PR: ἤ (What were you thinking?) *Are we trying to arouse the Lord's jealousy?* (1 Cor. 10:22)

8. Paul contends that because there are divisions among the Corinthians, they cannot be celebrating the Lord's Supper when they come together. They weren't even trying to include everyone, something Paul deemed especially unfitting for believers. Paul followed his exclamatory statement with further instructions about the proper way to conduct their fellowship meals (communion; see 1 Cor. 11:23-34).

   PR: ἤ (What?) *Don't you have homes to eat and drink in? Or do you despise the church of God by humiliating those who have nothing?* (1 Cor. 11:22)

The fact that Paul answers his argument in point 6 by saying, 'Yes, this was written for us' establishes that he is teaching the Corinthians the way they are to think on this matter. The same applies to the specific directions he gave for properly celebrating the communion fellowship meal following his rebuke of the way they currently practiced. This confirms his use of ἤ to instruct or correct the Corinthians in response to their wrong practice and thinking. ἤ introduces a statement or question geared toward urging the Corinthians to evaluate what they have done or said, nearly shaming them by making, 'Did you really think this through?'-type statements to expose their shortsighted and ill-considered ways.

Paul expertly leads them as a gifted teacher to help them first discern and acknowledge that their ways and thinking are in error. He then follows with an explanation on the proper behavior or thinking to replace that error.

Socratic Teaching Method

The method of teaching Paul employed in this letter is known as the Socratic method, which has been around for over two millennia. Aristotle credited Socrates with its inception. Socrates believed students would learn better if they were actively involved in the learning process rather than merely hearing a lecture. This method seeks to pull the correct answer out of the student by engaging in carefully directed questions that examine the student's belief systems. Socrates introduced this method to stimulate critical thinking and illuminate ideas.

This method initiates discussion "in which the defense of one point of view is questioned... The Socratic method is a *negative* method of hypothesis elimination, in that better hypotheses are found by steadily identifying and eliminating those that lead to contradictions... The basic form is a **series of questions formulated as tests of logic** and fact intended to help a person or group discover their beliefs about some topic."[31] Note that in the examples given, Paul employed this tactic as he followed each ἤ with this particular form of questioning.

This method allows the teacher to expose errors in thinking by helping the student move toward rational thinking and ideas supported by thoughtful analysis and logic rather than presuppositions and fallacy. "Most importantly, Socratic teaching engages students in dialogue and discussion that is collaborative and open-minded as opposed to debate, which is often competitive and individualized."³² This is an effective teaching tool to use when dealing with blind spots in understanding.

As an educated scholar, Paul would have been familiar with this tool. Teachers still use this method today because it has been shown to more effectively result in deeper understanding and retention. Questions guide the discussion to achieve specific learning objectives. Faulty logic and assumptions can be exposed, resulting in the student coming to the proper conclusion through the guided questions and direction of the teacher. Paul demonstrated this technique throughout this letter to address the sources of division this church experienced.

The Passage in Question

We observe Paul's next use of ἤ in the passage we are studying in this chapter. Paul introduces this discussion by saying each believer comes to the meeting with a word of instruction, etc.:

> *What then shall we say, **brothers and sisters**? When you come together, **each of you has** a hymn, or **a word of instruction**, a revelation, a tongue or an interpretation. Everything must be done so that the church may be built up.* 1 Cor. 14:26, NIV

[Note: Some dispute the translation of *adelphos* (Grk. 80) as 'brothers and sisters.' This translation is validated by Peter's address to the men and women gathered in the upper room after Jesus' ascension (Acts 1:12-14). 'Peter stood in the midst of the (120) believers and said, 'Men and *adelphos*, this Scripture had to be fulfilled... (vv. 15-16).' There are instances in the NT where the context is all believers regardless of gender, and others where it is strictly literal brothers in the male sense. The interpreter's preunderstandings have the power to influence whether we favor all believers, male and female, as addressed in certain passages, or just the men. When we look at words like *adelphos* and *anthropos* (Grk. 444, man or mankind) and interpret them as including both genders, it is not about being politically correct or biased—it is about being accurate.]

Paul spends the remainder of this chapter laying down instructions for orderly worship, concluding with:

> *Therefore, my **brothers and sisters, be eager to prophesy, and do not forbid speaking** in tongues. But everything should be done in a fitting and orderly way.* 1 Cor. 14:39-40, NIV

Paul begins this section by acknowledging that *each* believer came to their meetings with a word of instruction and concludes it by encouraging *every* believer to desire to prophecy, admonishing them to refrain from forbidding tongues. This hints at the chiastic structure of this portion of his letter (a literary device beginning and ending with parallel thoughts, with typically a main point in the central body; further discussion on chiasmus in the next chapter). Both men and women are being encouraged to teach and prophesy. Paul cites propriety and order in their meetings as the goal for his instructions.

Prior to these concluding remarks, Paul begins to address prophetic utterances (v. 29). The Bible gives us many examples of women prophets, as explained previously. Paul gives principles for prophets, namely that they should take turns so that everything is done in an orderly way to reflect God's character. So far so good.

In the middle of this chiastic argument, we are confronted with:

> [34] *Women should remain silent in the churches. They are not allowed to speak* (**laleo**), *but must be in submission, as the law says.* [35] *If they want to inquire about something, they should ask their own husbands at home; for it is disgraceful for a woman to speak* (**laleo**) *in the church.* 1 Cor. 14:34-35, NIV

As a visceral response, male believers read this and begin instinctively reciting the Talmudic prayer, 'Blessed are you, Oh Lord, our God, Ruler of the universe, who has not created me a woman,' and then quickly move on to chapter 15.

Women, on the other hand, are bewildered. 'Wait, what? i thought Paul just told us to participate in the meetings, because everyone is supposed to bring a word of instruction, a hymn, a revelation, etc. (v. 26). i was just getting over the guilt i felt for having short hair (1 Cor. 11:1-16) and for not being as dedicated to the Lord as the single women because i got married (1 Cor. 7:34). Now i'm told not even to speak, but ask my husband to explain scriptural issues at home? But he doesn't even read his Bible. And how can i be eager to prophesy if i can't speak in church? Is church a building, or is it anywhere believers are gathered? Do i have to take a vow of silence when i join the church?' (use of a small i for the personal pronoun intended).

Bringing the Passage into Conformity with the Whole of Scripture

In contrast to modern English, the ancient Greeks had no punctuation marks to make their meanings clearer. Because Paul is addressing the wrong thinking and practices of the Corinthians throughout this letter, we must consider the possibility that this discordant thought originated with the erring Corinthians—a mindset Paul wants to discuss and correct as he does with several other practices addressed in this letter. To disagree with this possibility due to the lack of quotation marks in the passage carries no weight because these were not used in *Koine* Greek.

First, we note that Paul's statement appeals to the law (v. 34). Why would Paul, who denied the OT ceremonial law (not the moral law written on the conscience of every person) and Jewish traditions (oral law) as binding on the NT Gentile believers, appeal to this law as an argument for rigid order in the NT church (e.g., Rom. 7:4,6; Gal. 3:1-3)? Second, where can we find this law in the Bible?

When Paul refers to Scripture elsewhere in his letters, he typically quotes at least part of the passage (e.g., see 1 Cor. 9:9ff). When he appealed to the Jewish laws dealing with oxen treading grain, he did so to make a spiritual parallel between feeding oxen as they work and spiritual leaders who labor on our behalf. He did not appeal to this law to establish NT doctrine regarding the fair treatment of oxen.

Some have made an appeal to Genesis to find this law, but one has to read a great deal of dialogue into the text to come to this conclusion. For someone to appeal to 'natural order' and some imagined law by reading between the lines in Genesis is a species of eisegesis. This is obvious to all except those seeking to establish support for Paul's appeal to the law as a legitimate basis for interpreting this passage at face value.

Furthermore, Luke recorded that Anna the prophet *never left the temple* and *continually spoke* (Grk. 2980 *laleo*) of Jesus to everyone she encountered (Luke 2:36-38). This is the same word Paul used in this passage, 'women are not to speak' (*laleo*). Why didn't the experts in the law resident in the temple silence Anna if the edict appeals to the creation order, enforced for all time?

> **Clearly no one who relies on the law is justified before God**, because "the righteous will live by faith." Gal. 3:11, NIV

We discover a more likely source in the oral law later recorded in the Talmud. The following statements taken from the Talmud closely resemble the 'law' Paul quoted in these verses:

> *A woman's voice is prohibited because it is sexually provocative.*[33]
>
> *To listen to a woman's voice is indecent.*[34]

[Note: I have seen other researchers quote the Talmud, Tractate Kiddushin, where Rabbi Merilla states, *"It is shameful for a woman to let her voice be heard among men,"* but could not verify this in a preliminary online search of the Talmud.]

From the pattern observed in this letter to the Corinthians, namely that Paul addresses issues and questions from the believers at Corinth with a reply of instruction or correction following, it is reasonable to believe he is addressing another practice/mindset of the Corinthians that requires correction. Rather than accept this as Paul's statement of his own views, the text more likely quotes the views of the Judaizers at Corinth, whose own oral law testifies to this view (see also 2 Cor. 11:13 and Gal. 2:4-5, which refer to the Judaizers' interference).

After Paul quotes what the Corinthians had written of their practice of not allowing women to speak, Paul responds using ἤ:

> (ἤ) *What? Came the word of God out from you? Or came it unto you only?* 1 Cor. 14:36, KJV

Notice how closely these remarks also fit the Socratic teaching method, as mentioned earlier. Paul counters their belief that women should not be allowed to speak by referencing (most likely) the events surrounding the outpouring of the Holy Spirit at Pentecost. He reminds them that the Word of God came to both men and women that day—the day the NT church was founded. The Word of God came to the women just as to the men when the Holy Spirit manifested as fire and wind in the house where they were gathered. The tongues of fire rested on *each one*, and *all* began to speak in other languages (Acts 2:1-4). The Word of God came out from each believer present.

This is reasonably the reference Paul makes to the Corinthian church. He is trying to engage them in the learning process by leading them to examine their beliefs and practice in light of truth and what God has already accomplished and established (cf. Acts 10:44-47; 15:8-9). Recalling the events of Pentecost would assist the Corinthians in this process. Just as he highlighted and corrected other divisive practices, Paul addressed this illegitimate practice as yet another source of creating division.

Every Believer Is Part of the Priesthood of All Believers

By asking the Corinthians whether the Word of God came only to 'them' (the men), he reminded the Corinthians that the Word of God was not given to men only but 'Jew and Greek, male and female, slave and free,' just as established at Pentecost. Peter proclaimed that the Spirit had been poured out on everyone in Christ, both the male and female believers, so that they could prophesy—a gifting that requires preaching and teaching. We are a royal priesthood that includes 'whosoever' (1 Pet. 2:9; cf. Rev. 1:6). Priests are expected to faithfully instruct others in the ways of God, which is also a duty of NT believers:

> **True instruction was in his mouth** *and nothing false was found on his lips. He walked with me in peace and uprightness, and turned many from sin.* **For the lips of a priest ought to preserve knowledge, because he is the messenger of the LORD Almighty and people seek instruction from his mouth.** Mal. 2:6-7, NIV

Paul wanted the Corinthian believers to resist false teaching as well as the Jewish customs and traditions that had no place in the new covenant for Gentile believers. Jesus rebuked the Pharisees for allowing their traditional practices to take the place of or nullify God's Word.

The interpretation offered here not only allows for a more natural flow to Paul's thoughts, it is in harmony with the progression, style, and content of the letter as well as Paul's own practice of including women in ministry. The evidence for this conclusion is compelling and far more objective than forcing the text to say something that is at odds with dozens of other passages in the Word.

Destroyed for Lack of Knowledge

Peter warned that some of Paul's letters were difficult to understand, particularly for the 'uninstructed and unstable.' Our discussion of those who break off bits of God's truth to erect a foundation of their own choosing leading to imbalance and unsteady footing applies here. This type of building, namely using one or two 'proof texts' through which to interpret other clear examples in Scripture, yields a very unstable inverted pyramid. We are to stand firmly on the solid Rock of God's Truth, seeking to understand God's Word as a harmonized whole. This alone gives us stable footing.

Both of the following English versions capture the essence of Peter's warning to us in interpreting Paul's letters. Even for the early church, some of the content of Paul's letters were not immediately clear, which implies that what he wrote at times had a complexity that believers unfamiliar with Scripture might distort. By his admission that the things Paul wrote were difficult to understand, Peter provides the reader with counsel to dig more deeply than what the surface meaning suggests to avoid misinterpretation.

> ***There are parts of his letters that are hard to understand,** and **some people give a wrong meaning to them**. These people are ignorant and weak in faith. They also give wrong meanings to the other Scriptures. But **they are destroying themselves by doing that**.* 2 Pet. 3:16, ERV

> *Indeed, he speaks about these things in all his letters. They contain some things that are hard to understand,* ***things which the***

uninstructed and unstable distort, to their own destruction, as they do the other Scriptures. 2 Pet. 3:16, CJB

Notice that those who are uninstructed in the meaning Paul sought to convey in his letters destroy themselves. Wrong interpretation and understanding can ruin not only our personal walk, but defile those we teach as well. In addition, these faulty interpretations can cause division. Regarding people who cause division, Paul counseled Titus to warn them twice and if they won't change, have nothing more to do with them (Titus 3:10).

Recall our discussion of the moldy (leprous) walls. Doctrines we hold that are at odds with the whole of Scripture cannot be ignored, lest we hear this indictment from the Lord:

> **My people are destroyed** *for lack of knowledge;* **because you have rejected knowledge, I reject you from being a priest to me.** Hos. 4:6a, ESV

Chapter 10

1 Timothy 2:11-15

> *Let a woman learn quietly with all submissiveness. I do not permit a woman to teach or to exercise authority over a man; rather, she is to remain quiet. For Adam was formed first, then Eve; and Adam was not deceived, but the woman was deceived and became a transgressor. Yet she will be saved through childbearing—if they continue in faith and love and holiness, with self-control.* 1 Tim. 2:11-15, ESV

Every time I have read this passage in the past, I've felt a knot in my stomach. A cloud of consternation hangs over this verse that is mind-numbing. I wondered, 'What is going on here, Lord? Why does Paul think women are so ignorant and worthless? Why does it look like he is recalling Eve's curse, when he teaches elsewhere that there is no longer any curse in Christ? How are the single women going to be saved if they don't have children? Aren't we saved by grace?'

> *When I was a child, I talked like a child, I thought like a child, I reasoned like a child. But when I became an adult* (OJB: 'mature'), *I set aside childish ways.* 1 Cor. 13:11, NET

In order to understand this passage, we have to put away naïve, childish reasoning. Thinking as a shrewd, mature believer requires digging more deeply when a passage at face value presents itself out of synch with Scripture as a whole. It also requires that we acknowledge the frailty of human translators who may have come up short in translating the Bible into English from the available Greek, Latin, Aramaic, and Hebrew manuscripts.

We will need some historical groundwork before we tackle this passage grammatically. We will also more closely examine Paul's relationship with Timothy. Each aspect contributes needed information that will uncover the true meaning of Paul's words to Timothy and bring this passage in harmony with the whole of Scripture.

Historical Context

First, let's look more closely at the relationship Paul and Timothy shared. Paul described Timothy as a faithful disciple from Lystra with a good reputation, brought up in the faith by his Jewish mother and grandmother (Acts 16:1-3; 2 Tim. 1:5). Timothy accompanied Paul as he delivered the decrees issued by the Jerusalem Council. They went to several cities from Lystra to Galatia, Troas, Samothrace, Neapolis, Philippi (where they were beaten), and finally to Berea, where Paul left Silas and Timothy (Acts 15; 16:3-12,22-24; 17:10-14). Paul sent for Silas and Timothy while preaching in Athens. They joined Paul in Corinth, where Paul records that Timothy participated in preaching (Acts 17:16; 18:1,5; 2 Cor. 1:19). The author of Hebrews implied that Timothy had been imprisoned at some point as well (Heb. 13:23).

Timothy delivered Paul's first letter to the Corinthian believers (1 Cor. 16:10). Paul confers co-authorship to Timothy for the second letter to the Corinthians (2 Cor. 1:1), as well as his letters to the Philippians (Php. 1:1), Colossians (Col. 1:1), Thessalonians (1 Thes. 1:1; 2 Thes. 2:1), and Philemon (Phile. 1:1).

Paul described Timothy as his co-laborer, his dearly beloved son, and a proven and faithful servant in the Lord (Rom. 16:21; 1 Thes. 3:21; Cor. 4:17; Php. 2:22; 1 Tim. 1:2; 2 Tim. 1:2). Paul trusted Timothy and sent him to follow-up on the churches that had been planted (1 Thes. 3:2-6). He mentored Timothy and carefully instructed him in the ways of the Lord, stating he had shown Timothy by his own life and teaching the proper conduct befitting believers entrusted with overseeing the flock (2 Tim. 3:10-11).

It is obvious that Paul spent a good deal of time and had a very close relationship with Timothy. Paul charged Timothy to stay in Ephesus to prevent the spread of false doctrine by preaching the Word faithfully to counter heresy (1 Tim. 1:3; 6:20; 2 Tim. 4:1-2). The closeness they shared as brothers in Christ was deepened by Paul's fatherly affection for this young man. Paul's letters frequently reflect these qualities. It is easily demonstrated that Paul and Timothy not only shared a common belief system, but also a common background of awareness regarding the cultures in which they ministered due to their shared experiences and encounters in their joint missionary travels.

Dr. Stacy E. Hoehl, Ph.D., professor at Wisconsin Lutheran College, wrote the following in her article on the mentoring relationship between Paul and Timothy:

> As Paul gained confidence in Timothy's competence as a minister, he employed Timothy in **one of the most challenging ministerial environments: the church in Ephesus**. Paul had spent a great deal of time developing the church in Ephesus, and was now concerned about the **spread of false doctrines and heresy** among its members. The city of Ephesus, located along the western coast of modern-day Turkey, was **famed for its cult and temple** dedicated to the **worship of Artemis**, around which a good deal of the **city's commercial interests** revolved... Ephesus presented the gospel with a **formidable challenge** in that it was a <u>center of pagan worship</u>... **Paul challenged Timothy's ministry skills** by placing him at the head of the church in Ephesus, a congregation that had **fallen ill with false teachings and heresies**.[35]

The common background Paul and Timothy shared as well as their likemindedness in matters of faith provided fertile ground for "high-context culture" communication as defined by anthropologist Dr. Edward T. Hall, Ph.D. (see Addendum). In this context, Paul needed fewer words to express his thoughts and counsel because of the closely-knit relationship he had with Timothy, their shared locus of beliefs, and their mutual knowledge of and experience with the culture at Ephesus. "In a higher-context culture, many things are left unsaid, letting the culture explain. Words and word choice become very important in higher-context communication, since a few words can communicate a complex message very effectively to an in-group (but less effectively outside that group), while in a low-context culture, the communicator needs to be much more explicit and the value of a single word is less important."[36]

Keep this in mind as we explore the cultural backdrop of the letters Paul wrote to his beloved son and co-laborer, Timothy.

The Climate at Ephesus

When Paul left Corinth, he made a brief visit to Ephesus, reasoning with the Jews in the synagogue (see Acts 18:18-19:41 for this discussion). Though they wanted him to stay, he departed and left the Ephesians in the capable hands of Priscilla and Aquila, who were later joined by Apollos—all three noted as teaching in the NT. When Apollos left for Corinth, Paul returned to Ephesus and met some Ephesians who had received the baptism of repentance but not the baptism of the Holy Spirit. He laid hands on them and prayed, and the Ephesian believers received the Holy Spirit.

Paul spoke in the synagogue there for three months and then left because they stubbornly refused to listen. He then took the believers and continued teaching in the Tyrannus lecture hall for roughly three years (see Acts 19:10; 20:31). Luke recorded that the fame of the Lord spread widely and grew in power because of the miracles done there and because of the incident with the sons of Sceva (see Acts 19:13ff).

During this time, a riot broke out at the instigation of tradesmen who were losing money because their idols of Artemis lost market share when Paul powerfully preached the one true God, discrediting all others. The tradesmen were zealous for their goddess Artemis, whose magnificent temple and chief shrine (noted as the seventh wonder of the world at that time) were nestled in Ephesus. The Ephesian economy received no small benefit from the many visitors who came because of Artemis and her temple.[37]

Sometime after Paul left, he sent for the elders at Ephesus and warned them (Acts 20:16-17,29-31), "**savage wolves will come in among you and will not spare the flock. Even from your own number men will arise and distort the truth** in order to draw away disciples after them. So be on your guard! Remember that for three years I never stopped **warning each of you night and day with tears**." Why was Paul so concerned about this particular little flock?

A brief look at the history of Ephesus unveils some of the deeply ingrained beliefs the Ephesian Gentile culture held. The threat this entrenched ideology posed for Gentiles struggling to grasp the truth in

God's Word required considerable attention to prevent the new believers from developing a syncretized belief system.

The Amazons and Artemis

The Amazons, viewed as both a mythological and historical group of warrior women, were believed to have founded Ephesus as well as other towns. These women were depicted as a dominating force in the region from Greece to the area surrounding the Black Sea. "In the *Iliad*, the Amazons were referred to as *Antianeirai* ("those who fight like men")... Herodotus [said], "No girl shall wed till she has killed a man in battle.""[38] These women lived under complete role reversal, even keeping male slaves for procreation. Artemis was the deity of choice, a goddess who excelled in strength and battle, forever a virgin and champion of women.

> Several Church Fathers speak of the Amazons as of a real people... Herodotus called them *Androktones* ("killers of men"), and he stated that in the Scythian language they were called *Oiorpata*, which he asserted had this meaning... They had initially set up wooden statues of Artemis... The deities worshipped by them were Ares... and Artemis, not the usual Greek goddess of that name, but an Asiatic deity in some respects her equivalent.[38]

The Temple of Artemis was also known as the Temple of Diana. While not purely the worship of the Greek Artemis or the Roman Diana, worship of the Ephesian Artemis included elements of both. Those who worshipped this goddess thought of men as inferior and in need of enlightenment from women. It becomes immediately apparent the appeal this cult held for the marginalized women of the day.

> Pausanias... attributed the earliest... [sanctuary] at Ephesus to the Amazons, whose worship he imagines already centered upon an image... of Artemis, their matron goddess. ... Pliny describes images of Amazons, the legendary founders of Ephesus and Ephesian Artemis' original protégés. ... [A] Roman edict of 162 AD acknowledges the **importance of *Artemesion*, the annual Ephesian festival to Artemis**... "one of the largest and most magnificent religious festivals in Ephesus' liturgical calen-

> dar."... Under Hellenic rule, and later, under Roman rule, the **Ephesian *Artemisia* festival was increasingly promoted as a key element** in the pan-Hellenic festival circuit. It was part of a definitively Greek political and cultural identity, **essential to the economic life of the region**. ... From the Greek point of view Ephesian Artemis is a distinctive form of their goddess Artemis... **[k]nown as the light-bearer**.[39]
>
> Artemis "becomes identical with the great **mother of Nature**, even as she was worshipped at Ephesus..." Artemis, while sitting on the knee of her father, Zeus, asked him to grant her... **the ability to help women in the pains of childbirth**. ... Most stories depict **Artemis as born first**, becoming her mother's mid-wife upon the birth of her brother Apollo.[40]

We note three things of use for our discussion here:

1. Artemis was known as the goddess of wisdom (title: "Light-Bringer").
2. She was born first (titles: "Leader"; "Best"; "Excellent"; "Of the First Throne"), which in this cult's eyes made her superior.
3. The women of Ephesus looked to Artemis for protection in childbirth in an era when mortality rates for both mother and child were high (titles: "Goddess of Birth," "Helper at Childbirth," and "Savior").[41]

There are other titles for Artemis useful for our discussion, including "Guardian," "Strong-Voiced/Lady of Clamors," "Of the Wolves," and "Of the Beasts."[41]

Paul, Beasts, and Wolves

In 1 Corinthians 15:32, Paul wrote that he 'fought wild beasts at Ephesus.' When the 'savage wolves' asserted their influence, as Paul had warned, Paul wrote his first letter to Timothy, the young elder of this church. 'Beasts' and 'wolves' are included in two of Artemis' titles. Do we know Paul to be a man who did things haphazardly? Don't we know him as the scholarly, clear-thinking apostle? The apostle who made every word count?

Plausibly, his use of 'beasts' and 'wolves' gives evidence that he is connecting the false doctrines of the Ephesian pagans with the false teaching he warned would enter the Ephesian church. After greeting Timothy, Paul urged him to stay in Ephesus 'so that you may **command certain people not to teach false doctrines** any longer' (1 Tim. 1:3).

Letter to the Ephesians

Paul's letter to the Ephesians predates his letters to Timothy. Paul spent time laying a foundation for the inclusion of Gentiles in the new covenant (Eph. 2:11-3:13). After urging this group of what seem to be primarily Gentile believers, Paul wrote that he insisted they cease from the worthless thinking of their former lives. Paul described the thinking of the Gentiles as futile and dark in its understanding of God.

This ignorance kept them separated from God because they were hardened to the truth (Eph. 4:17-18). When we have ingrained traditions, thinking, and practices established over a lifetime, it becomes very difficult to rid ourselves of those old ways and thinking. They become a part of us—second nature; our fall-back principles.

For example, people used to believe that if you left a loaf of bread in a dark room, it would turn into rats. People also formerly believed the world was flat, a concept that brought no small degree of outrage when it was challenged. The church used to believe the earth was the center of the universe, even branding people heretics if they believed differently. Church leaders refused to look into Galileo's telescope, thinking they would see something they shouldn't. Are we so confident and sophisticated today that we believe we haven't made any errors? Even the learned Sadducees were rebuked for not understanding the Word despite knowing it by heart (Matt. 22:29). We still only know in part... despite having Google.

Paul exhorted the Ephesian believers to cease from useless/corrupt speech as well as from anger, disputes, and slander (Eph. 4:29-31). Though they were once in darkness, Paul encouraged these new believers to live in the light by seeking truth and what pleases the Lord (Eph. 5:8-10). He urged them to be filled with the Spirit, 'speaking to one another with songs from the Spirit' (Eph. 5:18b-19a), reminding them to pray and keep on praying (Eph. 6:18). He was addressing this entire congregation, men and women alike.

> Then we will no longer be infants, tossed back and forth by the waves, and **blown here and there by every wind of teaching** and by the cunning and craftiness of people in their **deceitful scheming**. Instead, **speaking the truth in love**, we will grow to become in every respect the mature body of him who is the head, that is, Christ. Eph. 4:14-15, NIV

Paul Addresses False Doctrine

The context of this situation helps us more fully understand what Paul wrote in this first letter to Timothy. As stated in this section of the letter, Paul's first goal was that the Ephesian believers would be people of prayer (1 Tim. 2:1). He reminded Timothy there is only one God who wants everyone to be saved and understand the truth. Jesus is the only Savior who reconciled man to God and continues to mediate on our behalf. Paul then described himself as a true and trustworthy teacher of Gentiles (1 Tim. 2:1-7).

Notice that each point Paul made in this paragraph counters the deeply ingrained beliefs held by the Ephesian Artemis worshippers as well as the budding gnostic heresies. [Note: Gnostic heresies taught of 'secret' or 'hidden knowledge'; they seem to be a syncretized set of teachings combining Jewish mysticism, Christian thought, and pagan themes of a woman (Eve) who was created first and brings 'light' or understanding to deceived or ignorant men. They also taught the separation of a person's physical and spiritual self, some sects involved in rampant licentious behavior and others following asceticism.]

- There is only one God, not many.
- Unlike Greek and Roman gods that each had specific protectorates and functions, the one true God meets all our needs and desires everyone to be saved and understand truth.
- Artemis was primarily seen as the protectorate of women. Paul countered her title as "Savior," replacing the myth with the

> truth that Jesus is the only Savior and mediator. The newly converted pagans didn't have to pray to Artemis or any other god for favor, protection, etc.

Paul finishes this opening statement by reminding Timothy that he is and has been a truthful and faithful teacher for Gentile believers. They can trust his judgment and motives for the counsel he gives.

Paul then gives Timothy instructions on how to direct the believers to facilitate transformation from their paganistic worldview and practice to become a people of prayer grounded in the truth. Paul urged the men to stop their angry disputes (1 Tim. 2:8), similar to his instructions in his letter to the Ephesians. Remember, few people possessed any biblical writings, and fewer still had the entire OT. This would apply to these Gentile believers to an even greater degree.

He then urged the women to dress modestly rather than in the customary social garb of either the elite, prostitutes, or the Artemis temple worshippers (vv. 9-10). This type of immodesty only draws attention to the individual rather than the Savior, Jesus the Messiah, which is a subtle form of robbing God of His glory—or not so subtle in some cases.

There are various opinions on the origin and reasons for this extravagant dress habit. The idea that this statement rebukes the customs of Artemis worship is worth mentioning. Wade Burleson, head pastor of Emmanuel Baptist Church in Enid, Oklahoma, conducted research on this subject. He wrote in a blog post addressing this issue, "Heliodorus said, "Their locks of hairs carry their prayers." There were no sacrifices in this Temple. The women worshipped Artemis with their clothing, jewelry, and their words."[42] Paul addresses all three of these—clothing, jewelry, and disruptive speaking (1 Tim. 2:9-11).

Paul continues by addressing the problem they were experiencing with the false teachings circulating among these new believers. The Artemis followers in this region had been taught from childhood the tenets of the Artemis cult, e.g., that a woman was born first, that she brings 'light' (wisdom/reason) to men, and that prayers offered to her in childbirth would protect the mother and the child.

Keep in mind that this was the goddess the Amazon women worshipped—a goddess that met their need for a strong female figure; one whose dogma allowed for role reversal of the most extreme kind. Later in the letter, Paul gives an example of the doctrines of demons and seducing spirits he warned them about: doctrine forbidding marriage (1 Tim. 4:3). Not only did the Artemis cult advocate perpetual virginity, the ascetic proponents of proto-gnosticism also forbade marriage.

Recurring Themes

There must have been some very difficult, boisterous, intimidating, and/or controlling people at this church subverting Timothy's authority and teaching. In his second letter to Timothy, Paul encouraged Timothy not to be intimidated, but to persevere (2 Tim. 1:7). He instructed Timothy to entrust the teaching he had received and taught to the Ephesians to reliable people who would also be able to teach others (2 Tim. 2:2). The following are recurring themes in the second letter:

- study/teach the Word and handle it correctly, gently instructing those who oppose so they come to know the truth and escape the devil's snare; Scripture is from God for teaching truth and rebuking/correcting false doctrine so that believers will be properly equipped in the truth (2:14,15,25-26; 3:16-17; 4:2)
- warn the people to stop quarreling and to avoid godless talk, which Paul equates with false teaching; warn them to turn from myths (2:14,16-17,23; 4:3-4)
- urge the people to cleanse themselves from the common (teachings of that region) so they can be 'useful to the Master and prepared to do every good work' (2:20-22)

Grammatical Construction

Now that we have established the historical context of this passage, deciphering the grammatical construction helps build our case for how Paul intended this passage to be understood. Think back to our discussion of Paul and Timothy's close relationship and the likeliness that they shared a "high-context" style of communication. We will discover that the points Paul made in this letter demonstrate this style of communication with Timothy.

The Passage in Question

Let's read our English translation of Paul's words sent to help Timothy deal with the false doctrine spreading at Ephesus. Notice the similar nature of the phrases highlighted in bold. Keep this in mind as we discuss the chiastic structure of this portion of the passage.

> [11]**Let the woman learn in silence** with all subjection. [12]But I suffer not a woman to teach, nor to usurp authority over the man, **but to be in silence.** [13]For Adam was first formed, then Eve. [14]And Adam was not deceived, but the woman being deceived was in the transgression. [15]Notwithstanding she shall be saved in childbearing, if they continue in faith and charity and holiness with sobriety. 1 Tim. 2:11-15, KJV

Most women will admit this verse has bothered them at one time or another. None of the different arguments I had read gave the 'aha' feeling I was searching for. I remember one night in particular where I prayed, 'Please, Lord, help me understand this passage. I just don't see how it fits together or harmonizes with the rest of Scripture. Help me to see what You intended it to say, not what I want it to say.'

At 1:53 am the next morning, I received my answer—an inspiration to look for a literary device. My first thought was, 'Literary device? I'm not sure I even remember what the choices are.' I thought of Sherlock Holmes' note to Watson in *A Game of Shadows*. "Come at once, if convenient. If inconvenient, come all the same." God answered my prayer at *1:53 am*. My early morning search led me to a Greek literary device I had seen before—a chiasmus.

> *He has filled the hungry with good things but has sent the rich away empty.* Luke **1:53**, NIV

Micro-Chiastic Structure

This section is necessary but a bit technical, so get a cup of coffee, take a deep breath, and plow on.

Was Paul the scholar writing *ad hoc* (unsystematically or without planning) because this was a personal letter to Timothy? Or is this a carefully laid out, "high-context" response to the trouble Timothy faced at Ephesus?

Through this discussion, we will discover that Paul carefully constructed this letter with "high-context" points to make sure Timothy would follow his reasoning for the directives he gave him. Studied this way, we unearth the wisdom in this passage that also allows for harmony with the Word and Spirit of God.

The English language relies heavily on punctuation to give clarity. Notice the significant differences in meaning of these identical sentences. The only difference is the placement of punctuation, which results in identical words giving quite opposite meanings:

1. Woman: without her, man is lost.
2. Woman, without her man, is lost.

Because of its lack of punctuation, Classical Greek literature used different literary devices to accomplish the same task. One such device is chiasmus, a technique scholars have frequently noted in Paul's writing.

A chiasmus is a "rhetorical device used in ancient writings, including Biblical Greek, in which key words in a phrase, verse, or series of verses is repeated in an inverse pattern. It is sometimes called "inverse parallelism.""[43] They are often used to point out the emphasis or clarify the meaning of a passage (Ronald Man, as quoted in Slusser's article, following). Wayne T. Slusser wrote a very helpful article on the use of chiasmus in Paul's letters (see End Notes):

> The shortest chiasm consists of two lines. In a chiasm, the second line is inverted. While the parallelism is maintained, the author inverts the elements of the second line. Nils Lund observes that this inversion can be of "identical terms, but more often of similar ideas."[44]

By inversion, Slusser is describing a passage laid out in parallel fashion, with an initial **A** statement, followed by a **B** phrase, with (usually) a central or pivotal point in the middle (**C**). The inverted parallel can be seen in the phrases following, with a **B'** (similar to the **B** phrase but using synonymous words or parallel thought) immediately following the **C**, and finishing with **A'** (similar to **A** in thought or words).

If you want to more fully understand this concept, read the following; otherwise, skip ahead.

> **Classical scholars define chiasmus in terms of structure**. Some NT scholars, however, have extended the discussion of chiasmus to include pivotal theme or central idea as part of the definition... The ancients used chiasmus for a variety of reasons. To communicate clearly apart from the modern conventions of punctuation, paragraphing and typography, etc. **classical Greek writers structured their compositions much more carefully**... **Chiasmus can serve to divide a portion of text from the undifferentiated text around it**... Pivotal theme or central idea carries the main thought of the author. It is the focus of meaning around which the other parallel lines are constructed. **The structure of chiasmus accentuates this central idea with its formation of the two exterior complementary elements** (e.g., A and A') and its two interior elements (e.g., B and B'). The interior elements can act as the pivotal theme or they can point to a single central theme (e.g., C).
>
> Chiasmus in the New Testament plays an important role as a literary device to organize information. The use of **chiasmus can give cohesion to a passage** or **even to an entire book**. The emphasis placed within the center of the chiasmus is both valid and **necessary to properly understand** its contents. Although not all chiasms have a direct theological/doctrinal emphasis, they **may simply be used for a point of attention to the reader**.[45]

Slusser highlights the following to emphasize the need to recognize this important literary device in order to truly understand the author's intended meaning:

1 Timothy 2:11-15 | 163

> The purpose of chiasmus begs a discussion concerning the discipline of hermeneutics. Craig Smith notes, "[John] Breck is so convinced of the significance of chiasm in the New Testament that he calls the device a **'key to the Scriptures.'** He argues that **recognition of the figure makes it possible to discern the authorial intent of passages which may well have been misunderstood by those who failed to recognize their chiastic structure."**
>
> Smith notes, "If an author has gone to some trouble to say something a particular way, failure to note that will likely result in a **failure to understand precisely what the author intended to communicate."**[46]

In summary, Slusser argues that grammatical structure is just as vital as, if not more important than, word studies alone:

> [T]he New Testament exegete should not dismiss the importance of the structure of the chiasmus for interpretation. **Chiastic structures help to further validate the interpretation of the exegete**... As demonstrated in the discussion of this chiasmus, there is a **grammatical and structural basis** for the interpretation. Therefore, it is the **presence of this literary device that helps the interpreter to go beyond the lower elements of language (i.e. word studies, phrases, etc.) to come to a proper interpretation**. D. A. Carson suggests, "The heart of the issue is that **semantics, meaning, is more than the meaning of words. It involves phrases, sentences, discourse, genre, and style**." The interpretation of a passage is **not to be based solely on word studies but also on the literary structures that are present**.[47]

James M. Gibbs, Ph.D., also notes that the **parallel phrases 'may help to exegete each other'** (i.e., A and A', B and B', etc.).[48]

I believe Paul is employing this literary device here, breaking down vv. 11-12 as follows. I have used the basic Greek ordering of the words rather than our traditional English translations. In Greek, word order is less significant because the form of the word determines its use, not the order. I have also left *authentein* untranslated at this time.

A a woman in quietness (*gune en hesuchia*)

   B let learn in all submissiveness (*mantheneto en pase hupotage*)

      C but to teach a woman I not permit (*didaskein de gunaiki ouk epitrepo*)

   B' indeed not *authentein* of man (*oude authentein andros*)

A' but to be in quietness (*alla einai en hesuchia*)

[Note: The Greek word *en* (1722) means in, on, among. This chiasmus could also be constructed as **A** (*a woman in quietness let learn in all submission*)—**B** (*but to teach a woman I not permit*)—**B'** (*indeed not authentein of man*)—**A'** (*but to be in quietness*). This represents another acceptable chiasmus configuration and lends itself to a more parallel interpretation where A and A'/B and B' are concerned.]

<u>Part A</u>

'A woman in quietness' (*gune en hesuchia*)...

Gune (Grk. 1135; a woman or a wife) is in the nominative case and is therefore the subject of this sentence. The interlinear translation I studied had no definite article ('the') before *gune* in the Greek. Paul is addressing the conduct of men and women in this church, especially noting that the overall theme of this letter is the rampant spread of false doctrine. It makes more sense to translate this word as 'a woman.'

The word ***hesuchia*** (Grk. 2271), translated 'quietness,' is not speechlessness (more directly indicated by 4602, *sige*[49]) but rather the spiritual tranquility that God gives to the believer; "a God-produced calm."[50] The idea is to refrain from causing commotion or clamoring. Its use in the following passages demonstrates that speechlessness is not the main idea (translated word in bold):

- "Brothers and fathers! Listen to me as I make my defense before you now!" When they heard him speaking to them in Hebrew, they **settled down** more; so he continued... Acts 22:1-2, CJB

- *Such people we command and urge in the Lord Jesus Christ to **settle down** and earn the food they eat. 2 Thes. 3:12, NIV*

The adjective form of this noun, *hesuchios* (Grk. 2272), means the same: quiet or stillness. "[It] describes being "appropriately tranquil" by not misusing (or overusing) words that would stir up needless friction (destructive commotion),"[51] as seen in these passages:

- *[Pray] for kings and all who are in authority, so that we may lead a **tranquil and quiet** life in all godliness and dignity. 1 Tim. 2:2, NASB*
- *Rather, it should be that of your inner self, the unfading beauty of **a gentle and quiet** spirit, which is of great worth in God's sight. 1 Pet. 3:4, NIV*

Wade Burleson commented, "It never means "don't speak," but addresses the character of humility." The women in Ephesus were "coming out of a society saturated with the power, strength, abilities and even domination... through the Artemis cult" and needed to realize that they "had a great deal to learn about Christ and His kingdom."[52]

Part B

'...let learn in all submissiveness' (*mantheneto en pase hupotage*).

Paul instructs Timothy to 'let a woman learn in all submission.' A counter-culture thought in his day, Paul is advocating the instruction of women who were typically thought of as incapable of learning in some Jewish circles of the day and pervasively in the Greco-Roman culture. **Manthano** (Grk. 3129), to learn, is closely related to *mathetes* (Grk. 3101), from which we get the word disciple. Properly defined, the emphasis of *manthano* is 'learning key facts.'[53]

'In all (*pas*, Grk. 3956) submission' (*hupotage*, Grk. 5292). **Pas** "means 'all' in the sense of 'each (every) part that applies.' The emphasis of the total picture is on "one piece at a time.""[54] This is in keeping with discipleship, which requires being teachable and humble before our Teacher as He reveals truth to us and corrects the wrong ideas under which we have lived and acted, building precept upon precept. This directive, therefore, targets every relevant aspect of submission that pertains to the teacher-student relationship.

Hupotage means "to place in an orderly fashion under. In general, originally, it showed one's relations to superiors, either compulsory or voluntary subordination. If compulsory, the main idea may be that of either power or conquest on the one side or lack of freedom on the other. In the NT the verb **does not immediately carry with it the thought of obedience.**"[55] While the word does not directly equate with obedience, it does mean that we treat those over us with respect.

Paul directs the women to listen to sound teaching without clamoring, unlike Artemis, the 'strong-voiced lady of clamors.' Rather, the Ephesian women are instructed to learn quietly by settling down as a student submits to a teacher: without arguing, interrupting, or bringing up peripheral issues that would disrupt the teaching climate and/or cause confusion. The word *hupotage* makes room for someone to have a dissenting opinion as long as it is stated respectfully with support and appropriate timing. We remember that the Berean Jews were counted as more noble for verifying Paul's teaching with the Word. Students should never accept teaching blindly, but neither should they dishonor their instructors by the way in which they disagree.

Paul instructed Timothy that the Lord's servants (Grk. 1401 *doulos*, used of both men and women, e.g., Acts 2:18) must not be quarrelsome but **able to teach** (2 Tim. 2:24). In order to teach, one must be instructed first, which includes repenting of (turning from) wrong ideology. The fact that Paul gave instructions for the women to be taught indicates that he wanted them to come to a knowledge of the truth so they would be able to teach (cf. 2 Tim. 3:7; Heb. 5:12).

> Let the message of Christ dwell among you richly **as you teach and admonish one another**. Col. 3:16, NIV

Part C

'But to teach a woman I not permit' (*didaskein de gunaiki ouk epitrepo*).

In this part and in the phrase following, part B', there is no noun noted to be in the nominative case for our subject. We also note that no verb is in the Greek imperative mood (this mood gives instruction to the reader/listener, e.g., 'eat more vegetables'), so we conclude 'you' is not the understood subject.

This being so, we need to find a subject, perhaps a substantive (a pronoun, verbal-noun, etc. taking the place of a noun). For example, in English we have gerunds, an infinitive verb in the -ing form that can be used as a noun as well as a verb, e.g., swimming (verb: 'he is swimming'/noun: 'swimming is good exercise'). Verbs in the Greek infinitive mood can be subjects as well as direct and indirect objects, the possible answer for our need to have a subject.

To help me understand the grammatical construct of this sentence, I turned to and relied heavily on Corey Keating's (Th.M.) contributions to *Learning New Testament Greek* at ntgreek.org.[56] Much of the information in this section was gleaned from his explanations of various Greek word forms.

*didaskein***	*de*	*gynaiki*	*ouk*	*epitrepō**
Verb; no person or number given	**Conjunction**	**Noun**: dative case, singular	**Adverb**	**Verb**; first person singular
to teach	but	woman	not	(I) permit
1321	1161	1135	3756	2010

Notes: Information in this chart retrieved from biblehub.com[57]

    * first person singular present active indicative (see Addendum)

    ** present active infinitive (the present infinitive indicates ongoing or potential/possible action; infinitive verbs often act as nouns—'a verbal noun'—as either the subject or direct object)

Didaskein comes from the verb *didasko* and means 'to teach.' It was written in the present active infinitive form in this verse. There is no person or number indicated in its construction. Greek verbs have "five basic parts (or aspects) that are clearly defined or indicated by *every* Greek verb form. These five parts are: Person, Number, Tense, Voice, and Mood."[58] Because this verb construction does not indicate person or number, we reasonably suspect that this verb may be a substantive (used as a noun) as either the subject or the direct/indirect object in this phrase. If Paul intended to use this verb to describe the action of the woman, he would have ascribed *person* (third person) and *number* (singular) in its construction. In addition, he would have written *gune* (woman) in the nominative case (indicates the subject), not the dative (indicates the indirect object).

De is a Greek word that can be used in various continuative, copulative, or adversative functions, placed directly after the word that it is connecting with a previous thought (sometimes in the 3rd or 4th position in certain instances). In the passage currently under our review, it is placed directly after *didaskein*, connecting it with the previous thought, which is 'let a woman learn.'

Pastor William Wenstrom's article on *de* was very helpful. *De*, normally weaker than *alla* (used later in this passage), is translated 'but.' *De* can be used to contrast concepts or statements, or simply function as joining them. Pastor Wenstrom quotes A.T. Robertson, who stated, "The ordinary narrative use (continuative) I conceive to be the original use, the adversative the developed and later construction. The etymology confirms this explanation, though it is largely conjectural."[59]

De can provide a transition to something new, distinguishing it from the previous statement. *De* is also used to introduce an explanation, separating the explanation from the thing explained. Its function can be to contrast a preceding thought or give an expanded explanation.[60] It is this usage as an expanded explanation that seems most appropriate for this passage, namely, as an explanation for Paul's instruction for women to learn quietly. So how can we be more certain that he was providing further explanation of what these women were to be taught, rather than that he was contrasting women *learning* with women *teaching*?

The answer is found in the case Paul chose for the noun, *gune*, which can mean either 'woman' or 'wife,' as previously discussed. We will maintain the first definition, 'a woman.' **Gunaiki** is in the dative case, singular form. Because it is in the dative case, we know that it is the *indirect* object, a person or thing *indirectly* affected by the verb's action. Its primary use is to receive the direct object, informing us *to whom* or *for whom* something is done. In many English sentences, the indirect object often precedes the direct object, as in 'He (subject) bought (verb) his mother (indirect object) tickets (direct object)." The son did not buy his mother—he bought tickets that he gave to his mother. She is the recipient.

An indirect object can also be used to describe the means or location. It is unlikely that either of these two uses are meant here because of Paul's use of the word *de* after 'to teach,' indicating that he is linking the previous statement ('let a woman learn') with what he is now explaining. Since the content of the previous statement addressed a woman learning, this statement is to be understood as defining or explaining the teaching she is to receive. She is the recipient.

For an indirect object to exist there must be a direct object. The only choice we have for direct object so far is *didaskein*. This supports a translation 'to teach (direct object) a woman (indirect object),' or 'teaching to a woman.' She is the recipient of the teaching.

The next two words go together. **Ouk** is an adverb that modifies what comes after it by negating it, usually translated 'not.' For example, the word 'run' would become 'not run.' **Epitrepo**, which means 'to permit or allow,' immediately follows *ouk*. This makes the translation 'not permit' or 'not allow.'

The form of this verb, unlike the other verbs in this sentence, includes *person* and *number* (first person singular), rendering this verb form as 'I [do] not allow.' It is in the present active indicative form rather than present active infinitive (see Addendum for a brief explanation). Verbs in the indicative mood are statements of fact. Infinitive verbs are often treated as nouns or complement another verb.

Because *ouk epitrepo* looks like the most likely candidate so far for the subject and predicate, this half of the verse in readable English fashion would be: *I do not allow teaching a woman...*

It becomes very important that we understand why Paul inserted the conjunction *de* after 'to teach.' Because *didaskein* (to teach) is the direct object and left undesignated by person or number (as previously discussed), I believe the only appropriate and tenable choice we have is that Paul is explaining or qualifying the content of the learning he discussed in the previous verse. This leaves us with, 'And to teach (direct object) a woman (indirect object), I do not allow (subject-verb)...' But let's not be too hasty.

Part B'

'... indeed not man's *authentein*' (*oude authentein andros*)

I have placed man in front of *authentein* because the noun **andros** (Grk. 435), translated man, is in the genitive singular. The genitive case shows possession or limits the scope of a noun. Since there is no noun, it becomes readily apparent that the verb *authentein*, like *didaskein*, is being used as a substantive (used as a noun). With this information, we can be fairly certain that Paul was writing '*authentein* of a man,' or 'a man's *authentein*,' as opposed to anyone else's *authentein*.

The word **oude** (Grk. 3761) is a conjunction derived from the words *ou* (Grk. 3756: no or not) and *de* (Grk. 1161: and, but, moreover, indeed, as discussed previously). This portion could therefore be worded, 'indeed not *authentein* of man.'

The real difficulty surfaces when trying to define **authentein** (Grk. 831, a form of *authentes*), which appears in the Bible here alone. There isn't even a related derivative of this word present in the Bible. This verb is written in the present active infinitive with no designation of person or number, providing evidence that it is indeed being used as a substantive (a noun substitute), just as *didaskein*.

To further strengthen this argument, the fact that *andros* is in the genitive case indicates that this verbal noun (*authentein*) is conjoined to *andros*, which needs something to possess or a noun to limit in scope. If it was meant to describe something the woman was doing, *authentein* would have included *person* and *number* (third person singular in this case) in its construction along with tense, voice, and mood. In other words, the construction of this verb limits the way we can interpret how it is used in this passage. It is not an action the woman is doing. I believe it is being used as a noun to define what the genitive (possessive) form of *andros* is possessing.

The word *authentein* is typically translated authority, lord over, usurp authority, take authority, domineer over, etc., in various English translations. Since there are several other Greek words found in Scripture that carry the meanings noted, we have to wonder why Paul chose this word specifically instead of any of the other more conventional terms. Except where noted, definitions were retrieved from biblehub.com/greek.

- 1413 *dunastes*: possessor of power or authority; one who occupies high position [61]

- 1849 *exousia*: (from 1537 *ek*, out from, which intensifies 1510 *eimí*, to be, being as a right or privilege) authority, conferred power; delegated empowerment (authorization), operating in a designated jurisdiction [62]

- 1850 *exousiazo*: to exercise authority, having authority to act

- 2003 *epitage*: instruction, command, order, authority

- 2634 *katakurieuo*: (properly) to exercise *decisive* control (downward) as an owner with full jurisdiction; (passive) to be fully subjected to a master; to lord it over [63]

- 2715 *katexousiazo*: to exert authority downwards (oppressively); to strongly dominate (bring down; note the force of the prefix *kata*) [64]

- 5247 *huperoche*: superiority, excellence, preeminence, authority

With all these words at his disposal, why did Paul specifically choose *authentes* in his instructions to Timothy?

Dr. Linda L. Belleville, Ph.D., adjunct professor of New Testament at Grand Rapids Theological Seminary, conducted an in-depth study of Greek literary sources to see how this word was used contemporary to the writing of this passage. The meaning of 'authority' was not ascribed to this word until the third or fourth centuries A.D., about the time Jerome produced the Latin Vulgate.

> Lexicographers, for the most part, agree that the root of *authentes* is *auto* + *entes*, meaning "to do or originate something

with one's own hand." Usage confirms this. An *authentes* is **someone who originates** or carries out an action. During the sixth to second centuries B.C., the Greek tragedies used it exclusively of murdering oneself (suicide) or another person(s). The rhetoricians and orators of this period did the same. The word is rare in the historians and epic writers of the time, but in all instances it too is used of a "murderer" or "slayer."[65]

Biblestudytools.com supplied a similar definition for this rare verb (among others): 'one who with his own hands kills another or himself.'

Dr. Catherine Kroeger, Ph.D., a ranked adjunct professor of classical and ministry studies at Gordon Conwell Theological Seminary where she taught from 1990 until her death, concurs:

> Its earliest meanings are noteworthy, since they might provide a quite different understanding of a difficult text... Although the usages prior to and during the New Testament period are few and far between, they are briefs of murder cases and once to mean suicide, as did Dio Cassius. Thucydides, Herodotus, and Aeschylus also use the word to denote one who slays with his own hand, and so does Euripides. The Jewish Philo, whose writings are contemporary with the New Testament, meant "self-murderer" by his use of the term.[66]

Dr. Belleville found another set of meanings from antiquity worth consideration for our discussion:

> During the Hellenistic period, the primary meaning of authentes was still "murderer," but **the semantic range widened** to include "perpetrator," "sponsor," "author," and "mastermind" of a crime or act of violence. This is the case regardless of geographical location, ethnicity or religious orientation. For instance, the Jewish historian Josephus speaks of the **author** (*authenten*) of a poisonous drought... Diodorus of Siciliy uses it of (1) the **sponsors** (*authentas*) of some daring plans... (2) the **perpetrators** (*authentais*) of a sacrilege... and (3) the **mastermind** (*authentas*) of a crime... [67]

In the following, Dr. Belleville found *authentes* simply translated 'origin':

'All Jews [in Alexandria] shall be subjected to a registration... those who are registered are to be branded on their bodies by fire... and to register... in accordance with their [Egyptian] **origin** (*authentian*) of record.'"[67]

Inherent in the word *authentes* is the idea of origin or originator/author, as noted by Bellevile, and I believe the best fit for what Paul was communicating to Timothy. While there were certain elements of Amazon women being noted as 'man-killers,' the idea of defining this word as 'origin' seems to fit the entire context of the passage more adequately. This portion would read, 'indeed not man's origin.'

How can we have a greater degree of certainty that this word should be translated origin? I believe the answer lies with Paul's use of the Greek word *gar* (discussed shortly) immediately following the micro-chiasmus of verses 11-12.

Part A'

'... but to be in quietness' (*alla einai en hesuchia*)

This phrase essentially mirrors the opening phrase of this chiasmus, bringing Paul's immediate directive to a close. The chiastic structure would require that we interpret this parallel statement as we did its counterpart: these women need to learn by quieting themselves and settling down to receive teaching. This was altogether unlike the boisterous women of the Artemis cult who were accustomed to obstreperous expression of their views in their long-standing Ephesian tradition that women were the bearers of wisdom and understanding.

Paul Gives His Explanation for This Directive

> For (**gar**) Adam was formed first, then Havah ['Eve,' KJV]. Also it was not Adam who was deceived, but the woman who, on being deceived, became involved in the transgression. Nevertheless, the woman will be delivered through childbearing, provided that she continues trusting, loving and living a holy life with modesty. 1 Tim. 2:13-15, CJB

After completing the chiasmus, Paul uses the word *gar* (Grk. 1063; a conjunction; typically translated for), indicating that he intends to give the explanation for what he just said.

> While "for" is usually the best translation... its sense is shaped by the *preceding* statement—the "A" statement which precedes the 1063 (*gár*) statement in the "A-B" unit.[68]

In other words, the *gar* statement is the second half of a literary unit, providing the explanation for the first half.

Slusser examined Ephesians 2:1-9 as a micro-chiasmus in his article, breaking down the passage into the inverted parallel parts. He then stated that verse 10 was the conclusion, or explanation of the chiasm. This explanatory passage begins with the same word discussed here: *gar*.[69] As the author of both Ephesians and the letters to Timothy, we can see the consistency of Paul's literary style and use of Greek.

Wenstrom provides the following scholarship on the use of *gar* (either directly quoted or summarized):

1. **Gar introduces the reason or cause for the preceding statement**, or an explanation of a declaration, **often using proofs or examples**, "joined with other particles where **gar gives the reason of a clause to be supplied between *alla* and itself.**" (Liddel and Scott, as quoted by Wenstrom)

2. "[T]he **general is confirmed by the specific**... **expressing continuation or connection.**" (Bauer, Gingrich and Danker, as quoted by Wenstrom).

3. "More often *gar* **assumes a reaction on the part of the hearer** to some incident **and gives, in its clause, the reasons.**" (The Exegetical Dictionary of the New Testament lists these usages and meanings (volume 1, pages 238-239), as quoted by Wenstrom)[70]

Each of these reasons applies to the passage under scrutiny. Paul just told Timothy not to permit teaching that says a woman is man's origin. The general point Paul makes in Part C of the chiasmus—that he does not permit teaching a woman certain doctrines—is supported by the mention of the specific doctrines he wanted to correct in the Ephesians' thinking in the following verses. *Gar* introduces this explanation.

As the first use points out, *gar* supplies the reason for our *alla* statement, which is *alla einai en hesuchia*, 'but to be in quietness.' Paul knew there would be a reaction to this statement (third reason for *gar*'s use), indicating that he anticipated their puzzlement at such a directive, so he gives justification for his directive by initiating his explanation with *gar*.

Notice that the three proofs Paul uses to explain his reason for stating that 'he does not permit teaching a woman she is man's origin, but to settle down to learn' refute the Artemis and proto-gnostic teachings prevalent at Ephesus (see reason 1 for *gar*'s use). Paul's abbreviated reasoning as used here is in keeping with the "high-context" communication he and Timothy likely shared. Both were well-versed in the types of false teaching circulating at Ephesus as well as the boisterous and obtrusive conduct of women coming out of the Artemis cult.

1. **Adam** was created first, not Eve.

    Ephesian pagan dogma: woman was born first and was therefore superior

2. **Eve** was the one who was deceived.

    Ephesian pagan dogma: Artemis or Eve (gnostic) was the bringer of light (i.e., knowledge and wisdom) to Adam who was in darkness/ignorance

3. **God** will safely deliver women during childbirth through faith and trust in Him.

    Ephesian pagan dogma: Artemis protects and saves women through childbirth

Through his use of the word *gar* in verse 12, it becomes readily apparent that Paul referred to the Ephesian culture dogma that woman was the originator of man, as he refuted in the ensuing verses (vv. 13-15). His point was that these Ephesian women needed to learn the truth by submitting themselves to the teaching of those who had studied Scripture. He further explains that they had to relinquish their cultic beliefs and learn God's Word before they would be allowed to teach. Recall that very few people of this time period had the Bible in their possession, most of these few having only certain OT scrolls.

Recap

Paul wrote this letter to address false doctrine, particularly admonishing the Ephesians to stop quarreling over false ideas, godless myths, and old wives' tales. Paul emphatically implored Timothy to 'devote himself to the public reading of Scripture, preaching, and teaching,' and to 'watch his life and doctrine closely to save himself and his hearers' (1 Tim. 4:13,16). This was especially needed for counteracting the defilement of false doctrine and godless myths. Repeated reading of the Word would wash away the futile and indoctrinated thinking acquired from a lifetime of pagan religious practice.

Paul charged Timothy to keep his instructions without partiality or favoritism, stating that if anyone teaches anything that disagrees with sound doctrine, they are only promoting themselves and understand nothing. Their quarrels and interest in controversies only disrupt the church and cause envy, strife, and friction among people whose minds are robbed of truth. He finally instructs Timothy to oppose what is falsely called knowledge (gnosticism; 1 Tim. 5:15; 6:3-5,20).

Fighting heresy and error, Paul's stated focus in this letter, brought a specific injunction against the pagan influence on the teaching the Ephesian believers received. Unlike the Berean Jews who had grown up instructed in the Word, these believers were primarily Gentiles who did not have the Bible to verify teaching but only their own reason and culture clamoring to be heard above the witness of the Spirit.

Because Timothy listened to Paul's admonishment and faithfully discharged his duties, the climate in the Ephesian church changed. Under Timothy's perseverance and leadership, the Ephesians did quiet themselves to learn the Word. Jesus commended them for their labor and patient endurance—for testing false teaching and the false apostles who brought it and exposing them (Rev. 2:2).

Paul's admonishment could be accurately (though not precisely) summed up in the following way for our present day "low-context"

Western culture. While this may seem to be an example of 'reading a good deal of dialogue into the passage,' each statement can be supported by historical fact and/or documented scriptural thought found in this letter or elsewhere in the Word.

> *Timothy, the women coming out of the Ephesian culture have some wild ideas that are contrary to Scripture. Their cultural tradition provokes the women to assume they are the ones who must lead and teach to help the ignorant men understand wisdom. You can't allow them to promote their ideas or the entire church will be polluted with this mixture. Get them to calm down and receive instruction from the Word. I don't permit teaching a woman she is man's origin, as their former cult indoctrinated them. God's Word tells us Adam was created first. And Eve didn't waken Adam to enlighten him. In fact, she was the one deceived. It's okay for women to take the position as student, even if the only teacher available is a man. In Christ there is no distinction. Even a slave who is a mature believer can take a position to teach.*

> *I understand these women revered and relied on Artemis and have strong cultural and emotional ties to her as their protectorate. Tell the women that they don't need to turn to Artemis to be saved in childbirth. God will protect them—they need to place their faith and trust in Him. Persevere in teaching truth so they no longer believe godless myths and pagan doctrine.*

In summary, I would like to offer the following interpretation for your consideration. Encompassing its historical context, English grammatical equivalent and word order, and the "high-context" level of communication between Paul and Timothy, our controversial verse could more concisely be translated:

[I do] not allow teaching a woman [that she is] man's origin...

Using verses 13-15 as an appeal to the created order (i.e., man was created before woman and therefore the ruler) in Genesis contradicts OT and NT examples of female leadership as well as Paul's statements promoting women's roles in the NT church. Paul dismantles this type of thinking by saying that even as man was the source of woman, now man is born of woman, establishing there is no basis for superiority, for God is the source of everything (1 Cor. 11:3,11-12).

Creation was not pronounced 'very good' until the woman was standing beside the man. No one makes an appeal that mammals, created before man on the same day, are therefore first in order/authority. Nor has anyone come forward to argue that strength and a larger brain are the basis for authority and preeminence, for then we would have a sperm whale in charge. To the contrary, God gave man and woman—the last of His creation—His image as well as authority over the animals and all the earth.

> *Nevertheless, in the Lord woman is not independent of man, nor is man independent of woman. For as woman came from man, so also man is born of woman. But everything comes from God.* 1 Cor. 11:11-12, NIV

Closing Thoughts

The Lord often upsets our cultural paradigms to get our attention. The Ephesians were struggling to let go of the teachings they had heard all their lives in order to replace them with God's truth.

This can also be seen in OT culture. The firstborn son traditionally had preeminence. God's approval of Abel and not Cain caused conflict to erupt (Gen. 4:2-10). God's selection of Jacob over Esau was more than his father could accept (Gen. 27; see 25:23). God chose the Levites instead of the firstborn to serve Him (see Ex. 13:1-16; 32:26-29; Num. 3:12). Selecting David instead of Eliab surprised Samuel (1 Sam. 16:6-13). The Lord told Samuel (v. 17), "Do not consider his appearance or his height, for I have rejected him. The Lord does not look at the things people look at. People look at the outward appearance, but the Lord looks at the heart." This supports the following well-known passages:

> *"For my thoughts are not your thoughts, neither are your ways my ways,"* declares the Lord. Isa. 55:8, NIV

> *Who has known the mind of the Lord so as to instruct him?* 1 Cor. 2:16, NIV

As for the interpretation proposed in this chapter through substantial reliance on the grammatical-historical context, Paul's words to Timothy no longer feel like gears suddenly forced to grind in a different direction. In addition, we can make sense of the previously baffling reference to salvation through childbirth. The passage interpreted this way fits with the whole of Scripture and does not leave us with the, "Wait, what?" feeling that comes when something makes no sense.

Our eleven-year-old son was reading through his Bible, and when he got to this passage, he said, "I don't get this. What is he saying?" Someone with little cultural or gender bias easily saw the dichotomy this verse at face value posed with the rest of Scripture. But to those who are not negatively impacted by this verse, it becomes a proof text to which all other passages must comply, forcing those that demonstrate women in leadership, prophetic, speaking, and teaching positions to be reinterpreted and tooled to fit as 'exceptions to the rule.'

The troublesome nature of this passage has caused Bible students difficulty for generations. Our English translations, in my opinion, have prevented us from grasping Paul's intended meaning. I believe this may be a case of distanciation blindness, as Dr. Nebeker pointed out. The intellectual disturbance and 'cognitive dissonance' this presents in the minds of those who adamantly argued for silence of women and restrictions for teaching and authority needs to be addressed.

The church must prayerfully weigh the evidence and seek the witness of the Holy Spirit. Will we reject, avoid, or explain away the information offered here? Will we persuade ourselves that this does not change anything? Will we try to preserve our traditions, turning a blind eye so that we can keep the paradigm and order we have established?

Jesus, who is the Word, reminds us that He came to the world to help us understand God's truth, the only truth that will set us free. Amen.

> *Then Jesus told him, "I entered this world to render judgment— to give sight to the blind and to show those who think they see that they are blind." John 9:39, NLT*

Chapter 11

Shifting Paradigms

> *I have much more to say to you, more than you can now bear. But when he, the Spirit of truth, comes, he will guide you into all the truth... and he will tell you what is yet to come.* John 16:12-13, NIV

The Lord promised to be found by those who diligently seek Him. The wisdom harbored in God's Word is available to those who search for it as for hidden treasure. Filtering out the preunderstandings each translator or interpreter brings to the Bible has proved to be a difficult task and resulted in a diversity of thought and many denominations.

Some of what influences this diversity occurs through socialization. Dr. Nebeker stated, "[W]hen diversity of scriptural interpretations occur among Evangelicals, one way to account for this is by exploring various elements that can influence the accumulated knowledge that an interpreter brings to the Scripture." Secondary socialization, he argues, introduces biases that become so normative in a particular region that awareness of their existence can scarcely be consciously discerned. Dismantling their influence takes on a painful, surgical feel, leaving an unnatural sense in the mind and emotions about the new information. Like an old familiar building that has been demolished and then reconstructed in a different way, it takes some time for the new to become the normative and expected.

> As one enters into society, through education and wider social contacts, one's primary socialization is reinforced through "secondary socialization." In this process, **the values and ideologies of a particular system and social structure** (including class consciousness, orientation and values, racial attitudes, justification of stratification and economic distribution, etc.) **are inculcated so that the new member of society can internalize them and confirm them**. While such socialization may

reflect specific social location and forms of regional color, **its major goal is the integration of the individual into a social construction of reality so that the person believes it is the way things are**. In this way, "what is" becomes accepted as "what ought to be," and **world with all its inequities and biases, becomes canonized as "*the* world."**[71]

Contrary to past belief, young girls are just as vibrant and passionate about learning and exploring their environments as boys are. When girls first discover they aren't as valued as boys worldwide, or that historically girls have been denied education, privileges, and leadership opportunities, girls experience bewilderment and shock. They are insulted. Some get angry and others feel rejected, worthless, and second rate. Others try to ignore the traditional taboos and forge ahead. The individual responses can be attributed to a web of environmental factors, temperament, and personal support and relationships.

Whatever the case may be, girls demonstrate that though they may be physically smaller, their spirits and souls are just as large. Before they are exposed to the cultural paradigms that predetermine their status, girls are full of life and promise, eager to take on challenges and make their contributions expressed through the temperament and abilities residing within them. Accepting the place imposed on them by culture and society is *learned*, not innate.

These young girls aren't alone. When a woman becomes a believer and feels the stirring of the Holy Spirit, stepping out in faith to use the budding gifts the Lord has given her, she may find herself censored if that gifting doesn't comply with traditional roles and restrictions in certain churches. When first encountered, teaching that restrains a woman's participation is puzzling at best. There is no sense of the Holy Spirit 'moving as He wills' (John 3:8), but a barricade that incites a fear and caution to prevent intrusion or violation of the prescribed limit.

Relegating women to a different class without freedom to express their faith in the ways ordained for them may seem like a natural edict to some men, but it is at best perplexing to women when they first face the gender-based double standard. Within the spirit of every woman is the drive to accomplish something worthwhile with the freedom to use her abilities and gifting to the fullest extent. The fence erected in some churches that holds women back from full participation not only causes division, it demeans and cheapens the image of God placed in every women and insults the Spirit of grace.

Instead of freedom, women in churches that exercise restrictions on female participation become fearful they may tread on the bounds of propriety. Paul told the Romans that we are no longer slaves living in fear, but we have received freedom in the Spirit (Rom. 8:15). There can be no *koinonia* and freedom in the Spirit when half of our members are in strait jackets or walk out their faith with doubt and trepidation.

To label this restriction as part of 'God-ordained order' requires ignoring numerous other apostolic directives in Scripture as pertaining to female believers, as previously discussed. When interpreting Galatians 3:28 ('there is no Jew or Gentile, male or female, slave or free, for we are one in Christ'), do we view the verse as only pertaining to our equality as we stand before God for salvation and righteousness in Christ? Do we see equal opportunity for serving God in the body only for *male* Jews and Gentiles? For *male* free and slave? We must examine our beliefs to see if they are in compliance with the sum of God's Word.

Worldly Classifications Have No Place in the Church

I learned from this study that Paul is a brilliant scholar and we are slow to hear and understand, myself included. Many woman who have previously read the passages discussed in this book have felt cast aside; that even though the curse is lifted, she is still 'less than' and her place fixed because of the Fall; that she is and always will be relegated to the back of the bus.

Complementarians fix in their minds that this is not oppressive or demeaning, just God-ordained order. They do not discern the paternalistic condescension and subtle pride in some cases that accompany their reasoning. Neither do they discern the Lord's body, a condition that results in confusion and disorder. The body becomes weak and anemic. Christ is the head and all believers are His bride, whether Jew, Gentile, male, female, barbarian, Scythian, slave, or free. Our identity has simply become, 'in Christ.' He is the *only* head.

This same teaching of keeping people in worldly classifications convinced part of the church in the mid-nineteenth century that God had ordained slavery, using Scripture skillfully to defend their position. Only extremists hold this view today.

> *Keep reminding God's people of these things.* **Warn them before God against quarreling about words**; *it is of no value, and only* <u>ruins</u> *those who listen.* 2 Tim. 2:14, NIV

How many women's callings are being thwarted—*ruined*—by believing they are not to teach or even speak in church? The rules governing this type of thinking become more absurd the more one considers the impact this would truly have. As one practical issue after another surfaces, the more ridiculous the hairsplitting solutions become. For example: 'mothers can teach boys until the age of 13, the time they officially become men'; 'women cannot speak in the sanctuary, but they are allowed to do so in the side Bible class rooms or fellowship hall,' etc. Church becomes defined as the main sanctuary instead of how the Bible defines it as the meeting of any number of believers gathered anywhere. Single mothers can no longer teach their growing boys, contrary to King Lemuel's mother who taught him (Prov. 31:1).

We nullify the Word of God by our tradition and interpretation of Scripture. These are precisely the types of solutions offered by the Pharisees with regard to the Sabbath, dictating how far was 'too far' to walk, and how much was 'too much' to carry before the boundaries of the law had been encroached. Someone pointed out that leading worship includes elements of teaching doctrine in the lyrics, so women were banned from participating on worship teams in some circles. The solutions we offer to keep women in their place determine how much is 'too much' discussion or singing before it must be called teaching; how old is 'too old' for boys to be instructed by a woman; etc.

When we argue that the interpretations discussed in this book show flagrant current cultural bias and ignore the 'clear meaning' of the passage, claiming that we believe in taking the Bible literally (at face value) as opposed to those who seek to interpret Scripture in its grammatical-historical context, we do so at the expense of many more clear-cut teachings and examples in the Word in direct juxtaposition to the passages in question. This is blindness.

Further, some claim that taking these passages literally (based on an English translation) demonstrates their dedication to living the Word as it is written rather than seeking to 'water it down' by struggling to harmonize any given verse or topic in the Bible with the whole of Scripture. This is academic naïveté at best. While we agree that Scripture is inspired and without error in the original languages and documents, these presume that the English translators were infallible as well, something the translators themselves deny.[72]

Searching for scriptural harmony requires we exert the effort to discover what the biblical author intended to say to the people of his time. The differences the passages we've examined pose with the whole of Scripture are explained away by some, requiring that we dismiss solid examples or read extrapolated thought into other texts to accomplish this (e.g., 'as for Deborah, no man was available, so God had to choose a woman to do a man's job'). This is an abuse of Scripture and hints at a hidden agenda or a biased preunderstanding firmly rooted in the mind and heart that prevents us from seeing the truth.

Only by praying for guidance and instruction from the Holy Spirit in concert with diligence in studying the grammatical-historical perspective can we rectify what look like doctrinal divergences from the plain examples in the Word. Dr. Nebeker explains the complexity of hearing the voice of the Spirit above the clamor of our own ideas and paradigms:

> I am not suggesting that we are incapable of accurate interpretations of Scripture. Rather, the complexity of **the matter hinges on the role the Holy Spirit plays in helping us transcend that notoriously depraved network of compulsive attitudes and beliefs** in our hearts. In the final analysis, and so far as it is possible, cognitive interests and skewed motivations must be brought to light. Johnson suggests some necessary steps toward this end, *"A psychotherapeutic relationship, the prayer closet, the community of believers, the inner activity of the Holy Spirit and the Bible itself provide the necessary correctives for personal bias."*

By "psychotherapeutic relationship," Johnson is not referring to the interpreter's need for clinical counseling. Instead, in his words, *"The quest for personal insight needs an environment where fear is minimized and acceptance and freedom are predominant."* Do—or can—our Evangelical institutions and society meetings provide such an environment?[73]

Shifting Paradigms

As stated before, the Lord will often offend our minds and what we think 'should be' to expose the hypocrisy or misunderstandings we hold in our heart. Joseph was in a quandary when he found his betrothed to be with child by the Spirit of God (Matt. 1:19-20). The Pharisees couldn't believe the true Messiah didn't agree with their extrabiblical traditions and laws (Matt. 15:1-14). They were so angry they even plotted to murder this dissenter named Jesus. The Jews as a whole had difficulty accepting a Messiah who didn't immediately rescue them from their political oppressors according to their interpretation of prophecy (John 6:15; 12:13; 19:14-15; Matt. 27:22; Mark 15). The believing Jews in Jerusalem were shocked to find that God had given His Spirit not only to Jews but to Gentiles as well (Acts 10:45).

We need to shift our paradigms each time verifiable new information confronts us that contradicts the bases for our long held traditions. By way of comparison, consider the medical field, which requires constant updating due to the volume of ongoing research conducted. The findings presented by solid research tweak or may even contradict what we previously believed, affecting the way we view disease and therefore prescribe treatment protocols.

For example, in the 1960's we were told that neurons (grey matter) could not regenerate themselves, nor could our brains make more connections (white matter). Researchers convinced us that whatever brain matter we had developed by adulthood was what we had to work with for the rest of our lives. However, medical research over the past fifty years has proved this wrong. The long held dogma took a long time to die, but study after study gave conclusive evidence that the old model was incorrect.[74]

A Case Study: Apostle Paul

Before his Damascus Road encounter, Paul was *convinced* that people who followed Jesus were deceived and polluting Judaism (Acts 9:1; 26:9-11). He described himself as obsessed:

> *I too was **convinced** that I ought to do all that was possible to oppose the name of Jesus of Nazareth. And that is just what I did… I tried to force them to blaspheme. **I was so obsessed with persecuting them that I even hunted them down** in foreign cities.* Acts 26:9-10a,11b, NIV

The deeply held but contrabiblical conviction that women have no place in leadership or teaching is an example of the type of wayward obsession to which Paul confessed. I have read an account of men at a church leadership convention who turned their backs to one of the convention speakers because she was a woman. This happened to Anne Graham Lotz, daughter of Billy Graham. "When I stood in the lectern at the convention center, many of the 800 church leaders present turned their chairs around and put their backs to me. When I concluded my message, I was shaking. I was hurt and surprised that godly men would find what I was doing so offensive that they would stage such a demonstration, especially when I was an invited guest. And I was confused."[75]

I have also read about home Bible fellowship groups that insist their wives attend with their husbands, but the women are not allowed to speak during the meeting, not even to pray, until the meeting moves to the fellowship meal time—in the same room. I've read articles and books that essentially state the same, and I appreciate these believers' zeal to live according to the Word. But if even someone as super-intelligent as Paul could change his mind on matters he had formerly been convinced he was right according to his view of Scripture, perhaps these will also consider that holding these strict rules regarding women's roles in the church needs to be reexamined through the lens of the cross and the entire weight of Scripture.

We know Paul was highly educated, well-versed in the Scriptures, and zealous for God. Even so, by Paul's own admission he persecuted those who followed Jesus because he acted *in ignorance* and *unbelief*:

> Even though I was once a blasphemer and a persecutor and a violent man, I was shown mercy because **I acted in ignorance and unbelief**. 1 Tim. 1:13, NIV

God showed Paul mercy because he acted in *ignorance* and *unbelief*. Paul was not an ignorant man, as Pastor Wenstrom points out in the following excerpt. Governor Festus testifies to Paul's great learning as well (Acts 26:24).

> Paul's excellent education in Tarsus and in Jerusalem coupled with his tremendous study habits and genius IQ made him a great scholar. He was fluent in Aramaic, Hebrew, Greek and Latin. His genius can be deduced from his tremendous vocabulary, which he displays in his epistles along with a complete command of the Greek in all its dialects.
>
> Paul communicated in: Doric Greek, Ionic Greek, Aeolic Greek, Attic Greek, Hellenistic Greek, and the Koine Greek. His epistles also display Hebraicism's and Latinism's. He was a classical Greek scholar as witnessed to the fact that he quotes 2 minor Greek poets in Acts 17:28 and a Cretan poet in Titus 1:12.
>
> Quoting Plato or Homer was not significant but quoting minor poets reveals a comprehensive knowledge of Greek literature. His hometown of Tarsus was known for its great universities and scholars during the period of the Roman Empire. It was a center of Greek culture and philosophy ranking next only to Athens and Alexandria.
>
> Paul was also a Hebrew scholar. He studied alongside the greatest Rabbi in Israel in his day, Gamaliel, who taught in the famous Hillel school.[76]

Despite his impressive education and intelligence, Paul states he acted in: 1.) **agnoeo** (Grk. 50), which means to be unacquainted, to not recognize, to be unaware, to be mistaken, to err from lack of discernment,[77] sometimes with the idea of willful ignorance,[78] and in 2.) **apistia** (Grk. 570), faithlessness, unbelief, 'without divine persuasion.'[79] Can we prayerfully consider this may be the case for those whose doctrine imposes limitations on women in ministry?

'Offering a Service to God'

Jesus warned His disciples that those who opposed Him and His message would throw His followers out of the synagogues, which is precisely what Paul did before his eyes were opened to the truth (Acts 9:1-19). Currently, women who feel the call of God on their lives to pastor, teach, speak prophetically, or serve in leadership are given little chance to do so in some circles. Is this not also an example of the same *agnoeo* and *apistia* Paul demonstrated—ignorance and disbelief—that caused Jesus' followers to be thrown out of the Jewish synagogues?

> *They will put you out of the synagogue; in fact, the time is coming when anyone who kills you* **will think they are offering a service to God**. *John 16:2, NIV*

Many who require women to remain silent and deny them any type of leadership or teaching positions do so with the goal of being true to God's Word—'offering a service to God.' Others have not so much concern for the Word of God as they do maintaining control, especially favoring the subjugation of women in all things, because 'nearly two millennia of church tradition cannot possibly be wrong.' Regardless of the actual motives, however, the result is the same. Women are restrained in certain fellowships when the Holy Spirit empowers them with calling or purpose that exceeds the fortified enclosure erected to keep them within acceptable boundaries of culturally determined 'female' activity.

Discerning and Correcting Error

Most church leaders want to stay in step with the Holy Spirit, availing themselves to correction at any level. This is a mark of humility and the fear of the Lord. This is someone who 'trembles at God's Word.' Remaining teachable in the trustworthy hands of the Holy Spirit is the posture every believer strives after. The Lord wants to keep us from error so we do not defile ourselves or those we influence. Who can discern his own errors without the help of God's Spirit (Psalm. 19:12)?

> *Teach me, and I will be silent; and* **show me how I have erred**.
> Job 6:24, NASB

Paul taught that only the Spirit of God knows God's thoughts (for this discussion, see 1 Cor. 1:25-31; 2:10b-16; 3:18-23). Those without the Spirit of God are unable to understand spiritual truths because they appear foolish to them. People who rely solely on their own reasoning or reputation will miss God's truth. Believers, especially those in leadership, cannot become so hardened to correction that no change would be considered—even in the presence of the Holy Spirit's conviction.

We have been given the mind of Christ, and Christ is not divided. The sum of God's Word is in harmony as is the mind of Christ. John informed us that Jesus is the Word, and He is not conflicted. When we interpret the Word by consulting the entirety of what the Lord reveals on any given topic in the Word, we demonstrate wisdom. We are seeking the unity and harmony that the Spirit provides in the knowledge of God (Eph. 4:13).

Paul warned that those who think they are wise should not deceive themselves. This thinking caused the Corinthian church to align themselves with particular human leadership. In our day, many align themselves and put their confidence in male leadership alone. Might we consider that this is just another variation of being wise in our own eyes rather than allowing God to send whomever He wills? That such 'wisdom' only causes division? Did not Paul warn us to put no confidence in the flesh (Php. 3:3; 2 Cor. 11:18)?

Paul reminded the Corinthians that God uses those considered weak and foolish by the world's standards to shame those of status who consider themselves wise. God displays His strength through the lowly so that no one can boast before God. I would also like to add that I have met Ph.D.'s with greater humility than lay people. Some lay people have erected bulwarks in their minds regarding their personal views of Scripture that we can only shake our heads at and move on. They are not open to correction or even hearing another believer's point of view. There is no sense in casting pearls before pigheadedness, which results in being attacked by the one we sought to help.

While the reverse is also true regarding pride in the highly educated and humility in those who are not, I want to make sure to clearly state that humility can be seen in both great and small, as can arrogance and pride that is not open to correction. Many have found that the more they learn, the more they become acutely aware of the unfathomable amount of available knowledge that they don't yet truly understand. Taking our ignorance seriously places us on the path of humility and allows the Spirit of God to teach us.

> *For by the grace given me I say to every one of you:* **Do not think of yourself more highly than you ought,** *but rather think of yourself with sober judgment, in accordance with the faith God has distributed to each of you.* Rom. 12:3, NIV

Married Women with Authority

The idea that God could give a married woman more spiritual authority than her husband is established in the Word but creates a dichotomy in the mind of those who cling to man's tradition of keeping *all* women in subjugation to *all* men, not only in the husband-wife relationship. We make disparaging remarks about both the husband and the wife when such a dichotomy exists. We pity the man for his 'domineering' wife and label the woman 'Jezebel' for wearing the pants in the family, when, in most cases, nothing could be further from the truth.

How many women have given up their callings so as not to 'embarrass' their husbands or bring about his identity crisis, or to avoid being labeled a 'Jezebel'? How many capable, gifted women have we lost to the secular arena that welcomes her talent, creativity, and vision?

The tradition that seeks to keep all women in subjection to all men in all arenas displays ignorance of what God wants to teach us in the husband-wife relationship. The husband-wife relationship is a picture of Christ and the whole church. Just as the wife reverences her husband, every believer reverences Christ as their one husband. Men are in the same place of submission as women in the church as Jesus' bride. Men are the bride of Christ just as surely as women are the sons of God. Gender is not an issue in our relationship with God. It is only an issue in marriage as the spiritual parallel of Christ and the church.

Paul warned us about factions infiltrating the church, taking the body of Christ and dividing it into haves and have-nots, the privileged and those denied privilege, etc. There is no 'us' and 'them' in the body of Christ, whether based on gender, race, age, etc. This is a destructive teaching that has prevented the church from moving to a place of maturity. Paul warned us that these quarrels benefit no one and are useless (Titus 3:9).

> [T]here will be lying religious teachers among you. They'll smuggle in destructive divisions, **pitting you against each other.** 2 Pet. 2:1, MSG

Women's Vital Role in the Days to Come

When we look at the atrocities done to women in our time, we shudder and pray for deliverance from the underlying strongholds. The following quotes provide a glimpse of the gendercide we see today.

> The bias against girls is very evident among the relatively highly developed, middle-class dominated nations (Taiwan, South Korea, Singapore, Armenia, Azerbaijan, Georgia) and the immigrant Asian communities in the United States and Britain... As ultrasound imaging and other techniques increasingly allow early prediction of the child's sex, the more affluent families opt for an abortion, or if a girl is born, decrease her chance of survival by, for example, not providing sufficient medical care.[80]

> [T]he number of "missing" women has risen to more than 160 million... [M]ost of the missing females weren't victims of neglect. They were selected out of existence, by ultrasound technology and second-trimester abortion... The scale of that number evokes the genocidal horrors of the 20th century... [S]kewed sex ratios are associated with increased prostitution and sex trafficking.[81]

Beneath the surface of these atrocities, we might draw a parallel to two incidents in Scripture.

> **Exodus 1:15-22** Pharaoh instructed the Hebrew midwives to kill all male children born to the Hebrews. When they subverted his command, Pharaoh commanded the people to cast all male Hebrew babies into the Nile. *This happened precisely at the time God was bringing the Hebrews' deliverer, Moses, into the world.*

> **Matthew 2:16-18** Herod ordered all males two years old and under in Bethlehem and its vicinities to be killed *in an attempt to kill the recently born and prophesied Redeemer-King, Jesus.*

Our adversary is targeting women throughout the world for extinction, just as he did the males in Egypt and Bethlehem. Targeting women today parallels the strategy used to target the promised deliverers, Moses and Jesus, before they rose to fulfill their purpose in their appointed times. Women are not only eliminated through murder, sex-trafficking and the like, but also through negating her worth and dignity as an agent for meaningful and relevant influence. Through abusive patriarchalism, selective abortion, and sex trafficking in the East, and cultural traditions and denigrating church practices that keep her bound in the West, women are silenced.

Knowing this, I can't help but think women have a vital role to play in God's plan for the season upon us. The Lord said He would use the weak to confound the wise (1 Cor. 1:27). I believe there are many women God desires to raise up in this hour for the task of equipping the saints for the days ahead. This does not mean the role of men is devalued or eclipsed by the rise of women. Rather, it points out that men and women believers will be equally yoked partners with Jesus for equipping the saints and laboring in the harvest.

Love does no evil (Grk. 2556 *kakos*) to his neighbor (Rom. 13:10). *Kakos* evil includes unintentional harm. When churches keep women from fulfilling their callings, they will share responsibility for their negligence before God. Do we really think this verse applies only to how we treat men? I find it difficult to believe that we restrict women's activity and callings on the basis of a few proof texts taken at face value in the English translations that are discordant with the whole of Scripture, and then excuse male leadership for moral crimes committed against the never-changing laws ingrained in the conscience of every person (Rom. 2:13-15). This is leprosy on our church walls. The Lord is trying to get our attention.

Wisdom from the Past

Some of the first century Jews demonstrated the capacity to quickly change their ingrained paradigms when they witnessed God's activity.

When they *saw* that the Holy Spirit had also been given to the Gentiles, these believing Jews were quick to include them in their fellowships (prior to this, they had only been preaching the word to the Jews; see Acts 11:19). They set aside their former cultural distinctives and pride in order to stay in step with what the Holy Spirit was doing in their midst. God is infinitely creative and has not revealed everything to us. Remaining sober and watchful will prevent us from missing what He desires to teach us today or in the seasons ahead of us.

However, this was not so for many of the Jews Paul encountered. They became jealous and stirred up trouble when they heard the new covenant message and witnessed the inclusion of Gentiles (e.g., Acts 5:17; 13:45; 17:5). This upset their long-standing tradition that Jews alone were heirs of the covenants. The new information would disintegrate the social and religious platform that elevated them above other people groups. Jewish leaders were furious that the apostles were proclaiming Jesus as the Messiah and including Gentiles, and they wanted them silenced. They viewed this new trend as pollution to the Judaism they loved and the traditions to which they were accustomed.

Before his Damascus Road experience, Paul also wanted to rid Judaism of this new anomaly. It was dangerous to the status quo. He breathed out murderous threats to Jesus' followers and obtained permission from the Jewish leaders to pursue these wayward believers to punish them (Acts 9:1-2). Recall that the religious leaders were so angry with Jesus' teaching and the number of people who gladly followed Him that they plotted His murder.

Is this not the same fury that exists in some believers today that won't hear of a woman gifted with authority to teach or provide leadership in the church? If our reaction to this study is anger, outrage, intense obsession to discredit by any means, or any other fruit of the flesh, are we not convicted as unspiritual already? Did not Jesus remind us that the wisdom we exercise will be verified by the fruit it bears (Luke 7:35)? He said this in the context of being judged for not living up to what the Pharisees wanted. Claiming our anger is righteous indignation must be verified by the Spirit of God and the Word (see James 1:20).

> *The acts of the flesh are obvious... hatred, discord, jealousy, fits of rage, selfish ambition, dissensions, factions and envy... and the like.* Gal. 5:19-21a, NIV

Gamaliel, one of the Jewish leaders in the Sanhedrin of Paul's day, gave wisdom in the apostles' situation we should heed today. He cautioned the Sanhedrin to consider carefully what they intended to do. He advised them to leave the apostles alone, for if their activity was of human origin, it would fail, 'but if it is from God, you will not be able to stop them; you will only find yourselves fighting against God' (Acts 5:33-42). The parallel with what we are doing to women in the church is obvious. Do we want to find ourselves in opposition to God?

Put off the Old Ways of Thinking

The authors of the NT under the inspiration of the Holy Spirit exhort us to put off our old ways corrupted by deceptive thinking so we can be made new in the attitude of our minds (Eph. 4:22-24). We are warned to watch out for those who cause divisions and *put obstacles in our way that are contrary to the truth*, and to keep away from them.

> *I am telling you this **so no one will deceive you with well-crafted arguments**... And now I make one more appeal, my dear brothers and sisters. **Watch out for people who cause divisions and upset people's faith by teaching things contrary** to what you have been taught. **Stay away from them**. Such people are not serving Christ our Lord; they are **serving their own personal interests**. By smooth talk and glowing words **they deceive innocent people**.* Col. 2:4; Rom. 16:17-18, NLT

Rather than delivering the truth that will set people free, these well-crafted arguments keep people in bondage. Nineteenth century Bible commentator Albert Barnes stated they have "an appearance of great sincerity, and regard for the truth... People who cause divisions commonly make great pretensions to peculiar love of truth and orthodoxy; and put on the appearance of great sincerity, sanctity, and humility":

> "Flattery" is one of the most powerful means of forming parties in the church; and "a little special attention," or promise of

an office, or commendation for talents or acquirements, will secure "many" to the purposes of party whom no regard for truth or orthodoxy could influence a moment.[82]

Barnes described the innocent people mentioned in the previous passage as 'unsuspecting and without guile.' "The apostle means to designate those who are simple-hearted, without any disposition to deceive others themselves, and of course without any suspicions of the "designs" of others. He has thus drawn the art of making parties with the hand of a master. First, there are smooth, plausible pretences, as of great love for truth. Then, an artful mingling of attentions and flatteries; and all this practiced on the minds of the unsuspecting, drawing their "hearts" and "affections" toward themselves."[83]

Paul warns us not to be deceived:

> **See to it that no one takes you captive** through hollow and deceptive philosophy, **which depends on human tradition** and the elemental spiritual forces of this world rather than on Christ. Col. 2:8, NIV

Leaders in the church recognize that the Holy Spirit has been given to women, but many disallow that it could be in any teaching or leadership capacity. They seek to put limits on how they will recognize the ways in which God distributes gifts and callings. They ignore the precedents found in Scripture and have convinced many, including women, to accept the traditional hierarchy.

If this hierarchy holds our mind and emotions captive, consider the beginning of the new covenant. Were men the first people entrusted with telling the good news of the resurrection? Was the Great Commission given only to men? Did Joel prophesy or Peter preach that only men would prophesy, an action that includes teaching?

When we aren't sure of the right answer on a multiple-choice test, we have a greater chance of selecting the right answer if we can eliminate half the answers. In our churches, many have made easier the decision for choosing leaders by eliminating eligibility for some of the candidates based on gender alone. This is not Biblical. The Holy Spirit wants to show us God's choice, as He did when the early church fasted, worshipped, and prayed before choosing their leaders and missionaries (Acts 13:1-3).

Many people in the secular arena have experienced a loss of promotion not because they were less qualified, but because someone else received preferential treatment for unethical or at least questionable reasons. Put yourself in women's shoes for a moment. Have they been passed over in the church because of a lack of gifting, knowledge of the Word, or God-given authority? Are they less spiritual? Or have they been overlooked because of the doctrines of men? We have wasted the church's time and some believer's lives by convincing women they cannot minister by putting God and women in a box—a Procrustean bed that kills those forced to lie on it (see Addendum).

Paul reminds believers that love fulfills the law (Gal. 5:14). James, however, juxtaposes loving your neighbor as yourself with the practice of showing partiality, which he labels 'sin.' There can be no partiality or preferential treatment if we truly love others the way we love ourselves (James 2:8-9). The Bible speaks of God's nature as not showing partiality or favoritism (Deut. 10:17; 2 Chr. 19:7; Rom. 2:11; Gal. 2:6; Eph. 6:9; Col. 3:25; 1 Pet. 1:17). Though Peter wrote the following regarding Gentiles, I believe it applies for our discussion as well. God's nature never changes (Psalm 55:19; Mal. 3:6). While God does make selections of one person over another to fulfill a specific role or purpose (e.g., leadership), those selections are not 'predictable' by human standards or based on distinctions that appeal to our finite minds.

> *I most certainly understand now that God is not one to show partiality.* Acts 10:34, NASB

Women Leaders in the Closet

Many women know they are called to higher positions of authority but struggle to do so in order to avoid making waves or being rejected for gender issues. Others forfeit or hide their callings so they can be in compliance to the traditional interpretations of Scripture regarding their acceptable role in the church. Dr. Nebeker addresses the fear resident in believers who challenge the status quo:

Along with the fears resident within Evangelical subcultures, to one degree or another, fear may reside within the Evangelical interpreter himself. Fear of shoddy work, **fear of compromising cherished doctrines**, fear of a **lack of peer approval**, fear of **supervisory reprisals**, fear of producing less than fresh work, or "**scholarly politics**" are but several ways that **fear can sway our conceptual preunderstandings.**

Along these lines, Johnson makes a pertinent observation: *"Too often with Evangelicalism there is an emotional and political commitment to incomplete theological and hermeneutical models.* **Creative prophets are silenced, ostracized, or paternalistically tolerated.** *Fear of such responses* **cause many a prophet to surrender critical judgment for the sake of acceptance in the group."**... [W]hen scholars challenge cherished interpretive traditions because these traditions have veered away from Scripture, fear may creep in and persuade them not to voice their conclusions too loudly.[84]

When the Lord calls a woman to come up higher, she may dismiss the idea as coming from her own mind. The indoctrination that no woman can teach or have authority in the church clouds her ability to hear otherwise. The Lord had this to say about those who reject their callings, whether consciously or subconsciously:

> *The servant <u>who knows</u> the master's will and does not get ready or does not do what the master wants **will be beaten with many blows**. But the one **who does not know** and does things deserving punishment **will be beaten with few blows**. From everyone who has been **given much, much will be demanded**; and from the one who has been **entrusted with much, much more will be asked**.* Luke 12:47-48, NIV

In either case, the Lord is not pleased. We also find admonishments for the cowardly, whom the Lord stated would end up in the lake of fire (Rev. 21:8). Neither can the Lord stomach the lukewarm (Rev. 3:16). Believers must never be lacking in zeal (Rom. 12:11).

I want to add a note as a reminder that our own definition of what zeal looks like may not be the way in which it is expressed in another believer. One believer may express zeal in his or her calling by evangelizing everyone he or she encounters. Another may pursue the knowledge of God with every waking moment, surrounded by stacks of books, notepads, and pencils. Yet another may shut himself or herself in a closet for long periods each day to intercede for leadership, the church, and the nations. Each is demonstrating zeal in their respective calling.

It is not a trivial matter in the sight of God to bury our calling for whatever reason (see Matt. 25:24ff). Is it right to fear those who can only harm us in this age? Should not the fear of the Lord far surpass any fear we may have of men, even if those men are church officials (Matt. 10:28)?

The Lord has invested a great deal in His daughters, and He expects that His investment will bring a return. For women gifted in whatever area the Lord has chosen, the Lord expects them to walk in grace, boldness, and courage, using that gifting for God's glory and the equipping of the saints. Pastor Burleson gave this admonishment:

> God clearly reveals to us that Christian men and women should serve as they are gifted by the Spirit. Any imposed restrictions on women speaking, teaching, or leading in the assembly of Christ is contrary to inspired revelation of God's word. So if the New Testament teaches that men and women are gifted by the Spirit to do the work of the kingdom, why do some put a system of restrictions on women, a system totally contrary to the overall tenor and explicit teachings of holy Scripture? F. F. Bruce once wrote, "**Subjugation of a woman is a system of man's fallen nature. If the work of Christ involves... breaking the fall, then the implication of his work for the liberation of women is plain.**" Jesus Christ came to liberate subjugated women. The cultism in evangelicalism regarding women's behaviors will only be broken when people lay aside... false obedience to I Timothy 2:9-14 and realize the meaning of Paul's words to Timothy.[85]

Alleged Consequences

Evangelicals seem afraid that the humility of believing women will suffer if they assume a leadership or teaching role in the church, or that they will simultaneously morph into domineering man-hating feminists in the secular sense of the word. Worse yet, many fear this will open the door for all kinds of error. I find this somewhat amusing, considering the rampant sin, error, and pride in the church today under male leadership. Gary Nebeker addresses this unwarranted fear:

> One all too familiar way that fear plays itself out, both at the lay and academic levels, is **to resort to the argument of the slippery slope**. This informal logical fallacy contends that a certain outcome must eventually follow from a preceding event without any argument for the inevitability of an alleged consequential event. Since, event A has occurred (or will or might occur), therefore event B will inevitably happen... **The slippery slope argument is fallacious because there is no reason to believe that one event must inevitably follow from another** without a sufficiently convincing explanation for why such a claim must of necessity happen... In very general terms, **the slippery slope argument** of some Evangelicals **is sometimes based in a suspicion and an emotional conviction that if certain beliefs are taught and embraced, they will inevitably lead to the erosion of Evangelical doctrinal conservatism.**[86]

This unwarranted fear is seen in the opening paragraphs in the book of Esther. The king and his advisor feared the far-reaching effects of the queen's misbehavior, as discussed in chapter one—an exaggerated outcome scenario. The same fear resides in the church today.

I have heard arguments from those who believe that accepting women in leadership will inevitably lead to accepting homosexuals in ministry as well—a slippery slope argument. The basic flaw in this argument is the failure to discern the difference between moral issues and issues of religious practice. Homosexuality is a moral issue condemned in both old and new covenants (Lev. 18:22; 20:13; 1 Cor. 6:9-10; 1 Tim. 1:10; implied Rev. 21:8; 22:15). It is listed alongside lying, cheating, murder, stealing, adultery, greediness, drunkenness, abusiveness, idolatry, and all manner of sin.

The issue of women in ministry, on the other hand, is not a moral matter. It is clearly a religious practice issue. Nowhere in Scripture do we see women in ministry associated with sin or disinheritance. On the other hand, we do see that *'every evil practice'* follows anger, rage, envy, and selfish ambition (Psalm 37:8; James 3:16). These are the things we are told to watch out for—a true slippery slope based on the truth in God's Word and not on the inventions and fears of men.

No Christian woman I know wants to bellow, 'I am woman, hear me roar.' They just want the freedom and opportunity to use the gifts and abilities the Lord has given them to serve others in their sphere of influence, as the men now widely practice. The Christian women I know want to be obedient to the Word and the Spirit's call on their lives—no grandiose plan to take over what men currently control in some vengeful plot to swing the pendulum the other way. They merely want to be faithful in their obedience to the Lord in this age so they can be found faithful at Jesus' return.

These women are genuinely concerned for the other members of the body of Christ. They see the needy and have compassion for them as those who have the mind and Spirit of Christ should. They know these believers need care, mentoring, and discipling to keep them from wandering like lost sheep (cf. Matt. 9:36). They see that the church has many teachers but few who demonstrate the care and concern of a parent (1 Cor. 4:15). Bible commentator Adam Clarke said of this passage, "Many offer to instruct you who have no parental feeling for you."[87]

The teachers to which Paul refers are not spiritual parents, but rather teachers who have a burden to share with others the knowledge they have acquired. Some of these merely want to showcase their knowledge, which we are warned against doing (1 Cor. 8:1). We often call these types of individuals 'pastors,' but if the label is an indication of the calling and work, they are not pastoring but teaching.

The State of the 'Union'

The body is not healthy partly because we are ignoring the legitimate function of many members. The corruption in the body of Christ is profound: high divorce rates, gluttony, immorality among the male leadership on every level from pornography, adultery, and homosexuality to child molestation and rape; greed leading to embezzlement and fund misappropriation; deceptive propaganda to exaggerate productivity; denying membership to those who disagree with a specific view of peripheral doctrine or practice; denying counsel to those who don't practice 'fundamentals' as we have determined them (e.g., tithing); and so on.

When we cannot scripturally refute someone else's views, we turn to other tactics, such as seeking to discredit the person or resorting to name calling, labeling those of differing views as 'Absaloms' or 'Jezebels,' using anything but gentle, courteous language to vent our displeasure. This practice reminds me of a dialogue between Captain Kirk and Spock in *Star Trek Into Darkness*, where Spock says, "Reverting to name calling suggests that you are defensive, and therefore, find my opinion valid."

While many church leaders have genuine care and concern for their congregants and the lost, the institutionalized church at large is not widely known for its love but rather for its hypocrisy, prideful debates, greed, and immoral behavior that mirrors society at large. The mold has spread on our walls to the point where we may have to condemn the structure. Just as a slight deviation from the required trajectory would cause a spacecraft to completely miss a planet, the church is currently far from the mark set for it: a pure and spotless bride.

> *Do you still not see or understand? Are your hearts hardened? Do you have eyes but fail to see, and ears but fail to hear?* Mark 8:17b-18a, NIV

While recognizing where we are now, at the same time we keep in view what we will become. We do not base our hope on what is seen but on God's eternal truth. Jesus' High Priestly prayer will be answered, and He will return for a faithful and pure bride walking in unity with Him and each other. We cannot let our hearts and minds grow cold and calloused, causing us to miss what the Spirit is saying to the church in this hour (cf. 2 Tim. 4:3). This requires remaining teachable and turning from error and sin. For those who seek to see and hear with spiritual eyes and ears, God will provide understanding and the church will be healed of its present state (cf. Matt. 13:15).

Every believer has a part in working toward this end by using spiritual discernment to know and understand God's Word, His purpose in this hour, and the messengers He sends to equip and build the body. The Lord promised to give wisdom to those who ask and keep on asking. He desires to make His will and Word known to each of His children.

Paul continually asked God to fill believers 'with the knowledge of God's will through all the wisdom and understanding that the Spirit gives.' Knowing God's will and walking it out with wisdom and understanding results in honoring God's name and bearing fruit for His kingdom. Part of bearing fruit entails growing in the proper understanding of God's Word (1 Col. 1:9b-10). Paul also prayed:

> *[T]hat the God of our Lord Jesus Christ, the Father of glory,* **may give to you the spirit of wisdom and revelation <u>in the knowledge of Him</u>, the eyes of your understanding being enlightened; that you may know what is the hope of His calling**, *what are the riches of the glory of His inheritance in the saints, and what is the exceeding greatness of His power toward us who believe,* **according to the working of <u>His</u> mighty power**. Eph. 1:17-19, NASB

Chapter 12

Chayil Spirit of Women

> *And now, my daughter, don't be afraid. I will do for you all you ask. All the people... know that you are a woman of noble (**chayil**) character.* Ruth 3:11, NIV

Daughters of the King, read this passage as if the Lord is speaking to you personally. Even if you feel the *chayil* description doesn't apply to you, remember that the Lord can call things that are not yet manifest as if they were already present (Rom. 4:17). Gideon is a good example of this. God called this cowering man hiding in a winepress a *valiant* warrior. Gideon described himself as the least in all of his insignificant family (Jdg. 6:11-16). Yet by the hand of God, Gideon led the army to deliver the Israelites from their oppressors, the Midianites.

Previously we discussed the meaning of the Hebrew word *chayil* (Heb. 2428). This word is far weightier than narrowly defining it as excellent or praiseworthy. It literally means an army or a force. It can be translated as might, wealth, virtue, ability, noble, valor, strength, worthy. This is the word God prophetically called Gideon—a *chayil* warrior or champion. This is also what God calls His daughters.

Often employed poetically, *chayil* describes men and women alike. God's *chayil* spirit is imprinted on all of His children. He is, after all, *El Shaddai*, the Almighty God, and *Adonai Sabaoth* (*YHWH Tzva'ot*), the Commander of the hosts. All men and women have noble longings bound to their spiritual makeup by virtue of being created in God's image. While our lives do not always reflect pursuing and fulfilling those longings in God-honoring ways, our hearts yearn to demonstrate noble and valiant action for a just and righteous cause.

In the book *The Seven Longings of the Human Heart,* authors Mike Bickle and Deborah Hiebert describe the longings God placed in the spirit of every person.[88] These longings include our desire:

1. to be enjoyed by God
2. for fascination
3. for beauty
4. for intimacy without shame
5. for greatness
6. to be wholehearted
7. to make a deep and lasting impact

As the authors point out, each longing progresses toward fulfillment as we grow in our personal walk with the Lord. As fallen beings, we often try to satisfy these longings quickly in worldly ways by carnal means. In relationship with God, however, we can resist the temptation to gratify these longings with the short-lived, cheap substitutes the world offers by patiently waiting as the Holy Spirit satisfies them with something far more precious and eternal through our deepening relationship with God.

Three of these longings often additionally involve what we are called to *do* for God's kingdom—the longings: 1.) for greatness, 2.) to be wholehearted, and 3.) to make a deep and lasting impact. Eternity is written on the heart of every person (Ecc. 3:11), and believers are destined to reign with Christ (Rev. 20:4). Because of these longings, each believer has the desire and drive to accomplish something of lasting value and purpose in order to be found faithful at Jesus' return and receive the reward for which they labored.

Eternal Impact of Hindering Women

For the majority of women in the church, the restrictions imposed on female believers as a whole do not directly impact the ministry entrusted to each as an individual. Just as the majority of male believers are not called to fill what the church considers typical leadership or teaching positions, neither are these women called to such positions. The scope of their callings does not put them in a position to threaten traditional boundaries. For these women, ascribing priority to understanding these issues may not be as pressing. They can function in their callings whether or not the church modifies its stance on women in ministry.

For those women in the minority, however, who are called to pastor, teach, or lead in a wider scope, the restrictions imposed hinder them from being wholehearted in their callings as well as obstruct their God-given desire to make a deep and lasting impact in the way the Lord leads them to serve the community of believers and the lost. Only a small percentage of men unlettered by academia experience this type of frustration and hindrance in those situations requiring an official certificate to give them entrance.

Do we really want to explain to Jesus at the *Bema* seat why we hindered these believers from serving in the capacity they were called to fulfill?

> *We **must all appear before the judgment** (bema) **seat of Christ**, so that each of us may receive what is due us **for the things done** while in the body, whether good or bad.* 2 Cor. 5:10, NIV

Salvation is freely given by grace; rewards are given as a result of faithfully doing God's will. Though the context of the next passage does not have to do with a believer's calling *per se,* I want to use the principles in this passage and Paul's thoughts to breathe biblical language into expressing God's heart on this issue. Just as the Jews had to accept God's selection of the Gentiles in the new covenant, we must also accept the women the Lord raises to positions of authority.

> *You, then, **why do you judge your brother or sister**? Or **why do you treat them with contempt**? For we will all stand before God's judgment seat... So then, **each of us will give an account of ourselves to God. Therefore let us stop passing judgment on one another.** Instead, make up your mind **not to put any stumbling block or obstacle in the way of a brother or sister**.* Rom. 14:10,12-13, NIV

Job gave us a good example to follow. When confronted by the wisdom of God and the error of his thinking, we are impacted by the definitions of true humility and repentance in Job's response. If there was ever a passage of Scripture to memorize, this one will serve us well when we meet Christ:

> *I know that you can do all things; no purpose of yours can be thwarted. **You asked, 'Who is this that obscures my plans without knowledge?'** Surely **I spoke of things I did not under-***

> ***stand**, things too wonderful for me to know. "You said, 'Listen now, and I will speak; I will question you, and you shall answer me.' **My ears had heard of you but now my eyes have seen you**. Therefore **I despise myself and repent in dust and ashes**." Job 42:1-6, NIV*

The way we walk out our understanding of God's Word can obscure God's plans if we have understood incorrectly. The ramifications can have eternal impact. Paul's advice to the Roman believers is pertinent for us today. We are generally instructed to accept one another. In some instances, however, we are to turn away from those who cause division and hindrances.

> ***Accept one another**, then, just as Christ accepted you, **in order to bring praise to God**. Rom. 15:7, NIV*

> *Now I urge you, brethren, keep your eye on **those who cause dissensions and hindrances contrary to the teaching** which you learned, and **turn away from them**. Rom. 16:17, NASB*

Hope and Justice

In the movie *The Two Towers* (*Lord of the Rings* trilogy), Aragorn asked Eowyn what she feared. Her response echoes throughout the church in the hearts of women who have been prevented from fulfilling their God-ordained roles in the church:

> "A cage. To stay behind bars until use and old age accept them and all chance of valor has gone beyond recall or desire."

Aragorn, recognizing the *chayil* spirit in Eowyn, responds by saying:

> "You are a daughter of kings, a shield maiden of Rohan. I do not think that will be your fate."

Eowyn went on to defeat the Witch-King of Angmar, the deadliest servant of Sauron. The Witch-King knew there was a prophecy that said no man could kill him. What the Witch-King did not realize was that the warrior that stood before him was not a man but a woman. She removed her helmet and declared, 'I am no man,' as she thrust her sword through his helmet, killing him and turning the tide of the battle in their favor.

Every woman believer is a daughter of the King. Yet many have relinquished their fervency for God in order to gain the church's acceptance. They have watched the zeal of the Spirit ebb and all but disappear in their lives. They have forgotten who they are. They become a shell of what they once dreamed they would be and do for the Lord. The sense of promise the future held was replaced by complacency, or even worse, a sense of despair and dejection. They have accepted teaching that they are ever under the curse of Eve, that the curse is only reversed for men, and that they will always be second rate.

But the Lord speaks words of encouragement to his daughters:

> **A bruised reed He will not break,** *and a* **smoldering (dimly burning) wick He will not quench,** *till* **He brings justice** *and a just cause to victory.* Matt. 12:20, AMP

For the sake of justice, the Lord will move on behalf of His *chayil* women who turn to Him to plead their cause.

> *And will not God bring about justice for his chosen ones, who cry out to him day and night? Will he keep putting them off? I tell you,* **he will see that they get justice, and quickly.** Luke 18:7-8a, NIV

Many women are struggling to make sense of the calling they discern on their lives in view of the church's current rejection or, in some cases, condescending tolerance of women in positions of authority. Hoping for clarity, these women are praying for the Lord to show them the way to freedom, not unlike the Hebrews who were bound in Egypt as slaves. The lyrics to the song, "When You Believe" (co-written by Stephen Schwartz and Babyface) from the movie *Prince of Egypt* give voice to the longings in the hearts of many women in the church.

The setting takes place when the Hebrews were finally released from Egypt. They initially stepped out with apprehension, unsure whether the news of deliverance was actually true (recall that Pharaoh reneged on previous promises to release them). They glanced around nervously, half expecting to be put back in their place of bondage. But with each step they took and with every breath of freedom, they gained confidence. They no longer scanned their surroundings like prey, nervously cowering and waiting to be snatched by predators. They stood up straight, looked forward, and fixed their eyes on the goal of their freedom—to worship the Lord and serve Him as they had been called to do (Ex. 3:12; 7:16; 8:1,20; 9:1,13; 10:3,7).

Making God the center of our lives and being obedient to the call He has placed on our lives is an important aspect of worship. To worship God in spirit and in truth (Jn. 4:23-24) requires obedience—being a living sacrifice for God. Women restricted access to their callings because of tradition and doctrinal strongholds that set themselves in opposition to God's plan deprives these women of offering God worship through full obedience.

> *Therefore, I urge you, brothers and sisters, in view of God's mercy, to offer your bodies as a living sacrifice, holy and pleasing to God—this is your true and proper worship* ['spiritual worship,' HCSB]. Rom. 12:1

A Lesson from "Wreck-It Ralph"

There is a character named Turbo in the movie *Wreck-It Ralph*. He was the star of his racing arcade game. Kids flocked around his game day after day until a new game arrived. The arcade owner situated the new game directly across from Turbo's. Turbo became jealous of the new game's popularity as he witnessed the waning interest the kids held for his own game. Because of this, he left his game to enter the new one and take it over. This ruined both games, and they were removed from the arcade.

Turbo, however, secretly escaped so he could stay in the arcade. He entered another game, *Sugar Rush,* and disguised himself by rewriting his computer code. He became the 'king' of *Sugar Rush* by removing the lines of computer code for the real hero of the game, Princess Vanellope. Because the old Vanellope code had been locked away, no one in the game remembered that Vanellope had been the original star of the game. She was now known as 'the glitch' because her new lines of code were incomplete. Her image often disappeared or faded when she was nervous or upset.

The other racers ostracized Vanellope as incapable and inferior. King Candy villainized her. Before the viewer is made aware of his true nature, King Candy appeared to be the benefactor of everyone in the game, protecting the other characters from the damage 'the glitch' could cause if she ever raced. He led everyone to believe that if Vanellope raced, the game would be shut down for not working properly, and Vanellope would be trapped inside because she was a 'glitch.' He was only looking out for her best interests, after all. His sanctions were presented as being for everyone's good, especially Vanellope's.

As the story progresses, however, we find out the truth of what King Candy feared. If Vanellope raced and crossed the finish line, the game would reset. Vanellope would once again be the star, all the other characters would have their memories back, and he would be discovered for what he was—a fraud.

As a parallel, I believe our adversary has prevented us from remembering who women really are in the sight of God—that they are created in God's image and have a race to run alongside men (jasper and ruby) in whatever capacity the Lord chooses. In Eden, Satan targeted Eve because God created her as the type and shadow of wisdom. Without a unified team working together in wisdom, Satan knew man's efforts to govern the earth would become corrupt ('might makes right') and fail.

Anytime we think we can reach a God-given goal on our own, whether as a capable individual or a homogenous group (i.e., based on race, skill, denomination, socioeconomic status, gender, age, intellect, etc.), we reject wisdom to walk in our own reasoning and pride. We must surround ourselves with godly men and women whom God has gifted with ability and wisdom for leadership to fulfill His purposes in our generation.

Like Princess Vanellope, who believed King Candy's lie that she was defective and shouldn't even race, many women today have believed the lie that brainwashes them into thinking that they are less capable and less valuable than men in the body of believers. They have believed the teaching that they will harm everyone if they enter the race alongside the men.

By interpreting the Word as it was meant to be understood, we 'reset' our minds to the truth and come to the realization that women are co-heirs of all the promises and endowed by their Creator with the grace and strength to run their race in whatever authority the Lord has ordained, including leadership and teaching. It's time to 'reset the game' so it can work properly, as it was meant to.

Penny Chenery: A Modern Day Chayil Woman

In the movie *Secretariat*, we find themes that inspire us and remind us of our need to run the race the Lord has marked out specifically for us, no matter the opposition. It is based on the true story of the famous race horse, Secretariat, owned and raised by Penny Chenery Tweedy. The movie opens with this passage of Scripture:

> **Do you give the horse its strength** or clothe its neck with a flowing mane? Do you make it leap like a locust, striking terror with its proud snorting? **It paws fiercely, rejoicing in its strength, and charges into the fray. It laughs at fear, afraid of nothing; it does not shy away from the sword.** The quiver rattles against its side, along with the flashing spear and lance. In frenzied excitement it eats up the ground; **it cannot stand still when the trumpet sounds**. Job 39:19-24, NIV

As the story unfolds, we learn that Penny's father, Chris Chenery, invested in quality mares just as our heavenly Father invests in His daughters. He told Penny when she was young, "Penny, you run **your** race." Mr. Chenery did not want his daughter's life to be determined by someone else's expectations. Would our Heavenly Father desire anything less for His daughters?

Penny lived in Colorado where she and her husband were raising their four children. The movie begins with the death of Mr. Chenery's wife (Penny's mom) and his own failing health. Penny's father suffered dementia. With his wife's death, Mr. Chenery needed someone to look after him and make decisions in running the farm. Penny decided to stay temporarily in Virginia in order to help her father, trusting that her family would work together in Colorado in her absence.

She had many decisions in front of her, including her decision to fire the farm's dishonest horse trainer. This trainer tried to take advantage of Mr. Chenery financially just prior to his wife's death. Penny's brother, Hollis, berated her for this action, reasoning that no one would buy the farm if they didn't have a horse trainer in place. Hollis would have kept the trainer despite the trainer's dishonesty and unethical dealings. Hollis also wanted to put his father in a nursing home. He was the picture of expediency and pragmatism. He was decisive, a character trait often attributed to men, but his decisions were shortsighted, self-serving, and lacking in faith.

Mr. Chenery had two mares at that time pregnant by a famous stallion with the understanding that one foal would be his and the other would be given to the sire's owner, Ogden Phipps, determined by a coin toss. By now Penny was taking care of all her father's interests out of love and respect for him, and she represented him at the coin toss. She lost the coin toss, but still got the foal she wanted. She would get the older mare's foal—the one the wealthy horse breeder didn't want.

Under her very capable leadership, resourcefulness, and willingness to stick her neck out, her story became one of the most inspiring ever for me personally. While her brother was more concerned about the money their father's farm was losing, particularly in tax liability, Penny forged ahead to work things out. Hollis wanted the remarkable horse sold to pay off the debt. His decision was motivated by fear—he was afraid of losing everything. Penny's motivation was the love and respect she held for her father as well as her vision to remedy the complex situation despite the circumstances surrounding her.

Her husband was even less supportive than Hollis. He wanted her at home in Colorado taking care of their family. He focused primarily on how inconvenient their lives had become without Penny taking care of everyone's needs as well as the possible financial liability they could incur from her family's farm. One evening, when she was particularly struggling with discouragement, Penny reached out to her oldest daughter instead of her husband for the support she longed for.

Despite the lack of support, Penny was determined to honor her father and use the skill she inherited from him to turn their situation around. She stated with conviction, 'Our father's legacy to me isn't money; it is the will to win.'

'Big Red,' as he was called by everyone on the farm, was an unusual horse. Before his death, Mr. Chenery told Penny to 'let the horse run *his* race.' By now the tension between Penny and her husband had escalated. Penny recalled how full of promise she felt after college, 'like she could really accomplish something,' only to give up her career for her family. Many women have experienced this in the church because of wrong ideology. Paul's words to the Galatians can give wisdom for us to consider today:

> **You were running the race nobly. Who has interfered** in (hindered and stopped you from) your heeding and following the Truth? **This [evil] persuasion is not from Him Who called you** [Who invited you to freedom in Christ]... But **he who is unsettling you, whoever he is, will have to bear the penalty.** Gal. 5:7-8,10b, AMP

The course of events Penny had recently experienced inspired her to utilize all of her ability, training, and creative intelligence to persevere through challenges and come up with solutions. Penny was determined to honor her father through skillfully managing a horse she knew would race well. She solicited the help of her father's lifelong friend, Bull Hancock, even though it meant breaching etiquette by boldly meeting him at the gentlemen only club where he ate lunch every day. Instead of selling the horse, she got financial backing from the man who 'won' the coin toss, Ogden Phipps. She had singleness of vision that enabled her to enter a man's world and succeed in what she undertook.

Secretariat habitually won each race by coming from last place. The trainer remarked that it took the horse 'forever to find his stride,' similar to many believers who struggle to know their callings. Every race left Secretariat's jockey covered in dirt. Every award the horse won, Penny 'placed at her father's feet' to honor him.

Penny found time to support her daughters even though she didn't agree with their politics. It was the 1970's and her teenage girls were protesting the war. She wisely counseled them, 'Even though our ideas may change, our need to do what we believe is right never does.' Can we hear the Lord's advice for the church in that statement? There is no shame in changing our minds when new information is brought to light. It is our determination to do what is right that is praiseworthy. God can work with a person like that because once they become convinced of the truth, they will fight for it.

Penny demonstrated unconventional and creative thought throughout the story, never taking the easy way out but always sticking to her goal. This cost her emotional pain at times, especially when she had to miss family milestones. In spite of this, she kept focused on the goal set before her because, in the end, it would make all the pain she suffered worth the sacrifice.

Now three years old, Secretariat had just won the first two races at the Kentucky Derby and the Preakness Stakes, both in record time. There was one race left between Penny and the Triple Crown—the longest race at Belmont Stakes. Secretariat had never competed in a race of that distance.

The night before the final race, Penny and her family attended the Belmont Ball. At this gathering, Penny's children and husband praised her for standing by her vision for the past three years and accomplishing something extraordinary, despite their previous misgivings about her decision to undertake this challenge. Her eldest daughter remarked, 'I am so proud of you, Mom, [you're] all grown up.' Her husband conceded that all her effort had been worthwhile and that she had taught him something through all of this. He commended her for showing their daughters what it *really meant to be a woman*. At that point, Penny realized that her race had been won—she had accomplished the reason for all she had endured.

A calm came over her. She visited the horse in his stall later that evening and told Big Red, 'I've already won my race. Now you run yours.'

The trainer, Lucien Laurin, expressed his belief that the horse would be wearing wings during the Belmont race. The next day, Secretariat bolted out of the gate and immediately took the lead, unlike any other race he had run. He won the race with world record-breaking speed by thirty-one lengths—the first race his jockey wasn't covered in dirt because there was never another horse in front of him. This event took place in 1973, and to this day Secretariat's time and margin of victory have never been approached.

During the movie, Penny stated, 'You never know how far you can go unless you run.' Women of God, hear the Lord's voice in that statement. She ran despite the opposition she received from her husband, brother, and the men who looked down on her as 'a mere housewife.' She entered a 'man's world' and succeeded. As daughters of the one true King, can we exert any less effort to honor our Heavenly Father? Our Father's legacy to us is the will to run and win the race He ordained for us before we were even born. We have been appointed for this time in history and must discern what we have been placed in this season to accomplish for God.

Ironically, Big Red came to Penny by default. His mother, the *older* mare named Something Royal—twice as old as the mare Ogden Phipps favored—was ignobly associated with the tail side of the coin. Interestingly, the tail side of this coin was imprinted with an eagle, prophetically pointing to the 'wings' Lucien predicted Secretariat would wear in the final race at Belmont.

When Secretariat died, the autopsy revealed that his heart was roughly twenty-two pounds, or nearly three times the weight of an average horse. I believe there is a message here for those who want to finish well in Christ. The heart is often equated with love and generosity. The way to finish well is to run with all our might, undergirding everything we do and say with the love and generosity of God.

Women have often been relegated to the tail side of the coin—particularly older women. Similar to Secretariat, perhaps much of the energy, grace, and authority our Father has invested in His daughters will manifest in the final leg of the race. The women so designated will be wearing prophetic wings and will finish well by the grace of God in those churches that allow these women to run their own races.

Run Your Race

> *(The horse) paws the ground fiercely and rushes forward into battle when the ram's horn blows.* Job 39:24, NLT

Like the horse, God expects believers to run the race specifically ordained for them with zeal and vigor, unable to stand still when the trumpet sounds. Our heavenly Father has imparted His *chayil* spirit to each one of His children. His daughters must embrace this quality in their spirits and run the race the Lord has marked out for them, unrestricted by tradition and doctrines of men. They must do so without fear by walking in love—'perfect love casts out fear' (1 John 4:18).

> *For this reason I remind you to **fan into flame the gift of God**, which is in you through the laying on of my hands. For **the Spirit God gave us does not make us timid, but gives us power, love and self-discipline**... He has saved us and called us to a holy life—not because of anything we have done but **because of his own purpose and grace**. This grace was given us in Christ Jesus before the beginning of time.* 2 Tim. 1:6-7,9, NIV

Jesus told us to pray for workers to be sent into the harvest because there were too few (Luke 10:32). Paul stated that Jesus gave *each* believer a ministry calling, whether apostolic, prophetic, evangelistic, pastoral or teaching in whatever scope and sphere He has ordained. Through each believer doing his or her part, the body of Christ would be equipped and built up in love and truth. This would result in unity and maturity, safeguarding the body from deception so we can stand firmly in the days ahead (Eph. 4:7-16; cf. Matt. 24:10-12,24; 1 Cor. 1:8; 16:13; 2 Thes. 2:3).

The season for open doors of opportunity to minister in true freedom in the Spirit is upon us. As both male and female believers step into their

God-given callings, I believe we will see an unprecedented level of maturity and fruitfulness birthed in the church in the final hour before the Lord returns. Paul urges believers to live lives worthy of their callings in unity, love, and humility:

> *I urge you to live a **life worthy of the calling** you have received. **Be completely humble and gentle; be patient, bearing with one another in love.** Make every effort to **keep the unity** of the Spirit through the bond of **peace**.* Eph. 4:1b-3, NIV

Chapter 13

The Perfect Timing of God

> *A time to keep silence, and a time to speak.* Ecc. 3:7, NKJV

God reveals everything in its appointed time. The wisdom God chooses to unveil in any given time period is reflected in the understanding the Holy Spirit imparts to believers living in that particular prophetic season/generation (Amos 3:7). If the church knew everything there was to know, prophetic gifting would not be as urgently needed as Paul described. Prophetic gifting inherently includes timely declaration of the mysteries found in the Word of God by the illumination of God's Spirit. Only God can reveal deep and hidden knowledge (Dan. 2:22).

God has concealed mysteries in His Word, and those who diligently search for their meaning receive the honor of kings (Prov. 25:2). Job declared that God brings the things we have not understood out of darkness by shedding light on them (Job 12:22). Jesus restrained Himself from teaching the disciples everything He wanted to show them (John 16:12,25). There are hidden truths in the Word that God strategically planned to reveal at the proper times to the people He chooses (Matt. 11:25). Jesus taught that whatever has been concealed will be made known (Mark 4:21-25; Luke 8:16-18).

> *If you continue in My word, you really are My disciples. You will know the truth, and the truth will set you free.* John 8:31b-32, HCSB

The truth that sets us free often manifests when prophetic understanding of Scripture intersects with the timing of God and the readiness of His people. William Wilberforce was raised up for just such a purpose. He was divinely compelled to abolish slavery in his generation in England. He persevered through many obstacles and twenty-six years of opposition to see that the African slave trade was abolished. Many who supported the slave industry argued that slavery was justified as part of God's divine order. Nevertheless, the appointed time had arrived to restore the truth that God made men, but men made slaves.

Revelation at the Proper Time

> *For **the vision is yet for an appointed time**; but at the end it will speak, and it will not lie. **Though it tarries, wait for it**; because it will **surely come**, it will not tarry.* Hab. 2:3, NKJV

> *There is **an appointed time for everything**. And there is a time for every event under heaven.* Ecc. 3:1, NASB

When the Lord prepares His people as He is now preparing His female disciples, it is for a reason. The spiritual timing for releasing women into ministry in an unprecedented way is upon the church. While there have been extraordinary women in the past (Henrietta Mears, Corrie ten Boom, Maria Woodworth-Etter, Kathryn Kuhlman, to name a few), I believe the Lord is training an army of *chayil* women to take their place of authority in the body of Christ and the secular arena in the final generation before the Lord returns.

Until the last one hundred fifty years or so, women as a whole had little opportunity for education or other elevated pursuits. Someone had to attend to the bottom rung of Maslow's hierarchy. Daily chores easily surpassed the number of hours in a day unless one had servants. Each day held much labor to preoccupy the typical wife and mother, including spinning thread and yarn for making clothes, keeping a large garden, storing the food grown, grinding grain and making all bread and meals from scratch, tending livestock, making candles and soap, doing laundry by hand, tending the fire in the hearth, and teaching reading, writing, and arithmetic to her children when there was no school nearby. Women were already so weighed down with the care of their families that there was no room for added responsibilities or in-depth biblical study.

> *Arise, shine, for your light has come, and the glory of the LORD rises upon you.* Isa. 60:1, NIV

In our times, women have educational and vocational opportunities unlike any other time in history. The previously assumed intellectual difference between men and women has been proved false when women are given comparable education and opportunity. The timing for restoring God's truth about women as revealed in His Word has arrived in this generation.

Unfortunately, with their newly found opportunities and freedom, some women have chosen to pursue worldly success and social status rather than God's purposes or favor. Women have also allowed advertising gurus to dictate their life's focus, pursuing eternal youth and coveting the attention given to surgically-altered and Photoshop-enhanced cover girls in order to compete in a deceptive race that has no end. This empty pursuit depletes our time, resources, and self-worth as a child made in the image of God.

Paul's exhortation to the Romans reminds us that believers must think and act differently—a prerequisite for knowing God's will:

> ***Do not conform to the pattern of this world,*** *but be **transformed** by the renewing of your mind. **Then** **you will be able to test and approve what God's will is**—his good, pleasing and perfect will.* Rom. 12:2, NIV

Take a Stance for Truth

> *Be diligent to present yourself approved to God, a worker who does not need to be ashamed, rightly dividing the word of truth.* 2 Tim. 2:15, NKJV

Women now have the time to be like Mary, who sat at the Lord's feet to learn in much greater depth than previously attainable. Believers have the Holy Spirit to guide them into all truth and transform their character. Those who have filled their days with self-focused worldly pursuits must repent. We have been rescued from the dominion of darkness (i.e., deliverance from sin, ignorance, and the curse) and are free to pursue the knowledge of God in a much deeper way.

> *Christ redeemed us from the curse... For he has **rescued us from the dominion of darkness** and brought us into the kingdom of the Son he loves.* Gal. 3:13; Col. 1:13, NIV

Many women have and are fulfilling their callings exactly as the Lord intended within the current framework of the church. They are studying the Word, helping the needy, training and equipping the next generation, and interceding for the church and nation within the acceptable confines of traditional roles for women. Just as most men are called to serve in capacities other than 'pulpit' leadership, most women are called to serve in roles other than taking the reins of church leadership. Like the men, most women have a calling within their sphere of influence that doesn't trespass current restrictions.

These women must energetically and faithfully support and encourage other women who are called to positions of leadership and authority in the church and society. They must refrain from taking the easy way out by agreeing with traditional roles so they can personally win the favor of church leadership or other men who maintain restrictions on women in ministry. Seeking the approval of church leadership who refuse to accept women in leadership or teaching positions will only earn a rebuke from God because this strategy is self-serving and displays a willingness to sacrifice truth for personal gain. This precisely sums up the error of Balaam, about which we have been forewarned.

We have been appointed for this time to stand up for truth and God's purposes in our generation. 'If you remain silent at this time, relief and deliverance for the women will arise from another place, but you will miss your chance to be faithful. And who knows but that you have come to your position for such a time as this?' (adapted from Est. 4:14).

No matter the scope of the calling, however, every believer will necessarily teach to some degree. At the very minimum, we must have a ready defense—a form of teaching—for our hope and calling:

> ***Do not fear their intimidation,*** *and* ***do not be troubled,*** *but sanctify Christ as Lord in your hearts,* ***always being ready to make a defense*** *to everyone who asks you* ***to give an account*** *for the hope that is in you, yet* ***with gentleness and reverence.***
> 1 Pet. 3:14b-15, NASB

Timing Is Crucial

> *To act without knowing how you function is not good; and* ***if you rush ahead, you will miss your goal.*** *Prov. 19:2, CJB*

> *Being excited about something is not enough. You must also* ***know what you are doing. Don't rush into something,*** *or you might do it wrong.* Prov. 19:2, ERV

There will always be youthful or immature believers with great zeal who desire to be propelled into something 'significant' before sufficient maturity has been attained. Maturity in a believer's walk will preserve the individual from harming others and themselves through pride and ignorance. Patiently waiting for the timing of God can be very difficult but is a vital component of testing and maturity.

There are others, however, who are well-grounded in the truth, love the Lord and His purposes, and feel the love of God in their hearts and the zeal of His Spirit urging them to come up higher to train and equip newcomers in Christ. Many of these are women stirred to walk in a calling not accepted by the church at large. They have deep and broad training in the Word through the work of the Holy Spirit. These women feel like square pegs being forced to fit into round holes. They struggle to know what they are called to do, always keeping at the back of their minds the traditional church's taboo against women in leadership or teaching positions. Some may even be in agreement with those restrictions, causing confusion in their minds when they sense the Holy Spirit pressing them to move forward.

Other women have paid for seminary education only to discover on graduating that the very institutions that gladly received their tuition will not allow them to have a teaching or leadership position in their college or affiliated churches. These bewildered women are like race horses that were trained and taken to the starting gate only to find that when the race begins, their gates won't open. The locked gate forever bars them entrance to the race for which they prepared. They feel as though they are in a cage. Most desire only to do their part to prepare the body of Christ for the season ahead and to hear at Jesus' return, 'Well done, good and faithful servant.'

Admittedly, there are ambitious women in the church clamoring for attention that move in anything but a courteous spirit of humility. These women have little concern for unity or love; neither do they feel any parental concern for the people they want as followers. They want to be in front and in charge. They want to be heard and they want to be right, using whatever means are available to them, including manipulation, intimidation, ridicule, or a mean-spirited demeanor that destroys peace and unity. But are there not also male leaders in the church who demonstrate the same traits? Isn't this more likely the unsanctified ambitious bent of particular temperaments than a female issue?

The Lord is revealing in this hour His desire for women to take up their rightful place in the body of Christ, laboring as Paul did for the maturity of the church. Understanding the true meaning behind the passages we've discussed—meaning obscured for two millennia—demonstrates God's desire for this to be understood in our generation.

Recall that God did not reveal His intent to make Gentiles co-heirs with Israel until after Jesus' death, resurrection, and ascension (Eph. 3:4-6). This came as quite a shock to the Jewish population who had been taught for roughly two thousand years that they alone were God's chosen people; that only they had been entrusted with God's Word; that the covenants and promises were for no one but Israel. Many of the Jews were also forced to concede that their long held belief that the law was the path to God's promises had to be relinquished in light of the new information provided by Jesus' initiation of the new covenant prophesied by the OT prophets.

Is this not the same type of thinking we must overcome today, namely that men alone have been entrusted with leadership and teaching authority in the community of believers? We cannot cling to the belief that the world is flat when new evidence confirms that it is a sphere.

Adjusting our paradigms when presented with new information can feel very unnatural at first. The Lord told us in His Word that He does nothing without first revealing His plans to His servants. Amos stated, 'He who formed the mountains and creates the wind reveals His thoughts to mankind' (Amos 4:13). The Lord is looking for those who will tremble at His Word—those who fear Him and listen for the discernment of the Holy Spirit rather than presumptively rely on the church's traditions, their own reasoning and feelings, and the way things have always been.

> Surely the Sovereign LORD does nothing without **revealing his plan to his servants the prophets**. The lion has roared—who will not fear? The Sovereign LORD has spoken—who can but prophesy? Amos 3:7-8, NIV

> But to this one I will look, to him who is **humble and contrite of spirit**, and who **trembles at My word**. Isa. 66:2b, NASB

God's Strength Displayed Through Weak Vessels

The Lord often uses the simple to confound the wise. Many leaders have shunned the prophetic insight of those sent to them, rationalizing that if God wanted them to think and act differently, He would have told them personally. This same thinking caused the Pharisees to misinterpret John the Baptist, the prophet sent to prepare them for the promised Savior, and even worse, to reject the Messiah sent to redeem them. God still speaks through people the world views as weak and foolish to confound those who view themselves too highly. God resists the proud and hides Himself from those who have a lofty view of themselves.

> *I praise you, Father, Lord of heaven and earth, because you have **hidden these things from the wise and learned, and revealed them to little children.** Matt. 11:25, NIV*

In times past, the Lord patiently waited until the right time to reveal certain truths throughout history. There were things Jesus wanted to impart to the disciples that they were not able to bear at the time. Jesus promised that the Holy Spirit would reveal truth in the timing of God (John 16:12-13).

While it has been many centuries in coming, I believe the Lord has chosen this time at the close of the age to restore women to their place alongside men in the body. God has shown great patience with us as He restores truth because He 'wants everyone to come to repentance'—to turn from our former ways and thinking (2 Pet. 3:9; cf. Neh. 9:30). Paul warns us not to show contempt for God's patience, reminding us that God wants us to come to repentance (Rom. 2:4). He is giving us space to turn from the partiality we have shown in the church.

Moses reminds us that secrets belong to God, but the things revealed belong to us (Deut. 29:29a). Now that the Lord has revealed His truth regarding women, we must act accordingly no matter the offense this creates in our minds or the difficulty this presents when we consider the impact this will have on the way we run our churches.

The outcome will be worth the struggle. Our prayers will no longer be hindered and we will move one step closer to the elusive unity that Jesus prayed we would have (John 17:20ff).

> Now may the God of patience and comfort grant you to **be likeminded toward one another**, according to Christ Jesus, that you may **with one mind and one mouth glorify the God** and Father of our Lord Jesus Christ. Rom. 15:5-6, NKJV

A Gentle Tongue Can Break a Bone

> Through patience a ruler can be persuaded, and a gentle tongue can break a bone. Prov. 25:15, NIV

I cringe at the thought of women taking this message and instigating sharp debate in their churches. This is not the way of the Lord, who has demonstrated profound patience through His Spirit to each of us as He conforms us to the character of Christ and renews our carnal minds with His truth.

Consider the following examples:

When the tax collectors questioned Peter about whether Jesus paid the two-drachma tax, Jesus taught Peter a valuable lesson. Even though the children should be exempt from paying the tax, Jesus advised Peter to pay the tax for the two of them 'so as not to cause offense' (Matt. 17:24-27). From this we learn that there are situations where it is better to remain quiet and wait for the timing of the Lord to restore truth. On moral matters, we never compromise. On matters of religious ceremony and practice, we must practice diplomacy and forbearance within the confines of God's prophetic timetable.

We see another example to consider in Acts. When Paul appeared before the Sanhedrin, the high priest ordered one of the men to strike Paul. Paul, an expert in the law, replied, "God will strike you, you whitewashed wall! You sit there to judge me according to the law, yet you yourself violate the law by commanding that I be struck!" (see Acts 23:1-3). Paul knew he was right. Even so, look closely at what transpired.

The men standing near Paul knew the order to strike Paul came from the high priest. They rebuked Paul, saying, 'How dare you insult the high priest!' (v. 4). Despite having the law on his side, Paul responded with contrition, knowing the greater gravity of being disrespectful to those in higher authority:

> *Paul replied, "Brothers, I did not realize that he was the high priest; for it is written: 'Do not speak evil about the ruler of your people.'"* Acts 23:5, NIV

We have to seek the Lord as to what is more important in our situation: unity or taking a stand that may cause offense. There are times when the Lord wants us to cause offense in the minds of those who don't know truth. Jesus purposely did and said things that offended the Pharisees to expose their hypocrisy. However, *many times* our refutation of wrong thinking must be done in such a way that the one rebuked may not immediately know it was a rebuke (see 2 Tim. 4:2). Gently. Graciously. Diplomatically. Courteously. Respectfully. Humbly. In mutual submission. Undergirded by love. *In the timing of God.*

> *One who is wise can go up against the city of the mighty and pull down the stronghold in which they trust.* Prov. 21:22, NIV

Leo Tolstoy wrote in *War and Peace*, "The strongest of all warriors are these two—Time and Patience." Keeping in mind God's prophetic timetable, we must patiently wait for the discernment and the timing of the Holy Spirit. We bathe something like this in prayer, asking the Lord to open doors, soften hearts, remove veils, and create teachable spirits. The Lord wants everyone to turn from wrong thinking and embrace truth. However, it is naïve to think everyone will embrace truth if the change is counterintuitive to his or her worldview and tradition.

We should labor to avoid asserting ourselves in a way that will dishonor the Lord or the truth He wants to restore to His church. This would cause more harm than good in the goal of restoring women to their place in the body of Christ. Behaving as ambassadors with the dignity and strength God has instilled in His *chayil* women provides fertile ground for advancing God's purposes and bearing lasting fruit.

> *He who is slow to anger has great understanding, but he who is hasty of spirit exposes and exalts his folly.* Prov. 14:29, AMP

One thing we may have to keep in mind is that the Lord may want us to move on if we are not accepted. It is sometimes difficult to discern the Lord's voice in these circumstances because we may have family and friends that we cherish and with whom we have deep ties in our church. The Lord directed His disciples to shake off the dust from their feet in any place that did not welcome them or their message. This is not something to be done eagerly or with anger or scorn in our hearts. This action was meant as a warning to those left behind (Matt. 10:13-15; Mark 6:11; Luke 9:5; 10:11; Acts 13:51; 18:6).

The Lord is looking for those who will receive His messengers and His message. Doing so brings a prophet's reward to those who listen (Matt. 10:40-41). Scripture counsels the church to be sober and watchful for God's messengers and the prophetic messages entrusted to them. This can only happen if we actually believe the Lord still speaks today and if we truthfully want to hear what the Lord has to say to us.

Dream

I had a dream several years ago that I haven't forgotten. I was in a sizable church. A large group of men and women had congregated in the hall outside one of the rooms used for adult Bible classes. As I approached the group, I could see the people were very apprehensive about something, whispering nervously among themselves, some appearing quite angry.

I entered the room and saw more people at the back of the room. They were just as agitated as the group in the hall. No one had taken a seat—they were just standing in the back of the room. I asked, 'What's going on?' Several answered in hushed tones but with obvious distress, 'It's not fair!' 'He's making us take the test now and we aren't ready!' 'We weren't prepared for this test!' 'We weren't given enough time!' 'Why is he making us take a test we're not ready for?!' I thought how unfair this seemed. I was puzzled and said, 'This doesn't seem right.'

Just then, I looked up toward the front of the room and noticed the Teacher had His back to the class and was writing something on the black board. As I continued to watch, the Teacher turned around and looked directly at me with the most penetrating eyes I had ever seen. He spoke to me without moving His lips. 'I gave them every opportunity to prepare, but I have to move forward now—the prophetic clock is ticking and we must move forward.' In the dream, I knew immediately that the Lord was speaking. The peoples' perception that they hadn't been given enough time to prepare resulted from not heeding the warnings they had already been given.

Jesus' mission in His earthly ministry included freeing the captives. The Spirit of God often nudges us to think the right way, using the minimum force required to get us to change. Sometimes He waits because there are things we cannot bear presently. Sometimes He pushes harder because we aren't listening or because we are pushing back—resisting.

The countdown continues on God's prophetic timetable. The church is being nudged forward with the knowledge that men and women need to work side-by-side in whatever capacity the Lord ordains. The events lurking on the horizon will manifest soon, and those who are prepared and ready to work together will fare profoundly better. We quench the Spirit when we restrict God's chosen vessels. If we do not move forward together on this issue today, we invite not only rebuke, but quite possibly catastrophic loss in the days to come.

Grieving the Spirit of God must not be taken lightly. Paul admonishes us to 'always strive to do what is good for one another, not quenching the Spirit' (1 Thes. 5:15,19). How can we expect to have true unity or a move of God if we quench and grieve the Holy Spirit by restricting His activity through the weak vessels He chooses?

Can we hear the Father's plea to us in this hour to restore unity to the body? Paul wrote the following passage to reconcile Jews and Gentiles, reasoning that the 'wall of hostility' (the law as the means for inclusion in the covenant) had been removed by Christ. Can we consider that our God, whose character never changes, also desires to see the current barrier of gender division in the church—a wall of hostility between men and women—brought down as well; a wall that prohibits women from full inclusion in the church's mission and ministry?

> *For Christ himself has brought peace to us... he **broke down the wall of hostility that separated us**... by creating in himself **one new people from the two groups**. Together as one body, Christ reconciled both groups to God by means of his death on the cross, and **our hostility toward each other was put to death**.* Eph. 2:14,15b,16, NLT

Chapter 14

Closing Argument

> *So I said, "Wisdom is better than strength." ... The words of the wise heard in quietness are better than the shouting of a ruler among fools.* Ecc. 9:16a,17, NASB

Perhaps we will only know if we have interpreted these passages properly when we meet the Lord face to face. Choose which is more praiseworthy in God's sight: 1.) having an 'unpolluted' church where women are not allowed to speak, resulting in division and hindering believers from faithful ministry, or 2.) being part of a group of believers who are of one mind and heart, working together to accomplish God's purposes in their generation. Do we really want to be judged for hindering others and causing division?

> *Woe to you experts in the law, because you have **taken away the key to knowledge**. You yourselves have not entered, and **you have hindered those who were entering**.* Luke 11:52, NIV

Shouldn't we rather imitate Paul, who said, '...**we put up with anything rather than hinder the gospel of Christ'** (1 Cor. 9:12)? Didn't Jesus instruct His disciples to refrain from censoring others who were speaking in His name, even if they were not part of their particular group (Mark 9:38-41; Luke 9:49-50)? Recall that Paul also said that even when those of questionable motives preached, he rejoiced:

> *It is true that some preach Christ out of envy and rivalry, but others out of goodwill. The latter do so out of love... The former preach Christ out of selfish ambition, not sincerely... **But what does it matter? The important thing** is that in every way, **whether from false motives or true, Christ is preached**. And because of this **I rejoice**.* Php. 1:15-16a,17a,18, NIV

The important thing is that Christ is preached. This is one way we keep the main thing the main thing. While the one who does so out of improper motives will find that what he or she has built will be burned away, the point is that the Holy Spirit can still operate in the hearts and minds of those who hear the Word preached. This happens in spite of the preacher and his or her wrong heart posture.

The church needs both men and women to fulfill the great commission and labor for the harvest. Both men and women have the image of God impressed on their spirits, the jasper and ruby of God's appearance as discussed in chapter six. God created this partnership as fundamental to His original mandate for humanity. To neglect one or the other is to invite imbalance and reject the pattern of heaven, which is to establish righteous and just rule on the earth by wisdom.

> *Therefore, since we are surrounded by such a great cloud of witnesses,* **let us throw off everything that hinders** *and the sin that so easily entangles. And* **let us run with perseverance the race marked out for us, fixing our eyes on Jesus,** *the pioneer and perfecter of faith.* Heb. 12:1-2a, NIV

Judgment Notwithstanding Verdict

Regarding the role of women in the church and the verdict of complementarians to limit that role according to their own interpretations, I believe the Lord will issue a 'Judgment Notwithstanding the Verdict.' This is a practice where the trial judge may reverse a jury's verdict "when the judge believes there was no factual basis for the verdict or it was contrary to law. The judge will then enter a different verdict as "a matter of law." Essentially **the judge should have required a "directed verdict"** (instruction to the jury to return with a particular verdict since the facts allowed no other conclusion), and **when the jury "went wrong,"** the judge uses **the power to reverse the verdict** instead of approving it, **to prevent injustice."**[89]

The purpose of this type of verdict is to prevent injustice. The Judge of all the earth has directed the verdict regarding women in ministry by providing examples in the Word of valiant women chosen for noble tasks (case law). He inspired Paul to write that we are one in Christ and are no longer distinguished by earthly categories. Having Christ is all that matters because He lives in each of us, makes us one in Him, and richly blesses all who ask (Rom. 10:12; Gal. 3:28; Col. 3:11).

We have been admonished to 'no longer view anyone from a merely human perspective' (2 Cor. 5:16). Jude reminds us that those who follow 'natural instincts' (i.e., traditions and cultural norms) cause division because they are not following the Spirit (Jude 1:19). Jesus told us to stop judging by mere appearances (John 7:24), which includes ceasing from judging Scripture at only face value. These are the precedents handed down from the heavenly courtroom—decisions the lower court (the church) is obligated to honor.

When we make decisions, doctrine, or policy contrary to God's Word, the build-up of injustice requires that the Lord take action. He cannot deny Himself because the foundation of His throne is righteousness and justice. Building our theology on traditions or a few verses seemingly divergent (at face value in our English translations) from the main themes in Scripture yields very unstable ground on which to base our doctrine and practice. Worse, the injustice caused by such views attracts correction and quite possibly a rebuke from the heavenly courtroom.

> *If you address as Father the One who **impartially judges according to each one's work, conduct yourselves in fear** during the time of your stay on earth.* 1 Pet. 1:17, NASB

Each Believer Is Called to Ministry

Believers who have been given understanding need to pray for and implore church leadership to 'set the women free' from the chains imposed on them so that they may worship and serve the Lord as He intended—alongside the men as co-laborers in the body of Christ (cf. Ex. 8:1). Women have the same longings as men for wholeheartedness and making deep and lasting impact through their God-given callings.

The following passage, through a different interpretive lens, uses inclusive language (*hekastos heis*: each and every one), indicating that Christ has given **each** believer a calling to one or more of the four or five ministry gifts. This requires that each must be trained and equipped:

> *But to **each one** (hekastos heis) of us **grace has been given as Christ** apportioned it... And **He Himself** gave some to be **apostles**, some **prophets**, some **evangelists**, and some **pastors and***

*teachers, for the **equipping** of the saints for the work of ministry, for the **edifying** of the body of Christ, till we all **come to the unity** of the **faith** and of the **knowledge** of the Son of God, to a perfect man, to the measure of the stature of the fullness of Christ. Eph. 4:7(NIV), 11-13, NKJV*

[Note: An argument could be made for only four gifting since 'pastors' is linked to 'teachers' in a way different than the others. The others are linked by *tous de* (Grk. 3588 and 1161, 'and some'), a definite article and a conjunction. Pastors and teachers are linked solely by the word *kai* (Grk. 2532), which can also be translated 'namely,' without the definite article before 'teachers.' This would give us 'and some pastors, namely, teachers' or 'and some pastors-teachers.' This supports that those who are pastors must be able to teach, and those who are teachers must have parental feeling for those they instruct. But maybe this is splitting hairs...]

This interpretation is strengthened by Paul's tireless labor for maturity in believers so they would be able to equip others in the capacity the Lord has called them. Once we have been equipped through sound teaching, character transformation, and understanding God's will for our lives in this age (Col. 1:9-14), *each* is to take their place to equip the next generation—men and women alike. This pattern resembles God's charge to Abraham: to raise godly children after him who would walk in righteousness and justice so that God's promise would be fulfilled (Gen. 18:19). We need both fathers and mothers to equip the next generation (Prov. 1:8; see chapter 6).

Paul prefaced the following paragraph with a call to humility, patience, love, and unity, qualities desperately needed in the church today:

*Be completely **humble** and **gentle**; be **patient, bearing with one another in love**. Make every effort to **keep the unity of the Spirit** through the bond of peace. **There is one body and one Spirit**, just as you were called to one hope when you were called; one Lord, one faith, one baptism; one God and Father of all, who is over all and through all and in all. Eph. 4:2-6, NIV*

Dr. Nebeker agrees that humility is key for understanding the Word, closing his argument with the following: "To conclude, awareness of how our preunderstandings are shaped requires humility on our part, a **humility that is essential to our growth in the grace and knowledge of Christ**. Humility is a virtue that accords well with the integrity that should be the sum of all literary knowledge. Corduan says it well, *"Humility is called for by the interpreter's awareness that final truth may not always be in his grasp. But commitment signifies that the interpreter never give up in his quest to find the truth.""*[90]

God calls each believer to serve in some ministry capacity, whether apostolic, prophetic, evangelistic, pastoral, and/or teaching in nature. This gift may be expressed through a church, an academic institution, a home Bible study, a neighborhood 'coffee klatch,' a family group, the marketplace, prayer meetings, writing, mission work, music, fine arts, online community, a spirit-filled business lunch, weekly informal gatherings (not necessarily church sponsored), serving in rescue missions, or however the Lord leads. Many 'lay people' experience unrelenting hunger to serve and minister in a capacity greater than what they are currently allowed. Women are fully included members of the body of Christ, and we honor the Lord by releasing every believer into their callings, no matter the offense this may cause our unrenewed minds.

The other gifts of the Spirit (healings, miracles, tongues, words of wisdom, etc.; see Rom. 12:3-8; 1 Cor. 12:7-11) work through believers as the Spirit wills in different seasons and as the purposes of God require. These gifts can manifest while believers are in training or in the midst of walking out their primary calling in one or more of the four or five ministry areas. Believers must guard themselves against offense that can be created when we experience feelings of disapproval for the particular vessels the Lord chooses for His purposes.

Even though Job was a notably righteous man who loved God, his ordeal caused him to be offended and bewildered. Yet his ultimate meeting with God made him realize he did not know everything there was to know. In humility, he acknowledged that he had spoken of things he didn't truly understand, and that he had obscured God's plans by his display of ignorance (Job 42:1-6). James described this type of humility—acknowledging when we are wrong—as necessary for wisdom (James 3:13).

The Weak, Asthenes

> *You husbands, likewise, conduct your married lives with understanding.* **Although your wife may be weaker physically,** *you should respect her as a fellow-heir of the gift of Life. If you don't, your prayers will be blocked.* 1 Pet. 3:7, CJB

The Lord told Paul that God's strength was made perfect in weakness (2 Cor. 12:9-10). Paul spoke tongue-in-cheek when he told the Corinthians that they were wise, strong, and honored, while he was considered a weak fool and held in contempt (1 Cor. 4:10). But what had Paul been sent to do? He was sent to teach the truth to those who were 'strong and honored' by the world's standards but ignorant by God's.

At the opening of his letter to the Corinthians, Paul wrote that God deliberately chose what the world considers weak (*asthenes*) and foolish to shame and bewilder what the world judges as the strong and wise (1 Cor. 1:27). He used the same Greek word for weak that Peter used to describe wives in his instructions to husbands. In discussing spiritual gifts and our places in the body, Paul said that the parts we consider weaker or more feeble (*asthenes*) are actually the parts we cannot do without (1 Cor. 12:22). Men are physically stronger, but God has chosen the weak to shame the strong. We cannot let our enemy dupe us into thinking 'weak' women cannot carry God's authority.

But I Digress

My mind now returns to the midweek Bible study mentioned at the beginning of this book. The pastor continued, 'So you see, this is why we teach that male leadership must be present before a woman can be allowed to speak in the church...'

> *Sigh... Deliver us, Lord, so every believer can freely serve You as You have ordained and be found faithful at Jesus' return. Amen.*

Dr. Nebeker reminds us that discovering what Scripture really means to teach us may disrupt our long-held beliefs, as it did for the Jews and the pagan Ephesian Gentile believers of Paul's day. "If we can agree that Scripture serves a disruptive function in the lives of the people of

God, what might this look like within a sermon, or within any other small group context in the local church? A part of the church worker's task in teaching is to correct (and graciously so) the flawed preunderstandings that the people of God bring to the Bible."[91]

For some, what is written here may prove too outrageous to consider. They don't want to be confused by the truth because the worldview they have constructed comforts them (cf. Prov. 18:2). This could be one of the reasons the church is so anemic—we have not properly discerned the Lord's body, which is the body of all believers, including women. Paul wrote the following to the Corinthians in the context of teaching that they are one in the Lord and any practice they adopt that brings division is not from the Lord (1 Cor. 11:17-21).

> ***Your meetings do more harm than good****... For those who eat and drink **without discerning the body of Christ** eat and drink **judgment on themselves***. *That is why many among you are **weak and sick**, and a number of you have fallen asleep. But if we were **more discerning** with regard to ourselves, **we would not come under such judgment***. 1 Cor. 11:17b,29-31, NIV

Repercussions and Warnings from the Word

The Lord is moving ahead with His prophetic timetable. The church is currently in the grace period for turning from this error. In Romans 13:10-14, Paul exhorts believers to turn from darkness, which not only speaks of sin and the deeds of the flesh but of darkened understanding as well. He exhorts believers to 1.) wake up from their stupor, 2.) understand the spiritual season, and 3.) love and do no harm to one another, which requires that we cease from divisions and partialities.

Which is more scandalous, to move forward with better understanding by discarding old misinterpretations, or to be left behind in a building that has a spreading mold on the walls? When we turn from our faithlessness to truth, the Lord promised to give us shepherds after His own heart who will lead with knowledge and understanding (Jer. 3:14-15). If we refuse, consider the following from the OT prophets:

*For this is a **people without understanding; so their Maker has no compassion on them**, and their Creator **shows them no favor**.* Isa. 27:11b, NIV

Misunderstanding and misapplying truth can have very serious consequences. Some have embraced wrong doctrine through ignorance or immaturity. Others cling to wrong doctrine even when the error has been exposed. Sometimes it just takes time for the lure of the old wine to disappear. For others, pride and selfish ambition or vainglory (love of an elevated position) are the main obstacles. The fruit of this last condition is 'every evil practice' (James 3:16), which includes showing partiality.

*Where there is strife, there is pride, but **wisdom is found in those who take advice**.* Prov. 13:10, NIV

*Whoever trusts in his own mind is a fool, but **he who walks in wisdom will be delivered**.* Prov. 28:26, ESV

*He will surely **reprove you if you do secretly show partiality**.* Job 13:10, AMP

*Their respecting of persons and **showing of partiality witnesses against them**...* Isa. 3:9a, AMP

As a grim reminder, Solomon recorded the penalty for not turning to wisdom. Since God's nature does not change, we should consider that this penalty may await those in the church who refuse God's correction on this issue (bullets added for clarity/emphasis):

***If you will turn (repent) and give heed to my reproof**, behold, I [Wisdom] **will pour out my spirit upon you**, I will make my words known to you. Because I have called and **you have refused** [to answer], have stretched out my hand and no man has heeded it, and you **treated as nothing all my counsel and would accept none of my reproof**,*

- *I also will laugh at your calamity;*
- *I will mock when the thing comes that shall cause you terror and panic—when your panic comes as a storm and desolation*

> and your calamity comes on as a whirlwind, when distress and anguish come upon you.
>
> Then will they call upon me [Wisdom] but I will not answer;
>
> - they will seek me early and diligently but they will not find me.
> - Because they
>   - ✓ hated knowledge and
>   - ✓ did not choose the reverent and worshipful fear of the Lord,
>   - ✓ would accept none of my counsel, and
>   - ✓ despised all my reproof,
>
> therefore shall they eat of the fruit of their own way and be satiated with their own devices.
>
> For the backsliding of the simple shall slay them, and the careless ease of [self-confident] fools shall destroy them. **But whoso hearkens to me [Wisdom] shall dwell securely and in confident trust and shall be quiet, without fear or dread of evil.** Prov. 1:23-33, AMP

As harsh as this might sound, we must consider the ramifications for ignoring God's wisdom. Recall the consequences Jesus pronounced for those who would not turn from error—the Lord would burn away everything they have done (1 Cor. 3:13; cf. Rev. 2:21-23).

> *I gave her space to repent of her fornication* (adopting worldly ways/views); *and she repented not.* Rev. 2:21, KJV

Exhortation

> **Does not wisdom call out?** *Does not understanding raise her voice?* ...**Give careful thought** *to the paths for your feet... Say to wisdom, "You are my sister..."* ...**embrace her,** *and* **she will honor you.** Prov. 8:1, 4:26a, 7:4a, 4:8b, NIV

Paul admonished new believers to put on the 'new self that is being renewed *in knowledge in the image of its Creator,*' reminding us of our discussion of God's appearance as jasper and ruby. Paul explained that the knowledge of God's image on every person motivates us to free ourselves from former distinctions and partiality linked to race, gender, age, or any social strata. 'Christ is all and in all.' Our focus is rightly placed on Him alone, not earthly distinctions, and He works through us and is in each of us regardless of race, gender, age, or any other outward difference (Col. 3:9-11; Gal. 3:28). In order to accomplish this, the church must learn to make a distinction between the type and shadow marriage represents and the priesthood of all believers as the bride of Christ. Peter and Joel remind us that God's Spirit empowers men *and* women to prophecy—to speak in Jesus' name and explain mysteries. We cannot place in bondage those God has freed in Christ.

> *Therefore, as God's chosen people, holy and dearly loved,* **clothe yourselves with compassion, kindness, humility, gentleness and patience. Bear with each other** *and* **forgive one another** *if any of you has a grievance against someone. Forgive as the Lord forgave you. And over all these virtues* **put on love, which binds them all together in perfect unity.** Col. 3:12-14, NIV

It is time to remove the defiled stones from our spiritual dwellings and replace them with truth. Reconsidering our traditional translations and interpretations of 1 Corinthians 14:34-36 and 1 Timothy 2:11-15 as discussed in this book may require a paradigm shift in our thinking and practice. God's timing for restoring truth is not meant to merely provide us with information. We need to act on the revelation given.

> *This is what the Lord says:* **"Maintain justice and do what is right,** *for my* **salvation is close at hand** *and* **my righteousness will soon be revealed."** Isa. 56:1, NIV

For those women in whom the Lord has invested much in the Word and the Spirit, training them for a calling wider in scope—women who burn with a vision larger than themselves; women who have heard the trumpet sound and feel the Lord's call to come up higher; women who cannot be still with the message entrusted to them because it is like a fire shut up in their bones—I have adapted this passage from Job 39 for you. Read it as God's word to those who have misunderstood God's purpose and role for women in the body of Christ:

Do you give My daughters their chayil spirit,
or clothe them with dignity and strength?
Do you make them leap at My command,
igniting passion by their fierce love and loyalty?
They walk with sure feet,
rejoicing in My Word,
and charge into the fray.
They laugh at fear, afraid of nothing;
they do not shy away from the sword.
The quiver rattles against their side,
along with the flashing spear and lance.
With zeal for My name they eat up the ground;

They cannot stand still
when the trumpet sounds.

Draw me after You and **let us** *run…*
Songs 1:4a, NASB

Chapter 15

Restoring Women and *Koinonia*

> *Have salt in yourselves, and be at peace with one another.*
> Mark 9:50b, NASB

'Have salt in yourselves.' Salt represents the eternal truth in God's Word. Being rooted in the Word properly interpreted and integrated with the whole message and tenor of Scripture is vital for peace and unity. The Holy Spirit's guidance into all truth and grace provide the only legitimate means we have for reaching this kind of maturity.

Paul prayed that every believer would grow in the knowledge of God (Col. 1:10). He described himself as a servant sent to further believer's faith and knowledge of truth (Titus 1:2), knowing that God's people can be destroyed for lack of knowledge (Hos. 4:6). Paul taught that people can exchange God's knowledge to pursue a life of sin (Rom. 1:28). This can also happen when we pursue a life of self-centeredness known as the American dream.

The goal of every ministry gift must be to love and equip believers to mature so we can have unity in the faith and *in the knowledge of God* (Eph. 4:13). If the church does not adequately prepare and train the next generation, to whom will we pass the baton to continue the race? True maturity is not attained by organization, administration, money, numerical growth, advanced academic degrees, or even memorizing Scripture, though these are useful. It is attained through humility, grace, love, and walking in the Spirit as He teaches us what it really means to love God and one another. This is the way Jesus said the world would know we are His and that He had been sent by God.

Koinonia

The unity secular groups experience does not have the supernatural quality of the *koinonia* available to the body of Christ. *Koinonia* (Grk. 2842) does not only mean community in the English sense of the word. This word carries a component of intimacy and sharing that can only be achieved by joint participation as we labor together *in the Lord* and *for the Lord* as authentic members of His body. The bond that joins us to Jesus and the Holy Spirit becomes the same bond that joins us to every other believer. "The New Testament letters describe those bonds as so vital and genuine that a deep level of intimacy can be experienced among the members of a local church."[92]

The Lord has made every believer a joint-heir—a full partner in His ministry. Partnership defines another aspect of *koinonia*, a term often used of business partners in the Greek world. The following Wikipedia excerpts explain the practical, active aspects of this word (several excerpts follow in the narrative and refer back to this article; see End Notes):

> *Koinonia* embraced a strong commitment to "kalos k'agathos" meaning "good and good," an inner goodness toward virtue, and an outer goodness toward social relationships. In the context of outer goodness, translated into English, the meaning of *koinonia* holds the idea of joint participation in something with someone, such as in a community, or team or an alliance or joint venture. Those who have studied the word find **there is always an implication of action included in its meaning**...
>
> Only **participation as a contributive member** allows one to share in what others have. What is shared, received or given becomes the common ground through which *Koinonia* becomes real... *Koinonia* was used to refer to the marriage bond, and it suggested a powerful common interest that could hold two or more persons together... *[K]oinonia* **highlights a higher purpose or mission that benefits the greater good** of the members as a whole.[93]

Koinonia cannot be reduced to the mere camaraderie we feel when we eat fellowship meals or have Bible studies together. Even the unsaved have this in their shared activities. Meeting once a week to hear a message is not the *koinonia* the apostles described. "Fellowship is never passive in the meaning of *koinonia*, it is always linked to action, not just being together, but also doing together. With fellowship comes a close and intimate relationship embracing ideas, communication, and frankness, as in a true, blessed interdependent friendship among multiple group members."[94]

True Christian *koinonia* manifests when believers become like-minded in spirit and purpose with Jesus, rooted and grounded in His truth and love that goes beyond the human definition of love. It is simultaneously practical, tangible, and supernatural.

John the apostle spoke of this love very often in his letters. Our fellowship comes from walking in God's love and light (1 John 1:6-7). The light of God is Jesus, who is the Word. His truth will set us free to be like Him, to pursue real purpose, and to supernaturally love with abandonment both God and one another. If we do not understand and practice the truth, John reminds us that we are still in darkness and hinder our fellowship with God. There can be no *koinonia* in such an environment.

The source of our fellowship with each other is our communion (*koinonia*) with Jesus. Perhaps part of the problem in our fellowships today is that we have included so many who are not true believers. These are more attached to the world than to Christ, and it is far more difficult to have *koinonia* when there is rocky ground filled with thorns and thistles in our midst.

If we have a diverse mix of the uncommitted and committed, those who follow the world and those who follow Christ in our churches, *koinonia* will escape our grasp. This does not pertain only to the lay people. Many in pulpit ministry seek to define their success by the world's standards and revert to documented church growth tactics in order to bolster their numbers and feelings of success. This worldly mindset rubs off on those under their care. Church becomes a venue to showcase talent, put on a successful face for all to see, and judge every program's outcome as 'good, very good, or very, very good.'

Paul reminds us that without discerning the Lord's body as one—a body that is not divided—we do more harm than good in our fellowship meetings. Taking the Lord's Supper becomes a ritual for each believer alone, rather than partaking of the one loaf and one cup as a spiritual picture of our unity in Christ (1 Cor. 10:17). "[K]oinonia is viewed as much deeper... when the meal is associated with a spiritual purpose. Joining in the Lord's Supper is uniting oneself with other believers in the objective reality of Christ's death."[95]

Characteristics of Koinonia

The NT writers gave us many directives for our relationships with fellow believers if we are to experience the *koinonia* of the Spirit. Because the meaning of joint participation is included in the definition, the translators have interpreted *koinonia* as 'contribution' in passages where *koinonia* refers to believers taking part in the fellowship of suffering when poor believers are in need (Rom. 15:26; 2 Cor. 9:13). Rejoicing when another believer rejoices and suffering when another suffers, also known as empathy, is the fruit of true *koinonia*.

Contributions given out of compulsion, guilt, or as a good business practice do not represent the *koinonia* that is to characterize and prompt our giving. Those who tithe out of a sense of duty, with perhaps an eye on financial blessing or as insurance for financial stability, may benefit others with their giving, but it won't credit to their heavenly account. Only what is given out of love brings reward (1 Cor. 13:3).

True *koinonia* expresses the deeply ingrained belief that we are one in the Lord and hold all things in common because of that bond. This is the one way we are enabled to view our material goods as though they are not our own rather than entitlements. This is the only reason the emerging new covenant believers could take care of one another by selling what they had to benefit those in need (Acts 4:32-35).

The following are behaviors and attitudes associated with true *koinonia*, available only to those in fellowship with Christ by the Holy Spirit. Notice each trait has nonpartisanship as an underlying assumption, a quality that has its origin in God's unchanging nature.

- love one another (John 13:34; Rom. 13:8; 1 Thes. 3:12; Heb. 13:1; 1 Pet. 1:22; 1 John 3:11)
- teach one another (Col. 3:16)
- show generosity to those in need (Acts 4:32-35; Rom. 12:8; 15:26; 2 Cor. 8:7,13-15)
- be devoted to one another (Rom. 12:10)

- honor and give preference to one another (Rom. 12:10)
- be of the same mind toward one another (Rom. 12:16; 15:5)
- pursue the things which make for peace and the building up of one another (Rom. 14:19)
- accept one another (Rom. 15:7)
- admonish one another (Rom. 15:14)
- agree with one another (1 Cor. 1:10)
- have no division in the body, but have the same care for one another (1 Cor. 12:25)
- encourage and comfort one another (2 Cor. 13:11; 1 Thes. 4:18)
- serve one another in love (Gal. 5:13)
- submit to one another (Eph. 5:21)
- tell the truth, for we are members of one another (Eph. 4:25)
- be kind and compassionate, forgiving one another (Eph. 4:32)
- regard one another as more important than ourselves with humility of mind (Php. 2:3)
- build up one another (1 Thes. 5:11; Heb. 3:13; 10:25)
- seek what is good for one another (1 Thes. 5:15)
- motivate one another to acts of love and good works (Heb. 10:24)
- confess our sins to one another (James 5:16)
- pray for one another (James 5:16)
- live in harmony with one another (1 Pet. 3:8)
- show hospitality to one another (1 Pet. 4:9; 1 John 4:7)
- clothe ourselves with humility toward one another (1 Pet. 5:5)

These qualities will manifest in the church in greater measure as we mature and grow. This kind of growth takes place when we resolve to be conformed to the character of Christ while at the same time allowing the Holy Spirit to remove the desires and thinking of the world that have captivated our lives. The prescription for removing worldly pollution requires growing in the knowledge of God and walking in the Spirit.

Koinonia Leadership

Those who mentor and disciple us—who instruct us in the knowledge of God and contribute to our spiritual growth and training—deserve our honor and esteem. We submit to them as we are trained and equipped to walk in the ministry we are called to fulfill. These leaders serve to facilitate our spiritual growth.

True God-given leadership is not dictatorial, controlling our every breath and movement. It is *in Christ* that we live, move, and have our being, not in the church, its traditions, or its human leaders (Acts 17:28). While it is right and proper to respect church leadership, it is unbiblical to give any leader the allegiance Christ alone is worthy to receive.

A church that adopts a 'Moses model' of leadership usurps the authority of Christ and the priesthood of all believers. Moses prophesied that God would raise up another prophet like him. Jesus fulfilled that prophecy. None of the NT apostles claimed this kind of authority in the new covenant community. When problems arose, the community called together the elders and leaders to discuss the issues and the proper course of action based on testimonies of what God was doing, the Word, and the leading of the Holy Spirit (e.g., Acts 15).

Paul specifically reminded the Corinthians that the individual leaders to whom they gave too much honor were merely ministering servants. Leaders function to equip believers to be sent out to continue God's mission to reconcile the lost. They also labor for maturity in the saints.

For anyone to adopt a Moses style of leadership today might be viewed as a power grab. The one in charge makes all decisions regarding *his* church and the teaching *his* people receive. The heart of the one doing so may be moving in a spirit of obedience, but it is obedience *to tradition*. When tradition and the doctrines of men become second nature and necessary for a position of influence or inclusion in the group, it is nearly impossible to discern the Holy Spirit's voice.

Our Present Day Church Model

Our written or unwritten model for doing church often resembles the OT model for worship at the temple more than the new covenant practice of the early church. The OT model included gathering at a physically fixed temple, entering the gates with singing, bringing tithes and offerings, and allowing only the designated priest to minister at the altar. The high priest alone wielded authority to carry out this work, and everyone submitted to his authority. But is this the NT model demonstrated or taught by Jesus and the apostles?

The apostles remind us that *believers* are the church; they are the temple of the Holy Spirit (1 Cor. 12:27; 3:16). The priesthood includes all believers (1 Pet. 2:5-9; Rev. 1:6; 5:10). Each believer can speak in turn; each can bring a song, teaching, prophetic word, and encouragement (1 Cor. 14:26; Eph. 5:19). We give out of love and compassion as the Spirit guides us (1 Cor. 16:2; 2 Cor. 9:7). God puts the body together as He sees fit, and the Spirit moves as He wills (1 Cor. 12:7-11). No single believer has a monopoly. We are to submit to Christ as our Head (Eph. 5:24), to one another out of love and respect (Eph. 5:21), to our elders and those who have been in Christ longer than we have (1 Pet. 5:5), and to the leaders God provides to contribute to our spiritual maturity and equip us for our callings (1 Cor. 16:16; Heb. 13:17). Paul counseled Timothy to share his teaching responsibilities with those who were reliable and knew the Word (2 Tim. 2:2). This is a scriptural snapshot of what the church should look like.

God seeks to draw all people to *Jesus* (John 12:32), not a building, human leader, or specific brand of theology. Jesus counseled the weary and burdened to come to Him, not the temple or local synagogue. In contrast, some churches are trying to convince believers to come to them so the head pastor can further his personal or his denomination's vision/agenda rather than equip believers for ministry. Many seek the numbers that bolster their feelings of success, both the number of people and the finances they provide. Others pursue winning the hearts of the people in order to gain their loyalty and lifelong membership.

True believers, however, want to encounter the Lord. God's truth empowered by the presence of the Holy Spirit can set people free from the past and release them into their callings and purpose. *Koinonia* requires we promote Christ, embrace the Holy Spirit's leading, and equip the people God sends our way. If we are truly concerned about the spiritual welfare of the lost, we will not only promote our particular church. We will rejoice no matter which Bible-based church a new believer decides to join, trusting that the Holy Spirit will guide the youngling to the place the Lord has determined he or she should go.

Believers today have more biblical resources available to them than at any other time in history. When they discover they have gifts and can understand the Word by the guidance of the Holy Spirit, they often find little opportunity to express those gifts in the local church. The pastors and a handful of elders do it all. One pastor admitted that he preferred baby believers because they would accept what he taught without question or debate. He believed mature believers caused division because they questioned his doctrine. He saw them as rebellious and unwilling to submit to his authority rather than as hungry truth seekers or God's messengers sent to provide counsel, as Priscilla and Aquila did for Apollos. Humility remains the key ingredient for leadership.

In many churches, there is little avenue for functioning together in ministry unless it is to support the pastor in his ministry and focus. The message of the local church becomes painfully clear: the pastor is the head and the rest are his sheep. He determines the vision based on his personal calling, elevating the value of his gifting and ministry above every other calling represented in his congregation. Even the way he expresses his calling is viewed as the ideal for the sheep to emulate. If he is an extroverted, charismatic leader who loves giving people sound bites for sermons, he wants to see his people do the same.

The sheep are made to feel inadequate, or worse, to question their very salvation if their heart is not stirred by the same ministry focus that stirs the pastor's heart. No one feels appreciated or included unless he or she becomes like the pastor. This ignores the drive in every believer to be what *God* has called them to be, not a carbon copy of someone else. Some leaders expect the sheep to sit down, be quiet, listen, give money, submit, and help fulfill their personal ministry vision rather than equip these sheep to fulfill their own callings.

This model does not serve the pastor or the congregation in the long term. When authority rests only in the hands of the pastor, people clamor for his attention and time. The door to offense swings wide as the pastor fails to meet the expectations of every member of his church: the pastor didn't feed me; the pastor didn't visit me when I was in the hospital; the pastor didn't listen to my suggestions about the music; the pastor didn't return my call/email; I was gone for three weeks and he didn't call to find out how I was doing; I... me... mine...

Some who attend these churches think of the church as a place to have all their needs met, developing a sense of entitlement as long as they pay their dues. When we keep people in the pew to be spoon-fed, we lock them into a childish mentality of dependency instead of equipping and releasing them into ministry. This is not *koinonia*.

Rick Joyner, Founder and Executive Director of MorningStar Ministries and Heritage International Ministries as well as Senior Pastor at MorningStar Fellowship Church, is a prophetic voice for today's church. He sees a prophetic warning for the present day church in the following passage. When the disciples asked Jesus about His return and the signs that would accompany the end of this age, Jesus included the following remark in His answer:

> *"How terrible it will be in those days for women who are pregnant and for mothers with little babies!"* Matt. 24:19, GNT

Joyner has prophetically correlated this passage with those who are still 'nursing babes' in their congregations when the cataclysmic events on the horizon before Jesus' return manifest. Maturity in the body of Christ is desperately needed, more now than at any other time in history. No matter which eschatological viewpoint we personally agree with, the difficult days we have already entered require that as many believers as possible walk in mature faith and the knowledge of God for survival, and especially to bolster the immature faith of spiritual babes. These are also key ingredients for unity and therefore *koinonia* in the church.

No Cookie-Cutter Believers

Every believer is a unique blend of personality, temperament, history, vision, calling, depth in the knowledge of God, and ability, not to mention their current maturity level. No two are the same, and therefore each has a unique road to travel to take them to their place of maturity. There is no cookie-cutter definition of what a genuine walk with God looks like, though certain common elements will be present in each (e.g., the growing evidence of spiritual fruit, loyalty to the Lord and His truth, the absence of willful sin, etc.). The leaders of the church must discern this individuality. Without this discernment, we may become critical of or offended by those who don't follow the same roadmap to maturity that we followed and that makes sense to us.

Believers who find no place to rest in their quest to exercise their God-given gifts are sometimes labeled rebellious or equivocating little church hoppers. These believers can be the most difficult to understand. Pastors mourn when these restless ones move on, certain that they harbor offense or are deceived, rebellious, immature, unable to submit to authority, not listening to the Holy Spirit, and/or driven by consumerism. In some instances this might be so; we must examine ourselves to see if this is true of us.

In other cases, however, God prompts these believers to move on. They know the Word and search for something difficult to find—the presence of God, true *koinonia*, and the priesthood of all believers as practiced by the early church with opportunities to exercise the gifts the Lord has given them. I think most of these would settle for just one of these traits in a church. Some feel most at home when praying or studying the Word for the pure pleasure of getting closer to the Lord. The Lord is training these for depth in the ways and knowledge of God far from the fear of man and need for acceptance in a group. This describes the training many OT prophets experienced. While still involved in their communities, these definitely marched to the beat of a different drummer.

Though many in church leadership have overstepped the boundaries of true new covenant leadership as the NT defines it, those under this type of leadership must continue in a loving spirit of grace, unity, and honor while not sacrificing truth. Who knows if the Lord plants us in such churches to pray and speak truth in order for veils to be removed? On the other hand, the Holy Spirit might be directing us to move to a different fellowship that will honor His direction—one where believers are able to exercise their callings and contribute to the community with something other than money.

To be clear, we have to keep in mind that our specific callings are meant to bring a contribution to the fellowship of believers for the purposes of God. Though every believer is unique, we cannot understand our personal gifting in a vacuum but as part of the whole.

Getting Connected

Today's traditional church service provides little opportunity for believers to participate in their God-given callings. They do serve the purpose of providing needed teaching and, hopefully, updates on how the Spirit is directing the community of believers. Rick Joyner is teaching a timely series on *koinonia* that can be found on the MorningStar website (it is in progress at the time of this writing). He stated, "It is hard for anyone to discover their gifts and callings in the typical church service, much less have a place to function… [T]hese larger services can have an important part in the life of the body, but the real building of the church, which is the place where church life really happens, will be the smaller groups."[96] Joyner also points out that through the process of maturing, smaller groups can grow from functioning as 'special cliques' to finding their place as connected to the whole.

Being connected to the whole is necessary for survival. This is not only seen in the microcosm of small groups as they fit into a local church, but in the macrocosm of each individual church as part of the worldwide body of Christ. Viewed this way, the fear some leaders harbor toward dividing their congregants into smaller groups can be dispelled. We have the assurance of God's Word that Jesus will return for a bride walking in unity and purity. Joyner points out, "If we are overly fearful of small groups separating themselves, then we are not mature or secure enough in the Lord to be in leadership. Without a leadership that walks in faith instead of fear, *koinonia* will not happen. Without the freedom present that enables some groups to separate, the control spirit will be too great for authentic *koinonia*. Therefore, a secure and mature leadership is crucial for church life."[96]

Joyner further describes the process of and journey to maturity and *koinonia* and cautions against waiting until things are perfect before getting involved. Part of our growth into maturity as individual believers is to persevere through the trials by enduring the process in our local fellowship. "All relationships go through phases and challenges before becoming mature and stable. Churches do too. If we think that we will wait out the problems and jump in when things settle down, we will not fit in when we try to jump in. The process is essential. The more intense it is, the greater we can expect the purpose and *koinonia* to be. As we enter more deeply into the time when all of society is falling apart, the *koinonia* in the church is going to be a strong lifeline to many and become one of the most valuable treasures on earth. It will be well worth whatever price we have paid for it."[96]

Amen. To this I will only add that principles such as these are applicable ninety-nine percent of the time (this is not a literal figure; it is probably more like 99.9%). There are always those few who are like John the Baptist, living 'outside the camp' and waiting in the wilderness until the Word of the Lord comes to them. They are not avoiding church because they disagree doctrinally or don't like the programs or the difficulty in striving for unity and maturity. Most of these really like church and other believers, despite all the faults and shortcomings. Neither do these mature believers spend all of their time outside the church. They do, however, require a good portion of their time to be spent disengaged from the typical Western church with its customary concept of ministry to devote their energy and focus directly on God.

These wilderness believers are not driven out of the church through offense or disagreement with the way things are being done. If anger or offense describes our attitude toward the church we have left, then we are outside the church for the wrong reason. Those in the wilderness by the prompting of the Spirit are there because they are driven to seek God in a depth, breadth, and height unattainable in the typical church atmosphere of clamoring and activity. They are not there to get away from church issues but to get closer to God.

During these retreats to spend time alone with God, they are cleansed from the muddied waters of traditional church practice and thinking. They are enabled to go deeper in their knowledge of God through these times of solitude. They can rise above the sectarian spirit in the church to survey a broader view. When God sends them forth, they interrupt the scene by their timely presence and message—without the baggage of the battle weary or the mindsets of the traditional. Their presence can be like a cool cup of water to the parched and burned-out who are sincerely seeking God. In the Spirit's timing, these wilderness-trained messengers can act as catalysts for the imminent moves of God.

This concept resembles the difference between those who work and live in urban areas with those who operate large farms. Population data shows that far more people live in metropolitan areas than on farms. Urban dwellers spend a lot more time with other people, both at work and in their neighborhoods. While those who work farms spend less time with people, their function is vital for the sustenance of humanity. Without them, there would be no food to preserve the larger populations residing in our cities.

Whether our calling resembles those who must continually labor within the church for maturity or those who balance time between church and 'wilderness retreats' to hear more clearly from the Lord, it is all Christ. We must discern our function and calling unpolluted and unhindered by what others think we should be doing or our own guilt for not doing what church leadership describes as normative. Neither can we allow ourselves to become plagued by doubt about the legitimacy of a calling that defies the current standard. When each member discerns and supplies their specific part in the timing of God, the body is built up and experiences *koinonia*.

Believers Must Use Their Gifts

As faithful stewards, we desire to use the abilities and spiritual gifts we have been given to serve one another, not ourselves. Nor do we leave them in the box dormant, excusing ourselves from ministry for reasons that will not hold up in the court of heaven.

> God has **given each of you a gift** *from his great variety of spiritual gifts. Use them well* **to serve one another.** 1 Pet. 4:10, NLT

Rev. Bob Gilliam, Th.M., president of T-Net International, wrote the following on the importance of fellowship in the NT church:

> [F]ellowship is not just doing anything together. It is only doing God's will together. Quite obviously, our fellowship with others is only as good as our fellowship with Christ, our unity.

> Fellowship is a relationship of inner unity among believers that expresses itself in outer co-participation with Christ and one another in accomplishing God's will on earth... [T]he indispensable means of accomplishing the God-given purpose of the church... is to show to the world the... many-faceted wisdom of God.
>
> [O]ur purpose is to show God's glory to the world in all the many ways He has instructed us in the Bible. We participate together... to glorify God, to do it His way, and to do it together.[97]

Rev. Gilliam offers the following practical advice to those who aren't sure what their gifts or calling are or how to get involved:

> You can practice fellowship by taking an active part where you can best help with this goal. You can discover where you can best help by recognizing your spiritual gifts and natural abilities and by knowing the needs of [the] church. Then help where you can make not just yourself, but the church as a whole, to be the most fruitful.
>
> If you do not know your spiritual gift, pitch in where you have a natural ability. As you work with others, your gifts will surface and you'll find places you might function in [the] church according to your gifts and abilities...
>
> With the unity of the Holy Spirit and a divine purpose, we must all put our shoulders to the plow until God's plan is complete. So let's pull together. Let everyone practice fellowship as naturally as did those on the day of Pentecost that the many-faceted wisdom of God might be made known through [the] church.[98]

The early church practiced *koinonia* as a community of believers with all things in common and unity of mind and heart—'common unity.' When we move in a spirit of unity, we transcend challenges as a higher level of purpose emerges. An environment where every member is valued and can contribute leads to supernatural vision and creativity. There is no stifling of gifts or the Holy Spirit. In this environment, believers can overcome division and wounds to move forward in wholeness and maturity—a true family of love and mutual support.

This leads us to consider another point. True *koinonia* requires bonds of family and friendship that surpass what we can achieve through hierarchical command structures. It is much more organic in nature. Leadership in such an environment more closely resembles facilitation than control. "*Koinonia* creates a... bond which builds trust and, especially when combined with the values of Wisdom, Virtue and Honor, **overcomes two of humanity's deepest fears and insecurities: being betrayed and being demeaned**." I can assure you that women who are held back from full participation feel demeaned.

The goal of *koinonia* is "to propel their community forward, to share their understanding with others so that all ships would rise on a rising tide. Thus loftier goals and dreams are more easily manifested in the mind and achieved in reality." New covenant *koinonia* is the key to manifesting the greater purposes of God in our generation.[99]

Women Must Be Included

I have taken the time to read many comments and blogs from women who are crying out for more. The women who wrote expressed their frustration with the typical women's ministry offerings. Often, women feel that they are not taken seriously as students of the Word; that the church would prefer that they be herded off to a separate area for the 'little ladies' to learn only how to be good wives and mothers. Not only are the women placed in a 'church ghetto' by such thinking, women who are not wives or raising children are further marginalized by the teaching focus.

While I appreciate the churches who have taken measures to include women in leadership, some do so only if the women fit certain physical requirements that appeal to the people the church hopes to attract. Attractive younger women are sought after as worship leaders or ministry heads to give the right 'image.' Older women feel marginalized by the youth- and beauty-driven church that targets for leadership only those who mirror those attributes. Those with experience, training, true compassion, and wisdom are cast aside in favor of those who reflect the external image the church wants to sell.

Women Are More than Emotional Beings

Women's ministry too often becomes merely a place for women to heal emotionally rather than grow in the knowledge of God and the fellowship of Christ. In 2007, Amy Simpson, editor of *Gifted for Leadership*, wrote the following to capture the frustration many women experience in the church:

> Too often, we seem to buy into the world's lie that we are purely emotional beings, at the whim of fantasy and hormones, and not smart enough to go deep. God created us to feel and to think. Our souls hunger not only for the presence of God, but also for knowledge of his truth. Ministries that focus only on women's emotional needs or that stay on a shallow level are doing a disservice to their women and to the larger body of Christ. And they're failing to reach many women, who will never be engaged by a ministry that does not challenge their intellect.[100]

So what is the core reason behind this frustration? Simply, women have the same Holy Spirit as the men, and therefore long for serious spiritual growth. Sarah Bessey created quite a stir with the following blog post in 2011. She is a wife, mother, and author who yearns for true community in the church (emphasis her own):

> Some of us are drowning, suffocating, dying of thirst for want of the cold water of real community. We're trying really hard—after all, we keep showing up to your lady events and we leave feeling just a bit empty. It's just more of the same every time...
>
> **We need Jesus.** We are seeking deep spirituality. We are seeking fellow travelers. We are hungry for true community, a place to tell our stories and listen to another, to love well. But above all, point me to Jesus—not to the sale at the mall.
>
> You know what I would have liked tonight instead of decorating tips or a new recipe? I would have liked to pray together. I would have liked for the women of the church to share their stories or wisdom with one another, no more celebrity speakers, please just hand the microphone to that lady over there

that brought the apples. I would love to wrestle with some questions that don't have a one-paragraph answer in your study guide. I would like to do a Bible study that does not have pink or flowers on the cover. I would have liked to sign up to bring a meal for our elderly or drop off some clothes for a new baby or be informed about issues in our city where we can make space for God. I would like to organize and prioritize, to rabble-rouse and disturb the peace of the rest of the world on behalf of justice, truth, beauty and love. I'd love to hear the prophetic voice of women in our church.

Please may we be the place to *detox* from the world—its values, its entertainment, its priorities, its focus on appearances and materialism and consumerism?

So here is my suggestion: **Please stop treating women's ministry like a Safe Club for the Little Ladies to Play Church.**[101]

Wow—poignantly accurate. In her concluding remarks in the following excerpt, notice the tangible longing for significance. If the church would listen to the deep cry in her heart—the cry of all God's *chayil* women—we would begin working today to remedy the division caused by mindsets hardened to the truth. We would set the women free to function without restrictions in their God-given callings and gifts.

We are smart. We are brave. We want to change the world... **We have more to offer to the church than our mad decorating skills.** I look around and I can see that these **women can offer strategic leadership, wisdom, counsel and even, yes, teaching.** We want to give and serve and make a difference. We want to be challenged. We want to read books and talk politics, theology and current events. We want to wrestle through our theology. We want to listen to each other. We want to worship, we want to intercede for our sisters and weep with those who weep, rejoice with those that rejoice, to create life and art and justice with intention.

Let's be a community of women, gathered together to live more whole-hearted, to sharpen, challenge, love and inspire one another to then scatter back out to our worlds bearing the mandate that my friend Idelette wrote, we are women who love. "Let us RISE to the questions of our time. Let us SPEAK to the injustices in our world. Let us MOVE the mountains of fear and intimidation. Let us SHOUT down the walls that separate and divide. Let us FILL the earth with the fragrance of Love. Let us be women who Love."[102]

Amen, Sister. In the blog post immediately following this one, Sarah Bessey confessed that she had left the program-driven church for a season, not only because of her burnout, but also because she no longer believed church programs were effective for training disciples of Jesus. "I believe that we are at a crossroads as a global Church, shifting and changing, just as we have done for centuries."[103]

When we scrutinize cultural influences on the church, shouldn't our priority be those cultural laxities that violate the moral code, with only secondary consideration for those that encroach our religious traditions and ceremonial practices? Our stance on moral issues never changes. These are the laws written on the conscience of every person unless that conscience is seared by habitual sin or constant cultural imposition. These are serious issues where compromise is unacceptable.

But on matters of religious practice and tradition, we must be more thoughtful. After all, the early church decided in favor of relinquishing the ceremonial laws and extrabiblical Jewish traditions as binding on the newly-included Gentile believers. We must determine whether the things we do as a body of believers today are actually found in the Word. In some cases, I think we will find that our traditional practices and policies have more to do with previously accepted cultural norms than God's Word. Some believers have demonstrated an unwillingness to admit this—even when the Word points out the error—because we like or derive some profit from these culturally-based practices.

New Covenant Liberty

> *Now the Lord is the Spirit, and where the Spirit of the Lord is, there is liberty.* 2 Cor. 3:17, NASB

Jesus came to proclaim liberty to the captives, including those held captive by racism, class distinctions (e.g., slavery, income strata), and gender bias (Isa. 61:1; Luke 4:17-21; James 2:1-4). True Christianity requires the presence of God, and where God's presence is there can be only liberty. Discrimination and oppression have no place in the body of Christ.

Jesus valued women. Even when it meant losing points with His host, a local religious leader, Jesus spoke kindly and graciously to the former prostitute who ministered to Him. He judged not by what He saw with His eyes or heard with His ears in this situation, but in righteousness judged the woman as walking in greater love (Luke 7:36-50; cf. Isa. 11:3-4). Like David, she was willing to be more undignified than Jesus' host could stomach in order to express her deep love for her Savior.

> *I will become even more undignified than this, and I will be humiliated in my own eyes...* 2 Sam. 6:22a, NIV

Women followed Jesus, caring for His physical needs and sitting at His feet to learn (Matt. 27:55; Mark 15:41; Luke 8:1-3; 10:39; 23:49,50). They faithfully stood by Him at the crucifixion when most of the male disciples denied Him and fled. Despite the gruesome nature of and the intense circumstances surrounding the crucifixion, these women endured the strain and demonstrated unswerving loyalty by remaining and witnessing the unspeakable while the things they beheld carved deep pain and sorrow into their souls.

These same women were the first ones to hear and spread the good news of Jesus' resurrection (Matt. 27:55-61; 28:1-10; Mark 15:40-16:10; Luke 23:27,49,55-24:10). They were among the faithful in the upper room waiting for the outpouring of the Holy Spirit (Acts 1:14).

Oppressing faithful women of God has no place in our church gatherings. True *koinonia* will only be realized in the church when we view every believer as 'in Christ' rather than base our judgment on the temporary tent God has given each to wear in this age. Jesus rebuked the religious leaders of His day for judging by mere outward appearances (John 7:24). Striving to know one another by the discernment the Holy Spirit gives requires maturity and time. The church needs to view women as God does: they are joint-heirs and co-laborers in Jesus' ministry—full partners in the *koinonia* of the church.

> *So speak and so act as those who are to be judged by the law of liberty.* James 2:12, NASB

The authentic bond between believers establishes an environment of *koinonia* where every other member is valued, recognized, and respected as full and accepted partners—co-heirs. For this bond to be genuine, believers must consider the needs of others and do what they can to help those who are suffering. "Fellowship creates a mutual bond which overrides each individual's pride, vanity, and individualism, fulfilling the human yearning with fraternity, belonging, and companionship... When combined with the spiritual implications of *koinonia*, fellowship provides a joint participation in God's graces and denotes that common possession of spiritual values."[104]

Previously, we mentioned that *koinonia* creates a bond that builds trust. Anything we do that demeans or betrays another believer destroys that bond. Relegating women to restrictive roles demoralizes those women called to greater degrees of authority. This practice also dishonors the Holy Spirit who gave them the desire and gifts in the first place. Their talent, drive, creativity, and vision are debased and deemed fleshly in origin because to admit it is from God would destroy the paradigm under which much of the church has operated. This narrow-minded thinking adheres to the traditional view that women have no place in leadership, which prevents these from hearing the guidance, discernment, and selection of the Spirit of God. In the minds of those so inclined, the desire these women have to seek such a position could not have been given by God.

Is this not one way we quench the Spirit and ruin our ability to attain unity? The church degrades women by regarding their contributions as less significant, at least in the arenas of leadership and teaching. Like Gideon during the time of the Judges, many valiant women are in hiding wrestling with the Word in secret. They long to be included and have ever so much more to offer than what they are currently allowed.

Everyone has moved in error on some issue at some time. Remaining teachable and correctable allows us to grasp what the Holy Spirit seeks to impart to us in this hour. God did not teach the church everything on the front end—He waits until we are ready, timing the restoration of truth to suit His purpose.

> *Include prayer for us, too, that God may open a door for us to proclaim the message.* Col. 4:3a, CJB

Women believers who have leadership and teaching gifts are often denied full participation in the church for expressing those gifts and callings. Jesus stands outside the church with them, knocking at the door. For those who grant them entrance, I pray the Lord brings showers of great grace and *koinonia* to advance His kingdom and fulfill His Word that in the place of true unity He has commanded His blessing (Psalm 133). This, in turn, will transform the church, our communities, and the uttermost parts of the earth.

> *My prayer is … that all of them may be one, Father, just as you are in me and I am in you. May they also be in us so that the world may believe that you have sent me.* John 17:20-21, NIV

Epilogue

Prophesy to the Mountain

We have taken a lengthy journey to understand God's view of women and the roles He intended them to fulfill in the body of Christ. Having this knowledge and understanding bolsters our faith and enables us to remain resolved and unmoved in the face of opposition. It also frees us from the anxiety and instability of double-mindedness. This freedom provokes us to run with vigor the race that has been set before us.

Even so, it would be naïve to think there will not be any opposition. In the Bible, mountains are used as poetic metaphors for governments and kingdoms as well as for obstacles. The obstacles before women that hinder their ability to take their place as God purposed in the body of Christ may seem as formidable as a mountain. These obstacles are not specific people or institutions, but ideology that opposes the true knowledge and will of God.

> *We demolish arguments and every pretension* ('every proud obstacle' NLT) *that sets itself up against the knowledge of God, and we take captive every thought to make it obedient to Christ.* 2 Cor. 10:5, NIV

When we try to overcome these obstacles in our own strength, we will most likely fail or run ourselves into the ground with the amount of exertion required. Recovering from a season of burnout can be costly in terms of being fruitful for God's kingdom. The result of this type of striving is discouragement, frustration, depression, or even anger that seeks revenge.

If any of these describes you, I urge you to seek the Lord for healing, and, if applicable, relinquish offense and bitterness and repent for using carnal means to accomplish God's purposes. I believe every believer has at some time tried to accomplish God's purposes in his or her own strength when he or she experiences zeal to serve the Lord. Think of Moses killing the Egyptian before he became Israel's deliverer, Peter cutting off the servant's ear to fight for Jesus in a worldly way, or James and John vying for the best positions in God's kingdom.

If we wait patiently for discernment to move God's way—in His timing and strategy—the mountain-obstacle before us will be cast into the sea. This takes place through prayer, standing firm in our faith that God will finish what He has started in us, guarding our hearts against offense, and breaking our agreement with the enemy's lies. Jesus taught the disciples that mountains can be removed by the word of prophecy spoken in faith:

> *Truly I say to you, whoever says to this mountain, 'Be taken up and cast into the sea,' and does not doubt in his heart, but believes that what he says is going to happen, it will be granted him.* Mark 11:23, NASB

While in the process of writing this book, the following thoughts came to mind as I sat before the Lord early one morning, and I would like to share them with you. The entire stream of thought is actually an adaptation of an ordered set of phrases and verses from the Word. As I contemplated the mountain of tradition and opinion that has exerted itself between women and the race God has called them to run, my mind led me to adapt the following words from Scripture:

> *The word of the LORD came to me: Son of man, set your face against the mountains (obstacles) and prophesy against them.*
>
> > *I am against you, you destroying mountain, you who destroy and hinder My daughters, declares the Lord. I will stretch out My hand against you.*
>
> *Is not My word like a fire, like a hammer that shatters the rock in pieces? See, I will make this word into a threshing sledge, new and sharp, with many teeth. It will thresh the mountains and crush them.*
>
> > *What are you, O great mountain, before my daughters? You will become a plain. I will go before you and will level the mountains. Every valley shall be raised up, every mountain and hill made low.*
>
> *Truly I tell you, if you have faith and do not doubt, you can say to this mountain, 'Go, throw yourself into the sea,' and it will be done. But whoever has doubts is condemned because everything that does not come from faith is sin.*

(Wording based on Ezk. 6:1-2; Jer. 51:25; Jer. 23:29; Isa. 41:15; Zech. 4:7; Isa. 45:2; Isa. 40:4; Mark 11:23)

Prophesy to the mountain in faith, and the Lord will open a door for you to run your race with the light, wind, and fire of the Holy Spirit.

Without Love, We Are Nothing

As a closing thought, remember that nothing written in this book and nothing any believer does is worth anything before God if it is not infused with and pursued out of love.

> *If I have the gift of prophecy, and know all mysteries and all knowledge; and if I have all faith, so as to remove mountains, but do not have love, I am nothing.* 1 Cor. 13:2, NASB

Father, deliver Jesus' bride by infusing her with the knowledge of Your will with all wisdom and understanding. Transform her by Your truth and the power of Your love. Help her to love You and love others through the practical outworking of the gifts You have given to each member. Raise up leaders who will not shy away from declaring truth as it is written in Your Word, and who will spend themselves on behalf of Your people to bring them to maturity by the power and strategy of Your Spirit. Raise up those who have zeal and vision to see each believer trained and equipped for their individual callings. Give us more of Your Holy Spirit for discernment as well as grace for unity and true koinonia.

Release the preparation ministries and open doors for unhindered work. Bring the church to a place of purity and maturity so she will experience the love, unity, and peace that will allow her to fulfill Your plans and purpose for this hour in history, so the world will know she is Yours and that You are with her.

Amen.

Make haste, my Beloved.
Songs 8:14a, NKJV

Addendum

On intelligence/brain comparison:

1. "Human Intelligence, Cleverer Still." Dec. 22, 2012. http://www.economist.com/news/science-and-technology/21568704-geniuses-are-getting-brighter-and-genius-levels-iq-girls-are-not-far. Retrieved 01.20.2014.
2. Babak A. Ardekani, Khadija Figarsky and John J. Sidtis. *Sexual Dimorphism in the Human Corpus Callosum: An MRI Study Using the OASIS Brain Database.* September 10, 2013. Abstract. http://cercor.oxfordjournals.org/content/early/2012/08/09/cercor.bhs253.full. Retrieved 01.23.2014.
3. Steinmetz H, Staiger JF, Schlaug G, Huang Y, Jäncke L. "Corpus callosum and brain volume in women and men." *Neuroreport.* May 9, 1995; 6(7):1002-4. Abstract. http://www.ncbi.nlm.nih.gov/pubmed/7632882. Retrieved 01.23.2014.

High-context and Low-context Cultures

"Anthropologist Edward T. Hall's theory of high- and low-context culture helps us better understand the powerful effect culture has on communication. A key factor in his theory is **context**. This relates to the framework, background, and surrounding circumstances in which communication or an event takes place. The following summary highlights the problems facing low-context North Americans when they interact with people from high-context cultures.

"**High-context cultures** (including much of the Middle East, Asia, Africa, and South America) are relational, collectivist, intuitive, and contemplative. This means that people in these cultures emphasize interpersonal relationships. Developing trust is an important first step to any business transaction. According to Hall, these cultures are collectivist, preferring group harmony and consensus to individual achievement. And people in these cultures are **less governed by reason than by intuition** or feelings. **Words are not so important as context**, which might include the speaker's tone of voice, facial expression, gestures, posture—and even the person's family history and status. A Japanese manager explained his culture's communication style to an American: "We are a homogeneous people and don't have to speak as much as you do here. When we say one word, we understand ten, but here you have to say ten to understand one." High-context communication tends to be **more indirect and more formal**. Flowery language, humility, and elaborate apologies are typical.

"**Low-context cultures** (including North America and much of Western Europe) are logical, linear, individualistic, and action-oriented. People from low-context cultures **value logic, facts, and directness**. Solving a problem means lining up the facts and evaluating one after another. Decisions are based on fact rather than intuition. Discussions end with actions. And communicators are expected to be straightforward, concise, and efficient in telling what action is expected. **To be absolutely clear, they strive to use precise words and intend them to be taken literally.** Explicit contracts conclude negotiations. This is very different from communicators in high-context cultures who depend less on language precision and legal documents. High-context business people may even distrust contracts and be offended by the lack of trust they suggest." (Brian G. Wilson, College of Marin, Business Instructor. Chapter 1 Lecture: "High-context and Low-context Culture Styles." College of Marin. http://www.marin.edu/buscom/index_files/Page605.htm. Retrieved 03.08.2014.)

After reading these two descriptions, I think we have another factor that reveals why it is so difficult for the church in the West to experience true *koinonia*. We are a low-context culture with heavy reliance on personal intellect and individualism. Even our social contacts today tend to be more sterile with the advent of email, facebook, texting, twitter, etc. The church was meant to function more as a high-context culture, something we have difficulty attaining in our personal achievement oriented society. This could also explain why we tend to favor a predictable college lecture style church format rather than a fellowship where each member in some way contributes to the discussion and gathering. For many, it is much easier and less disturbing to stare at one face in the spotlight on a platform and the backs of innumerable heads than it is to engage in meaningful conversation with something valuable to contribute.

Notes on NT Greek

In Greek, a gender designation of a word is grammatical (as in Spanish), and therefore most often arbitrary, i.e., not necessarily associated with the actual gender, although that can be so.

A verb in the active voice means that the subject is the one doing the action, e.g., 'He taught Gamaliel.' Passive voice, where the subject is acted upon by another, would change this sentence to, 'He was taught by Gamaliel.' Middle voice, where the subject is acting on himself, e.g., 'He taught himself.'

> It is an important distinction to understand, as discussed below, that **the only place in which 'time' comes to bear directly upon the tense of a verb is when the verb is in the <u>indicative mood</u>**... The 'time' aspect of the tense of a verb really only comes into affect when the verb is in the indicative mood. When a verb is outside of the indicative mood, then the aktionsart ('kind of action') of the tense is usually emphasized and should be carefully noted, and its bearing upon the passage should be considered... For instance, **outside of the indicative mood it is often customary to use the tense that implies a 'simple occurrence', the <u>aorist tense</u>**... If the writer does not wish to emphasize or focus on the progress of the verb's action (whether continuous or completed) he will use the aorist tense. The term 'aorist' means 'unspecified' or 'unlimited'. It signifies nothing as to the progression or completeness of an action... If one has the mistaken concept that aorist tense means past time, many passages of the New Testament will be very confusing if not altogether nonsensical. (Only in the indicative

mood does the aorist indicate past time). Many times the action of a verb in the aorist subjunctive or aorist imperative forms, for instance, will actually take place at a future time, not a past time... **For action happening at the present time, only the 'present tense' is available.** Whether the writer is wishing in any particular instance to emphasis the progressive aspect of the verb or just indicate a simple occurrence at the present time, there is only one choice of tense to use. Therefore, **one must consider the context** and the basic meaning of the verb **to determine whether the emphasis is on the continuous aspect of the action or merely on the present time** element. It may be that no real emphasis on progressive action is intended but, for a statement requiring the element of present time, there is no choice but to use the 'present tense'. (Of course **outside the indicative mood** the emphasis almost certainly will be on the progressive element of the verb, since the aorist tense could readily be employed). (Corey Keating. "Greek Verb Tenses (Intermediate Discussion)." http://www.ntgreek.org/learn_nt_greek/inter-tense.htm. Retrieved 01.31.14.)

Procrustes

"[I]n Greek legend... [Procrustes] had an iron bed... on which he compelled his victims to lie. Here, if a victim was shorter than the bed, he stretched him by hammering or racking the body to fit. Alternatively, if the victim was longer than the bed, he cut off the legs to make the body fit the bed's length. In either event the victim died... The "bed of Procrustes," or "Procrustean bed," has become proverbial for arbitrarily—and perhaps ruthlessly—forcing someone or something to fit into an unnatural scheme or pattern." ("Procrustes." http://www.britannica.com/EBchecked/topic/477822/Procrustes. Retrieved 01.22.14.)

End Notes

CHAPTER 1

1. Spiros Zodhiates, Th.D. *The Complete Word Study New Testament (WSNT)*. AMG Publishers. Chattanooga. 1991. 2nd Edition 1992. p. 894.
2. Dr. Gary L. Nebeker, Ph.D. *"Who Packed Your Bags?": Factors That Influence Our Preunderstandings.* Posted October 11, 2004. https:// bible.org/article/%E2%80%9C who-packed-your-bags%E2%80%9D-factors-influence-our-preunderstandings. Retrieved 01.20.2014.
3. Loren Cunningham and David Joel Hamilton. *Why Not Women? A Fresh Look at Scripture on Women in Missions, Ministry, and Leadership.* YWAM Publishing. Seattle. 2000. p. 60.

CHAPTER 2

4. Susan Cain. *Quiet: The Power of Introverts in a World that Can't Stop Talking.* Crown Publishers. New York. 2012. pp. 5,22,26.
5. Billy Hallowell. *5 Possible Reasons Young Americans Are Leaving Church and Christianity Behind.* October 5, 2013. http://www.the blaze.com/stories/2013/10/30/5-possible-reasons-young-americans-are-leaving-church-and-christianity-behind/. Retrieved 02.05.2014.
6. Lenny Bruce. *The Essential Lenny Bruce,* as quoted at "Church Quotes." http://www.notable-quotes.com/c/church _quotes.html. Retrieved 02.05.2014.
7. Bruce H. Wilkinson, Executive Editor. *The Daily Walk Bible*. Tyndale. Wheaton. 1988. p. 191.

CHAPTER 3

8. Nebeker. Ibid. Retrieved 01.20.2014.
9. "Fruit Tree Pollination." Subhead "Apple." Wikipedia. Ibid. Retrieved 03.11.2014.
10. Dr. Eric H. Chudler. "The Blind Spot." Neuroscience for Kids. http://faculty. washington.edu/chudler/chvision.html. Retrieved 03.11.2014.

CHAPTER 4

11. Nicholas D. Smith, Ph.D. "Plato and Aristotle on the Nature of Women." *Journal of the History of Philosophy.*Vol. 21, Num. 4, October 1983. pp. 467-478. http://muse.jhu.edu/login?auth=0&type=summary&url=/journals/journal_of_the_history_of_philosophy/ v021/21.4smith.pdf. Retrieved 03.18.2014.
12. "Statements on Women by Church Fathers, Doctors, and Saints." Theology Library at Spring Hill College. http://www.shc.edu/theolibrary/resources/women.htm. Retrieved 03.18.2014.
13. Marie I. George, Ph.D. "What Aquinas Really Said About Women." *First Things*. The Institute on Religion and Public Life. http://www.firstthings.com/article/2007/01/what-aquinas-really-said-about-women. Retrieved 03.18.2014.
14. "Natural Law." http://en.wikipedia.org/wiki/Natural_law. The Wikimedia Foundation, Inc. Retrieved 03.18.2014.

15. "Thomas Aquinas." http://en.wikipedia.org/wiki/Thomas_Aquinas. The Wikimedia Foundation, Inc. Retrieved 03.18.2014.
16. Jan Edward Garrett, Ph.D. "Aquinas on Law." Western Kentucky University. http://people.wku.edu/jan.garrett/302/aquinlaw.htm. Retrieved 03.18.2014.
17. Scott Barry Kaufman, Ph.D. *Beautiful Minds*. "Men, Women, and IQ: Setting the Record Straight." July 20, 2012. http://www. psychology today.com/blog/beautiful-minds/201207/men-women-and-iq-setting-the-record-straight. Retrieved 01.18.2014.
18. Christopher Badcock, Ph.D. "The Incredible Expanding Adventures of the X Chromosome." *Psychology Today*. Sept. 06, 2011. http://www.psychologytoday.com/articles/201109/the-incredible-expanding-adventures-the-x-chromosome. Retrieved 04.05.2014.
19. Comment by J. Kemp. *Human Intelligence: Cleverer Still*. December 21, 2012. http://www.economist.com/news/science-and-technology/21568704-geniuses-are-getting-brighter-and-genius-levels-iq-girls-are-not-far. Retrieved 01.22.2014.

CHAPTER 6

20. Rebbetzin Tziporah Heller. "Men and Women: Jewish View of Gender Differences." Jan. 30, 2000. http://www.aish.com/ci/w/48955181.html
21. Spiros Zodhiates, Th.D. *The Complete Word Study Old Testament (WSOT)*. AMG Publishers. Chattanooga. 1994. p. 2380.

CHAPTER 7

22. "Precedent." http://legal-dictionary.thefreedictionary.com/precedent. Retrieved 03.25.2014.
23. "Precedent." http://en.wikipedia.org/wiki/Precedent. The Wikimedia Foundation, Inc. Retrieved 03.25.2014.
24. Zodhiates. *WSNT*. Ibid. pp. 952-953.
25. Zodhiates. *WSNT*. Ibid. p. 953; particular reference to Eph. 2:20; 3:5; 4:11; 1 Cor. 12:28.
26. Marie N. Sabin, Ph.D. "Women Transformed: The Ending of Mark in the Beginning of Wisdom." ttp://www.thefreelibrary.com/Women+transformed%3a+the+ending+of+Mark+in+the+beginning+of+wisdom.-a020968459 OR http://www. crosscurrents.org/sabin.htm. Retrieved 03.20.2014.

CHAPTER 8

27. John Wijngaards. "Greek Philosophy on the Inferiority of Women ." http://www.womenpriests.org/traditio/infe_gre.asp. Retrieved 03.29.2014.

CHAPTER 9

28. Nebeker. Ibid. Retrieved 01.20.2014.
29. ἤ (e). http://biblehub.com/greek/strongs_2228.htm. Retrieved 01.29.2014.
30. Cunningham and Hamilton. Ibid. pp. 190-191.
31. "Socratic Method." http://en.wikipedia.org/wiki/Socratic_method. The Wikimedia Foundation, Inc. Retrieved 03.16.2014.
32. Heather Coffey. *Socratic Method*. UNC School of Education. http://www.learnnc.org/lp/pages/4994. Retrieved 03.16.2014.
33. Babylonian Talmud: Tractate Berakoth, Folio 24a. http://www.come-and-hear.com/berakoth/berakoth_24.html. Retrieved 01.30.2014.

34. Babylonian Talmud Nashim, Kiddushin: Tractate 70a. http://halakhah.com/rst/nashim/30b%20-%20Kiddushin%2041a-82b.pdf. Retrieved 01.30.2014.

CHAPTER 10

35. Stacy E. Hoehl, Ph.D. "The Mentor Relationship: An Exploration of Paul As Loving Mentor To Timothy And The Application Of This Relationship To Contemporary Leadership Challenges." *Journal of Biblical Perspectives in Leadership 3*, no. 2 (Summer 2011), 32-47. 2011. School of Global Leadership & Entrepreneurship, Regent University. pp. 38, 44. http://www.regent.edu/acad/global/publications/jbpl/vol3no2/JBPL_Vol3No2_Hoehl_pp32-47.pdf. Retrieved 03.08.2014.
36. "High- and Low-Context Cultures." http://en.wikipedia.org/wiki/High-_and_low-context_cultures. Ibid. Retrieved 03.08.2014.
37. "Ephesus." http://en.wikipedia.org/wiki/Ephesus. The Wikimedia Foundation, Inc. Retrieved 01.24.2014.
38. "Amazons." http://en.wikipedia.org/wiki/Amazons.The Wikimedia Foundation, Inc. Retrieved 01.31.2014.
39. "Temple of Artemis." http://en.wikipedia.org/wiki/Temple_of_Artemis. The Wikimedia Foundation, Inc. Retrieved 01.31.2014.
40. "Artemis." http://en.wikipedia.org/wiki/Artemis. The Wikimedia Foundation, Inc. Retrieved 01.31.2014.
41. Titles for Artemis found at http://www.theoi.com/Cult/ArtemisTitles.html. Retrieved 01.31.2014.
42. Wade Burleson. "Artemis and the End of Us: Evangelical Errors Regarding Women." Blogpost. February 22, 2013. http://www.wadeburleson.org/2013/02/artemus-and-end-of-us-evangelical.html. Retrieved 01.22.2014.
43. *The Apologists Bible Commentary.* "Glossary of Grammatical, Philosophical, and Theological Terms." http://www.forananswer.org/Glossary.htm. Retrieved 02.03.2014.
44. Wayne T. Slusser. CHIASMUS IN PAULINE WRITINGS? The Significance of the Micro-Chiasm for Exegesis. 2002. p.4. http://www.slusser.us/papers/Chiasm%20paper-web.pdf. Retrieved 02.03.2014.
45. Slusser. Ibid. pp. 7,8,9,12.
46. Slusser. Ibid. pp. 12-13.
47. Slusser. Ibid. p. 29.
48. James M. Gibbs, Ph.D. *Chiastic Structuring: An Introduction.* http://newtestamentresearch.com/NT%20Research-Mk%202/chiastic_structuring.htm. Retrieved 02.03.2014.
49. *Hesuchia.* Thayer's Greek Lexicon. 2002, 2003, 2006, 2011. Electronic database by Biblesoft, Inc. Retrieved at biblehub.com 02.01.2014.
50. Helps Word Studies. *Hesuchia.* Helps Ministries, Inc. 1987, 2011. Retrieved 2.1.2014 at biblehub.com.
51. Helps Word Studies. *Hesuchios.* Ibid. Retrieved 02.01.2014 at biblehub.com.
52. Burleson. Ibid. Retrieved 01.22.2014.
53. Helps Word Studies. *Manthano.* Ibid. Retrieved 02.01.2014 at biblehub.com.
54. Helps Word Studies. *Pas.* Ibid. Retrieved 2.1.2014 at biblehub.com.
55. Zodhiates. *WSNT.* Ibid. p. 964.

56. Corey Keating's contributions to *Learning New Testament Greek* at http://www.ntgreek.org/learn_nt_ greek/grkindex.htm. Retrieved 02.02.2014.
57. 1 Timothy 2:12, Greek construction. http://biblehub.com/text/1_timothy/2-12.htm. Retrieved 02.01.2014.
58. Keating. "Greek Verbs (Shorter Definitions)." Ibid. Retrieved 02.02.2014.
59. A.T. Robertson. "A Greek Grammar of the Greek New Testament in the Light of Historical Research." pp. 1183-1184, as quoted by William E. Wenstrom, Jr. Bible Ministries. *De*. http://www.wenstrom.org /downloads/written/word_studies /greek/ de.pdf. Retrieved 02.02.2014.
60. Wenstrom. Ibid.
61. Zodhiates. *WSNT*. Ibid. p. 908.
62. Helps Word Studies. *Exousia*. Ibid. Retrieved 02.01.2014 at biblehub.com.
63. Helps Word Studies. *Katakurieuo*. Ibid. Retrieved 02.01.2014 at biblehub.com.
64. Helps Word Studies. K*atexousiazo*. Ibid. Retrieved 02.01.2014 at biblehub.com.
65. Ronald W. Pierce, Rebecca Merrill Groothuis and Gordon D. Fee, editors. *Discovering Biblical Equality: Complementarity Without Hierarchy*. Linda Belleville, Ph.D. "Teaching and Usurping Authprity." InterVarsityPress. Downers Grove. 2005. pp. 211-212.
66. Catherine C. Kroeger, Ph.D. "Ancient Heresies and a Strange Greek Verb." http://godswordtowomen.org/kroeger_ancient_ heresies.htm. Retrieved 01.31.2014.
67. Pierce, et al. Ibid. Belleville. Ibid. p. 212.
68. Helps Word Studies. *Gar*. Ibid. Retrieved 02.02.2014 at biblehub.com.
69. Slusser. Ibid. pp. 20-27.
70. Wenstrom. *Gar*. Ibid. Retrieved 02.03.14

CHAPTER 11

71. Nebeker. Ibid. Retrieved 01.20.2014.
72. See the section titled "The Translators to the Reader" in the translator's preface of the 1611 King James Bible at http://www.kjvbibles.com/kjpreface.htm
73. Nebeker. Ibid. Retrieved 01.20.2014.
74. Bruno Dubuc. "History Module: The Growth of New Neurons in the Adult Human Brain." http://the brain.mcgill.ca/flash/ capsules/histoire_bleu05.html. Retrieved 01.23.2014.
75. Cheryl Schatz. "Anne Graham Lotz and 800 pastors' shame." Oct. 8, 2008. https://strivetoenter.com/wim/2008/10/24/anne-graham-lotz-and-800-pastors-shame/. Retrieved 03.26.2014.
76. William E. Wenstrom, Jr. Bible Ministries. "The Apostle Paul." 2006. http://www.wenstrom.org/downloads/written/people/new /paul.pdf. Retrieved 02.13.2014.
77. Zodhiates. *WSNT*. Ibid. p. 879.
78. *Agnoeo*. http://biblehub.com/greek/50.htm. Retrieved 02.13.2014.
79. Helps Word Studies. *Apistia*. Ibid. Retrieved 02.13.2014 at biblehub.com.
80. "Missing Women of Asia." http://en.wikipedia.org/wiki/Missing_ women_of_Asia. The Wikimedia Foundation, Inc. Retrieved 01.30.2014.
81. Ross Douthat. "160 Million and Counting." *The New York Times*. June 26, 2011. http://www.nytimes. com/2011/06/ 27/opinion/27douthat.html?_r=0. Retrieved 01.30.2014.

82. Albert Barnes. *Notes on the Bible*. 1834. http://biblehub.com/commentaries/barnes/. Retrieved 01.27.2014.
83. Barnes. Ibid. Retrieved 01.27.2014.
84. Nebeker. Ibid. Retrieved 01.20.2014.
85. Burleson. Ibid. Retrieved 01.22.2014.
86. Nebeker. Ibid. Retrieved 01.20.2014.
87. Adam Clarke. *Commentary on the Bible*. 1831. http://biblehub.com/commentaries/clarke/1_corinthians/4.htm. Retrieved 01.27.2014.

CHAPTER 12

88. Mike Bickle with Deborah Hiebert. *The Seven Longings of the Human Heart*. Forerunner Books. Kansas City. 2006.

CHAPTER 13

89. "Judgment Notwithstanding Verdict." http://dictionary.law.com. Retrieved 02.18.2014.
90. Nebeker, Ibid. Retrieved 01.20.2014.
91. Nebeker. Ibid. Retrieved 01.20.2014.

CHAPTER 14

92. "Koinonia." http://en.wikipedia.org/wiki/Koinonia. The Wikimedia Foundation, Inc. Retrieved 03.01.2014
93. "Koinonia." Wikipedia. Ibid.
94. "Koinonia." Wikipedia. Ibid.
95. "Koinonia." Wikipedia. Ibid.
96. Rick Joyner. "Worth the Price—The Great Commission, Part 12." Week 12, 2014. http://www.MorningStarministries.org/resources/word-week/2014/worth-price-great-commission-part-12#.Uzcn69jQe00. Retrieved 03.26.2014.
97. Rev. Bob Gilliam, Th.M. "The Importance of Fellowship in a New Testament Church." May 26, 2004. https://bible.org/seriespage/importance-fellowship-new-testament-church. Retrieved 03.01.2014.
98. Gilliam. Ibid.
99. "Koinonia." Wikipedia. Ibid.
100. Amy Simpson. "Ideas for Women's Ministry." Blog posted Sept. 28, 2007. http://www.giftedforleadership.com//2007/09/ideas_for_womens_ministry.html. Retrieved 03.01.2014.
101. Sarah Bessey. "In which I write a letter to Womens' Ministry." Blog post Oct. 1, 2011. http://sarahbessey.com/in-which-i-write-letter-to-womens/. Retrieved 03.01.2014.
102. Bessey. Ibid.
103. Sarah Bessey. "In which I write a bit more about womens' ministry and invite your thoughts." Blog post Oct. 3, 2011. http://sarahbessey.com/in-which-i-write-bit-more-about-womens/. Retrieved 03.01.2014.
104. "Koinonia." Wikipedia. Ibid.

www.ingramcontent.com/pod-product-compliance
Lightning Source LLC
Chambersburg PA
CBHW032103090426
42743CB00007B/220